Awakening and Healing

the Rainbow Body

by the same author

Books

Non-Fiction

Awakening and Healing the Rainbow Body
Companion Guide to Self Mastery
(forthcoming in this series)

Fiction

The Lineage of the Codes of Light

The Brotherhood of the Magi

The Priestess and the Magus
(forthcoming in this series)

Audio Compact Discs

Deep Trance Shamanic Journeys
Volume I: Pachamama's Child

Deep Trance Shamanic Journeys
Volume II: Right Relationship

Deep Trance Shamanic Journeys
Volume III: Reclaiming Our Power
(forthcoming in this series)

AWAKENING AND HEALING THE RAINBOW BODY

by
Jessie E. Ayani

HEART OF THE SUN
2004

Awakening and Healing the Rainbow Body© by Jessie E. Ayani. Printed and bound in the United States of America. All rights reserved. No part of this book may be reproduced in any form or by any electronic or mechanical means without permission, in writing, from the publisher, except by reviewers, who may quote brief passages in review.

Published by Heart of the Sun, P.O. Box 495, Mount Shasta, CA 96067
First Edition
First Printing 2004
Ayani, Jessie E.
Awakening and Healing the Rainbow Body / Jessie E. Ayani - 1st Heart of the Sun Edition
ISBN# 0-9648763-5-3
1. Spirituality 2. Enlightenment 3. Metaphysics 4. Self-Help 4. Shamanism

Cover Art:
Tetrahedral Heart Drawing by Francene Hart
P.O. Box 900, Honaunau, HI 96726
www.francenehart.com hartart@haii.net

Cover Design and Illustrations:
Silverlining Designs, Leanne Krause
P.O. Box 1346, Talent, OR 97540
www.silverlining-designs.com leanne@mind.net

Editing and Typesetting:
Heart of the Sun

Published by
Heart of the Sun
P.O. Box 495
Mount Shasta, CA 96067
www.heartofthesun.com info@heartofthesun.com

To the Masters, San Pedro

and Beloved Sananda

Thanks

The author wishes to thank the following for their participation in the manifestation of this book. Very special thanks, and endless love and respect, go to Dr. Mike I., in the Twin Cities, for being an extraordinary support person, and a cheerful but ruthless guide during seven critical years of my own healing and awakening. My love and gratitude move through the dimensions to my birth parents, both of whom passed during this writing. To my soul parents, Don Pasqual, Master of Energy, and his wife, Doña Dominga, my second mother to pass during this writing, I send all of the *munay* my heart is capable of generating. Heartfelt gratitude goes to my ongoing group in Santa Fe, New Mexico for being the pioneers who validated this work through their own dedication to liberation. *Munay* goes to my *wayki* and son-in-law, Javier Casapia, for introducing me to the Master, San Pedro. I send gratitude to my readers/editors, Suzanne James, Thea O'Brien, Janine and John Thompson-Stokell, Neddy Thompson, and Emma Casapia Salas for friendship and steadfastness on the path as well as great editorial support. To magical artist and soul sister, Francene Hart I send love and gratitude for the gift of awakening through sacred art. Great appreciation for ever-increasing expertise in design and layout goes to Leanne Krause of Silverlining Designs. And last, but never least, love and gratitude go to all of my students around the world, and to those who have traveled with me on sacred journeys, for their self-motivation, and dedication to their own awakening and healing.

JEA

Table of Contents

Forward: Introduction   11

PART ONE
Awakening the Rainbow Body

1. The Path of Liberation   17
2. Awakening Memory   31
3. The Rainbow Body   57
4. The Art of Moving Energy   85

PART TWO
Healing the Rainbow Body

5. Physical Fitness   99
6. Etheric Fitness   125
7. Emotional Fitness   139
8. Emotional-Mental Fitness   159
9. Intellectual-Mental Fitness   183
10. Spiritual-Mental Fitness   207

Epilogue: The Penthouse   227

Glossary of Terms   231

liberation!

INTRODUCTION

    Welcome to the path of liberation. Each of us walks a uniquely beautiful path to enlightenment - self-realization. However, there are universal truths that bind all paths together. There are certain passages, portals of awareness, transited by all those who seek higher consciousness. Those drawn to the path I describe herein have chosen an autonomous path to God – one without guru, priest or hierarchy. Yet, the wisdom, truth, and technique this path holds are applicable to any path.

    If you are inclined to self-reliance, welcome aboard. If you prefer to follow a spiritual guru, enrich that path with this wisdom. In any case, take what is yours and leave the rest behind. Please remember this is not about giving your power to anyone else. This is about your personal relationship with the Divine. My task is to awaken truth within you – the rest is up to you.

    This path was not laid out before me. I have never received direct teachings from the Andean Elders who continue to be my guides, though the energetic transmissions they have imparted have been powerful awakeners. I was blessed to work with Américo Yábar who is a bridge to the Q'ero nation in Peru, and who has, in the past, brought the Andean teachings to us in the United States. Additionally, I have studied many paths and healing modalities during my earthwalk. All of them contribute in some way to this work because some of the truths upon which those paths were founded worked for me. I do not channel, or generally recommend channeled material, because it accesses the astral. However, I do suggest that we can learn to connect with our higher self, a part of us capable of guiding us from wisdom, truth, and the frequencies of mastery.

This is a path that walks in the world, moving energy on behalf of the greater Mission – that shift into higher consciousness that we all came to participate in. I see goodness and grace in all religions and new age movements. I also see the flaws inherent in all institutions - the loss of freedom, human frailty, and now days, the marketing strategies that dominate our materialistic world. As a disheartened young adult, turning away from religion, I received a very strong message from my internal guidance system – "never join anything." I have adhered to that guidance and have not regretted it for a single moment. Consequently, this path cannot be "joined." However, it can be embraced in part or in its totality.

It is life itself that has given me this path and continues to guide me as I walk it. Life, once an adversary, is now the teacher. Admittedly, I have been gifted in two ways. Firstly, since childhood, I have cultivated the art of observation – one of many keys to success on this path. Secondly, I have always known my truth and have allowed it to guide me. Likewise, your own gifts will have given you unique keys to mastery that will become important to you on your journey to higher consciousness. Don't be afraid of that which is inherently yours. Cultivate and use your gifts.

Within the pages of this book and all of the related material, the intent is to weave the filaments of magical transformation - a way of holding space for you while you do your spiritual work. It is what I would do in circle with you, drawing on the support of your higher self, your guides, and all the masters of consciousness who have gone before us. If it feels right to you, intend that connection for yourself each time you pick up the material. Ask to be guided towards your truth, your Essence, and your mission.

Introduction

As we work our way through this book, we will see that enlightenment – indeed, life itself – is all about light/energy. We will come to understand energy and its relationship to our multidimensional bodies of light/energy. This book, *Awakening and Healing the Rainbow Body*, works at the level of thought form – the fourth dimensional matrix and blueprint of this reality. My hope for you is that self-realization will be attained. Self-realization, to be explored further throughout this text, is a stage of enlightenment often called "lightbody." I will also refer to it as fourth dimensional mastery.

A second book, *Awakening and Healing the Rainbow Body Companion Guide to Self Mastery*, will soon follow this publication. In this guidebook, you will find chapter by chapter guidance, with further examples, detailed exercises, and additional, less formal teaching. This companion guide, written in the second person, to you, will support and expand your understanding of the work. In the guidebook, there will be instructions to access web support for those working on their own or in their own groups.

Additionally, the shifts in frequency within the *Deep Trance Shamanic Journey* compact disc audio series open the doors to the fourth dimension. You will find references to these important journeys in the text. Accessing fourth dimension, the unconscious, after we have completed the cognitive work in this reality, is critical to complete healing. The third compact disc in the journey series, *Reclaiming Our Power*, will complete the journeys necessary for this fourth dimensional work. Its publication will follow the companion guide.

Awakening and Healing the Rainbow Body opens us to fourth dimensional awareness and takes us to the portal of fifth dimension. The work contained in this text, and the companion guide, is tremendously empowering and capable of activating gifts that we were meant to bring to earth. It may take years to complete this work – or lifetimes. We all have a timing that deserves our respect. If our soul designed that we become enlightened in this lifetime, it will happen. It is our choice whether to attain that self-realization with pain and suffering (the dark night of the soul) or ease and grace. This is a path of responsible hard work, but it is with ease and grace that we approach it.

Awakening and Healing the Rainbow Body

To avoid the loss of motivation so necessary for the work, I suggest periodically reading the Spiritual-Mental Fitness chapter at the end of this book to reconnect with the vibrations of attainment. It is good to remember where this part of the journey ends. In addition, it is not expected that key words or phrases be instantly remembered and recalled in this work. A comprehensive glossary of extraordinary key words and phrases is located at the end of the book. Please use it.

If you are carrying light codes of consciousness for this time of planetary ascension, they will be activated and released as you do your work. These codes are embedded in the rainbow body scaffolding, and what it takes to activate and release them is *the work*. Anyone who has walked a path to self-realization understands that there is no substitution for *the work*. On that note, with grace and ease, let us begin.

Jessie E. Ayani
Witsun, Full Moon in Gemini
June 3rd, 2004

PART ONE

Awakening the Rainbow Body

Let us remember...

We are the Sons and Daughters of the Kings and Queens of Light.

Enlightenment is our attainable inheritance.

THE PATH OF LIBERATION

We are beginning to walk a path of direct connection to God. It puts us in the driver's seat of our own enlightenment. Though religion has given us a moral foundation that supports brotherly love, faith, and hope, it has also led us to believe that God can be inaccessible, fearsome, and judgmental. Though upholding the need to live by ethical and moral codes, this path contradicts all of the fear-based beliefs acquired through religious experience, and asks us to live to our fullest potential as a vital and aware part of God.

Those of us attracted to this path have missions that require us to work in the world rather than to hold light for the planet in a monastic setting or a mountain cave. We are being asked to embody the Divine – right down to the soles of our feet. This means that the lower energy centers (constituting the first three chakras in the Hindu teaching), where the nitty-gritty of life takes place, must be prepared to hold Divine Light. This is our work together of awakening and healing the rainbow body.

Few paths described and practiced on this earth delve deeper than the higher energy centers (constituting the throat, third eye and crown chakras in the Hindu teaching). Meditation and metaphysical thought have their place on the path to self-realization, but holding the Divine only in the higher centers is not the same as embodying the Divine on earth, which is the greater Mission. Focusing energy in the higher centers not only ignores the heart, our central energy center, it can lead to a loss of grounding in the earth's field, a vastly expanded spiritual ego, and a desire to be elsewhere – "home." This is home. The Mission is here and now.

This path of liberation has some powerful attributes. Among these are autonomy, detachment, surrender, fluidity, fearlessness, impeccability, and attention. This path asks us to live heaven on earth with every breath and step we take in our lives, and with our whole heart and soul. It requires consciousness and commitment. It promises liberation and light.

Autonomy

Let's look at each of those hallmarks in depth, beginning with autonomy. Autonomy is defined as self-government. When we allow others to govern us, we voluntarily give our power to them. We do this every day because we are connected to the experience of humankind that is embedded in the collective unconscious. Humans have not been fully autonomous since long-ago times when a powerful amnesia swept over the beings of the earth. What our legends call "The Fall" left humanity subject to death, karma and reincarnation – third dimensional awareness.

As a result, we have been slaves of body, mind, and spirit to forces we have not been able to conceptualize. These forces exist in the fourth dimension – the unconscious. The leaders of old served yet another hierarchy of the gods. There was a time, an ancient time, when autonomous beings arrived and left the earth in fifth dimensional consciousness – of their own accord. Those levels of autonomy will come again to earth as we raise our consciousness beyond the limitations of the amnesia.

On this journey together, we will explore the tragic loss of power experienced as part of that amnesia, but also the conscious art of disconnecting from the unconscious controlling forces. We will walk the path of reclaiming our rightful ascension – in life or death. This book is meant to be a consciousness guide for the inevitable journey through the fourth dimension – a journey essential to the eventual reclamation of our inherent God-Self.

In this book, we are interested in how to reclaim that inherent power, how to lift the veil of that amnesia and live consciously upon the earth. The task, in fact, is to bring heaven to earth – to embody the Divine, which is our birthright. This work is very much about remembering and reclaiming who we already are. Autonomy is key to this reclamation because the accomplishment of this task requires that we listen to our higher self - our inner truth and guide – and take responsibility for our own lives. That is what self-governance is all about.

Taking responsibility for our lives means that we cease to blame others for the circumstances or events of our lives. The simple truth is that we planned it all. We chose our parents, siblings, friends, foes and all we have experienced with them for the growth of our soul. When we take responsibility for ourselves, we are able to transform. As long as we hold ourselves in patterns of blame we, as well as those we blame, are in "the box" – the limitation of third dimensional reality where the amnesia exists. We are subject to limitation, and that is not autonomy.

In ceasing to blame others, we not only reclaim our own power, we free them to their own path of awakening. One of the most powerful acts of mental "black magic" is to hold another person in judgment, which must, necessarily, be in place before one can blame another. The act of judgment, faced in depth in a later chapter, places limitations on others and self. It is a defining factor in "the box." We will work with judgment when exploring the mental body. For now, we will hold an awareness that our need to judge those we blame will have to shift to make autonomy one of our own qualities.

To sum up, autonomy is about taking responsibility for our actions and thoughts, and being free from the attachments to others brought on by those actions and thoughts. It is also about the art of self-observation and self-correction, a concept to be introduced and honed on our journey together. At higher levels of conscious existence, autonomy is essential to the connection with our own internal master – governance originating from higher self.

Detachment

The word detachment can make us feel nervous. It seems a normal reaction in a culture so materialistically bound, and emotionally entangled. Detachment brings forth our insecurities, which are driven by one of our deepest fears - survival. This fear has led us to develop very resourceful ways in which to get our needs met. Most of these survival techniques are manipulative of others. Taking responsibility for the ways in which we meet our needs is another matter. For any seeker of enlightenment, detachment represents the door through which we might escape from "the box."

Our traditional entry and exit from "the box" can be called birth and death. Within the rules of the physical world – "the box" – we come into this world alone and leave this world alone. Detachment is forced on us, whether we like it or not. Why wait until the moment of death to release our attachment to this reality? Why must we die in pain and fear? When the Tibetans speak of the bardos,[1] the wrenching and often frightening levels of consciousness that we pass through when leaving this reality, they are, in part, referencing the forced detachment from all of our life experience. The journey of death includes the passage through our own fourth dimension, our unconscious, which necessarily occurs in death.

In this ultimate detachment, a life review is forced upon the consciousness and all that we have stored as memory within our own unconscious (the repository of life experience), or have chosen to ignore or suppress in this reality, is revealed. To the ill prepared, the experience of death is the ultimate fear. Those who die suddenly have the added burden of shock – suddenly thrust into another reality without contemplation or preparation. Additionally, the inevitable confrontation with the collective unconscious, which is rich in the collective experience of mankind and every conceivable thought form within that experience, contributes to the bardo experience and to the endless cycles of karma that bind us to the fourth dimension and incarnation.

On the level of energy, the rules of "the box" do not apply. Those who leave the earth can be fully or partially entangled with those they have left behind. Death may look like an ending, but it is not. The attached beings must learn to detach from fourth dimension, and typically are soon incarnate once again to play out the dramas of life. Until we break the

The Path of Liberation

karmic cycle, jumping off the wheel of karma entirely by claiming our enlightenment, we are subject to this seemingly endless entrapment. This path is about breaking those cycles. It is, literally, preparation for conscious dying, which is an ascension.

Paramount in this preparation is the exercise of detachment. It does not mean that we are not connected to the people in our life or in death. It means we are not attached – not dependent. It does not mean that we cannot have material possessions. It means that they do not possess us. It does not mean that events of life will not go on. It means that we have no attachment to the outcome. When a child is born in the Andes, the father takes the child in his hands and, walking out upon the earth, offers the child to *Pachamama* (Mother Earth) and the *Apus* (the Mountain Spirits), as its true parents. In our culture, we begin making plans for the child's education and athletic success. Detachment means dropping agendas, giving space to a greater energy of guidance.

As this work unfolds, we will find it necessary to first recall and reclaim much of our life experience before detaching from it. This requires accessing memory, and the result is often soul retrieval – picking up the pieces of our consciousness lost in trauma in this lifetime. More correctly, it is the work of *reconnecting* with our souls by accessing and healing past experience. Retrieving our soul is not something we want to assign to someone else, though guidance is often helpful. We seem eager to give our power away for a quick fix, but, too often, doing so does not provide lasting healing.

We have our personal storage bin in fourth dimensional reality where we have stashed our experiences long forgotten. In death, those experiences must be claimed as the consciousness is released. Our work is to claim it now by taking responsibility for it, and detaching from it. This opens the fourth dimension to us – for mastery. We will find that the fourth dimension must be mastered (self-mastery) to access the fifth dimension where we enter training for the attainment of Christ Consciousness.

The sorcerers are masters of fourth dimensional reality. The have left us a legacy of that mastery that we can apply to our passage through fourth dimension to the higher dimensions. Though our intent is not to embrace sorcery, we will use many of their tools at this level of the work because they are highly successful. Before he died, Carlos Casteneda wrote an amazing book entitled *The Active Side of Infinity*.[2] There is a passage in Casteneda's book that refers to death. To paraphrase: At the moment of death we are sucked into the fourth dimension (the dark stream of awareness; also the collective unconscious), which takes from us our life force and our life experience. All that the fourth dimension wants from us is our experience, which is the ground substance (thought form) of the collective unconscious. If, in life, we are able to give that experience to the fourth dimension, there may come the opportunity to retain our life force at the moment of death. Note that this is my interpretation. To the sorcerers, the work of conscious dying is called preparation for touching the Infinite.

The work of giving our experience to the collective while still alive is called detachment. The Masters who ascended with their bodies had first to master this level of awareness. Because they had taken their consciousness in life to the higher dimensions, they are now part of fifth dimensional awareness and beyond. In other words, fourth dimension must be mastered for our consciousness to become fifth dimensional. This step frees us from the burden of the unconscious imposed at "The Fall."

Surrender

If detachment symbolizes the door leading out of " the box," surrender represents the hinges on that door. Detachment allows surrender to actually open the door. Surrender is the art and act of letting go. It allows magic to happen in our lives. It allows the Divine Plan to unfold. The Divine Plan aligns us with the purpose of our soul on earth. What stands in the way of this natural unfoldment is fear. To the average person, the game of life is not about the magical revelation of the soul's mission. To the average person, life is about survival, and beyond survival it is about comfort and the fulfillment of desire.

Survival requires that an enormous amount of available energy be allocated to control life. Even though this concept seems absurd to the initiate, the complexity of human behavior establishes control mechanisms in all layers of the rainbow body, and none of us have escaped the human experience. It starts the day we are conceived. This work is about liberation

The Path of Liberation

- about freeing our selves from restriction, and allowing surrender to take its course. We will examine the conscious and unconscious ways in which we get our needs met in this work. It is a wonderful way to begin understanding our lives.

The mechanisms of control and the restrictions that our desires impose on us are not just responsible for our emotionally based behavior patterns. They pollute our minds with endless dialogue, worry, and regret. Fortunately, there is, in this work, hope for liberation from this servitude. This freedom will not happen because God has shown mercy on us, or because our guru has agreed to eat it all up for us, but rather through the diligent efforts of conscious self-observation and self-correction. Surrender frees us of limitation.

What happens when the door of "the box" creaks open, giving us a glimpse of fourth dimension? Initially, the realm of fourth dimension reveals itself, and for many it is not easy to face the past. Fearlessness can help us own the totality of our experience. The resistance we feel is just the ego's investment in the status quo. We must be ruthless with ego in owning our experience. At the same time, we must learn the value of living virtuously in our everyday lives. If we can learn to inform ourselves from virtue rather than desire, we will accelerate our journey on the spiritual path.

Though all the virtues have value on the path, the most critical virtues to adopt while working through the fourth dimension are humility, acceptance and gratitude. Humility allows us to accept the ego pain that is part of self-realization. Acceptance is essential to owning the fact that we call all of the people and events of our life to us. Gratitude permits us to see beyond the discipline and hard work of the path. When we see beyond the illusion, we access aspects of ourselves that we have never previously known At the same time we have been in the bondage of the amnesia, we have always been free. We have always been masters longing for conscious connection.

Surrender is also one of the virtues. As surrender begins to replace control in our lives, magical things begin to occur. With surrender, we will find that our path defines itself, rather than we defining it. It will seem all to perfect a fit for us – the magic unfolding. Surrender facilitates our connection with our own Divine Plan guided by the Original Birth

Awakening and Healing the Rainbow Body

Template – the light-geometric architecture of the soul. What more encouragement do we need to surrender?

Fluidity

Let's examine the concept of flow. Just as detachment allows surrender, surrender allows fluidity. There is a flow to the Divine Plan - a timing and sequence unknown to us until we have merged with the wisdom of our soul's blueprint for this life – our Original Birth Template. Life stands between our third-dimensional consciousness and our soul. As we work to clear our lives – to own them, detach from them, and give them to the unconscious, we will draw our soul towards us and become more aligned with our original life blueprint. Casteneda refers to this alignment as our glow of awareness – the perfect alignment of our rainbow body with the soul's template and its concurrent flow of energy (my interpretation). We are born with our glow of awareness, then life eats it away – primarily through energy loss to fourth dimension and the consciousness lost to the living of life. As adults, we are in grace to have a glimmer of that awareness.

We must take a small diversion from fluidity to discuss the concept of predatory energy. The energy loss to the fourth dimension, described above, feeds energetic beings that the sorcerers refer to as predators. For now, the easiest way to imagine predators is as thought-form constructs capable of consuming human energies that are not properly (consciously) managed. Energies of emotional drama and mental obsession are two examples of predatory "food sources." Casteneda speaks extensively of predatory energy in *The Active Side of Infinity*, and we will discuss it many times over as this book continues. The predators are real in fourth dimension, most likely coming into being with the creation of the fourth dimension at the time of "The Fall." At that time the predators could have been opportunistic thought-form constructs that took advantage of the inception of a thought-field reality like fourth dimension. Alternatively, they could be the thought-form constructs of "those" who caused the human amnesia – "The Fall."

Perhaps the reason for "The Fall" was to imprison humanity through loss of memory to create an energy source for these thought-form constructs and whatever may be feeding off of them. In this work it

The Path of Liberation

is essential to recognize that they do exist. At the same time we must cease to give our energy away to them through unconscious living, which precludes the generation of fearfulness about their existence. The realization that we have been masters on this earth before, and can regain that mastery, is important. Applying ourselves to this work will help us regain our glow of awareness, and our mastery. The predators have no interest in energy that is difficult to obtain because there is so much easily obtained energy generated on the earth every second of every day. Anyone who has recovered all or part of their glow of awareness (who is or is becoming conscious) ceases to be a target for their predation.

Now, we return to fluidity. Much of what we will learn about our rainbow body has to do with fluidity because our multi-dimensional architecture must be fluid, in numerous ways, for us to maintain health and expand awareness. The application of a metaphor commonly used with the spiritual work is appropriate at this point. The metaphor is bamboo. We are hollowing ourselves out, making space for energy/light. After the gross innards of the bamboo have been removed, there comes the persistent honing of the core; the removal of limitations. Finally, there comes the meticulous removal of the fine, grasping fibers at each joint of the bamboo – a metaphorical way to put the elusive work of taming and integrating the ego. Water flows unobstructed through the empty bamboo. Similarly, the self-realized human becomes a conduit for consciousness – the glow of awareness. We are designed as energy conduits, but where is the energy going? How is it being lost? These are the kinds of questions to be asking as the work progresses.

Flexibility, another way to look at this attribute, is as important as the concept of fluidity. Obviously, it also requires the relinquishing of control through surrender. When we discuss our core beliefs, this will be reiterated and expanded upon. The beliefs that create our reality become our limitations. Flexibility at the level of mastery infers an ability to shift reality by changing our core beliefs without hesitation. Since those of us pursuing this path are no longer living oblivious or unconscious lives, the places where we plateau or get stuck with our work are our obvious limitations. With earnest work, our fortunes will change and limitations will be overcome; but not if we live in fear.

Awakening and Healing the Rainbow Body

Fearlessness

Love and fear cannot co-exist. Fear is the absence of love. If we have fear, then what we are calling love is something else. It is not love as it flows from the Divine. In the Andes, there is a word, *munay*, which translates loving power. *Munay* does not resemble love as our culture defines love. *Munay* is a force, or a force-field, that projects a fifth dimensional frequency. In the presence of *munay*, we feel loved by Source; we open our hearts; we love those around us in ways not previously experienced. Jesus had *munay*. *Munay* accounts for the magnetism present between Jesus and all of those who dropped what they were doing to be in his presence. When he asked people to give up their lives to follow him, he was asking people to open their hearts to live in love, not to physically follow him all over Galilee. To embody this love, one must be fearless. In our world, love comes with agendas. As we do this important work together, we will dig deeply to identify the fear-based core beliefs at the root of those agendas for they must be changed.

From the fundamental fear of survival two dominant fears manifest -- the fear of the unknown (death or the future), and the fear of alienation or separation (not being accepted, being abandoned or forgotten). Lesser fears are then projected from these two principal fears. Where do these base fears originate? They originate from incarnation. When we lost our ability to come and go from the earth as masters ("The Fall"), we became slaves to birth and death and the loss of memory that accompanies incarnation on the earth plane (third dimension). Survival becomes the overwhelming issue from the moment we initiate the birth process.

Though babies are most often born with their glow of awareness, the structures inherent within "the box" dim the lights immediately because they are born into a world dominated by fear. We live with images of a punishing God and human suffering. We cannot remember who we are, or why we so willingly agreed to incarnate on the earth. We compete, dominate, and exclude because of survival. All of the issues we are discussing in this text become global. The only pulse of pure love available to most of us is the newborn's glow of awareness and, energetically, we can devour it with a voracious hunger. We unconsciously possess our children in many ways, and take control of their lives. Our disconnection from true love can unconsciously lead us to rob our children of their soul's awareness.

This is but one example of the fundamental shifts necessary for global ascension. It does not paint a pretty picture of our world, but as long as humanity lives in fear, fear will persist and the destiny and potential mastery of humanity, our nations, and the earth will be thwarted.

This path progresses to heart opening. Fearlessness is necessary to break through the cage around the heart, smoothing one more section of the bamboo to allow the flow of love. Fearlessness also allows us to access courage and qualities like valor - personal bravery in the face of all odds. Valor carries the vibration of freedom and often opens the doors of liberation. Valor springs from a belief in the truth and a willingness to stand in it – to embody it. Such qualities would serve each of us well on this path.

In a similar vein, I am often asked how I feel about the state of the world we live in, and what I am doing to constructively promote peace. To these inquiries, I must reply honestly. Many ways exist to demonstrate good intentions, but good intentions have limited power. Intentions are thought forms - thought forms of peace, or love, or compassion. Thought forms have power in the fourth dimension, which can manifest in this dimension. However, our third dimensional reality is an illusion created by those thought forms and the translation of those thought forms into this reality is bound to be distorted by that illusion. If we want to move beyond the illusion into the higher frequencies, intent is the energy required to manifest the actual absence of fear and presence of love – the fifth dimension. This manifestation would naturally create peace.

If peace is our desire, then we must become peace, and the world will change accordingly. If we remove all conflict, judgment, opinion, criticism, suffering, and self-pity from our lives, we will become a force of peace upon the earth. Those who wage war are providing us with mirrors of the adversarial relationships which dominate our lives and our culture. We have been trained to face all of life as an adversary. It is obvious to see this in our competitive need to win and in our judgments and opinions. However, in a more abstract way we can detect an adversarial approach in the accepted stream of life. For example, our predominant medical system has, historically, created drugs to combat illness rather than utilizing the intelligent and gentle practice of prevention. Negative thought patterns predominate in our culture – a fact that is reinforced daily by our news media. Currently, as a collective, positive news would bore us.

Peace demands accountability. Accountability means that we walk our talk; that we embody what we say we believe in. The same is true for love, compassion, and any number of desperately needed positive energies on earth. Our ability to change the world rests on our mastery over our lower, unconscious self, and not on good intentions. We must reclaim our power (our consciousness) to fulfill our missions. Essential to the reclamation of that power is the quality of fearlessness.

Impeccability

To be impeccable is to be beyond reproach. For example, the impeccable person publicly advocating freedom and independence cannot privately exercise tight control over his family. Impeccability demands that we walk that talk, that we live in our truth, and that we are accountable for our actions. Webster's dictionary defines impeccable as being incapable of sin, but sin is the creation of fear-based religion. That will not work for us here. Here we are speaking of a truth beyond religion – the same truth that would illicit valor. It is a truth born of Essence, untouched by the world and the controls imposed by the status quo. It manifests as integrity and authenticity. Authenticity, simply put, is living a life in keeping with the soul's values, truth and purpose.

Impeccability demands that accountability; the willingness to take responsibility for our every thought and action. It is a hard-won attribute for the best of us, yet we are quick to demand it of those to whom we give away our power. Why would it be any different than peace, love or compassion? If we want impeccability in leadership, we must embody it ourselves. Our world is simply a reflection of our selves. If we want change, we begin at home.

Finding and aligning with our truth is the most difficult aspect of embodying impeccability. If we are not born knowing our truth (as few are), life becomes an exercise in discernment, until we gradually come to know what does and doesn't resonate with us. Once we understand this aspect of the work, we can open to truth through the signals in the body that announce its presence - the shiver up our spine, or our hair standing

The Path of Liberation

on end, for example. Soon, truth becomes our ally. Discernment and the processing it requires is no longer necessary. A "knowingness," very much connected to feelings, takes its place.

Attention

Attention is being present. It does not ruminate over the past. It does not have a plan of the future. It is now. We live in a world of distractions, not the least of which are our internal dialogues and our external dramas. To become self-realized, we must, ultimately, still the mind and emotions to arrive at a state of serenity - peace.

For stillness too occur, ego must yield to higher self. Though the focus of later chapters in this book, it is good to mention ego here because it is difficult for some of us to conceptualize, much less understand. Until we come to know ego better we will think of it as self. Self is a simplistic definition but relevant, since we live in world of near consummate self-absorption. The wants, needs, and desires of self prevent us from attaining the stillness. It is how our world has become and what we most need to change about it. To change our world, we must focus intent - attention. In the case of those lost to self-absorption, any attention at all would be a huge awakening.

If we attune to the emotional work and succeed in clearing away our past, we will find ourselves with a lightness of being. If we clear the mind of internal dialogue by consciously and energetically clearing the mental field of thought patterning, we will arrive at the silence. It is, for example, an amazing state of grace to be free of criticism and opinion. Then life, itself, becomes a meditation.

What sort of consciousness leap does it take to chip away at our self-absorption? It takes awareness and vigilance – attention. Attention encompasses self-observation and self-correction – major skills required to walk this path. Because it allows us to be truly present for others with heart energy flowing, attention is a highly regarded attribute of the path. However, attention is rarely understood because those who have attained that level of awareness value invisibility over recognition. Invisibility is higher self's way of keeping the ego in check. Those who are invisible do not seek recognition, praise, attention, or credit for what they do or who they are. They are content with anonymity, with being part of something

Awakening and Healing the Rainbow Body

much greater than self. This creates a space where energy can be moved without obstruction on behalf of the greater Mission.

In the space of the now moment, being wholly present, we can find the God within us and pass through the blazing portal of self-realization, what I will call the eye of the needle, to open our hearts. Our journey through the fourth dimension will lead us to the needle's eye. All of the attributes thus described will be needed to successfully pass through. It is a small death followed by a resurrection into the eternal love of an open heart.

---

[1] The Tibetan Book of Living and Dying, Sogyal Rinpoche, Harper San Francisco, 1992.

[2] The Active Side of Infinity, Carlos Casteneda, Harper Perennial, 1998.

AWAKENING MEMORY

To awaken is to activate memory. At some consciousness level, we know who we are, but our birth into the human family causes a great amnesia of that truth. To awaken is to lift the veil of that amnesia to remember our true nature. Who are we? We are everything and nothing. We are human and Divine. We are the earth, and we are the cosmos. Enlightenment is a process of gradually expanding consciousness to embody our God-self. If we could become conscious of ourselves as God we would never feel alone again.

It is not difficult to accept that a few limitations have to fall by the wayside on this quest – not the least of which are beliefs that it is not possible for us to become God-realized. One of the great steps along the way is self-realization, the awareness of our own presence and place in the grand scheme of things. Self-realization, the mastery of the fourth dimension (the unconscious) opens the doors to higher consciousness. Mastering fourth dimension is the work we are here to do together.

It is time to begin thinking of our selves as light/energy. As this text progresses we will likely abandon any other way of knowing our selves. All of the limitations existing for us appear, energetically, as a rigid

Awakening and Healing the Rainbow Body

luminous body, which holds our energy and consciousness within a tightly compressed field. Eliminating the limitations allows expansion of our luminous bodies, which map the limit of our awareness. All of the baggage picked up in this life is stored in our energy bodies, adding weight to the inertia. Herein, the tools will be given to change our lives – to cast away everything that limits us from being who we came to earth to be. We will clear away the heavy baggage to make way for light – actually coming to embody light. Coming into "lightbody" is a multilevel experience paralleling our journey through the fourth dimension.

Frequency and Ascension

When most of us hear the word ascension, we immediately conjure up the picture of Jesus rising into the clouds, free of earth's suffering and pain forever. We have, in our mythology, the notion that heaven is "up there" somewhere and that hell is "down there" somewhere. In reality, the dimensions (heaven being a reference to the fifth dimension) are everywhere because the universe exists as a hologram. Our luminous fields are holographic microcosms of that universe projected by levels of conscious awareness. We will learn that our soul consciousness creates our third and fourth dimensional bodies. We are light/energy, as is all of creation.

There are many steps in the ascension process, which is the raising of frequency through the embodiment of light. In conscious death there can be an ascension – the soul freeing itself from the grasp of the lower astral of the fourth dimension. We will learn that those who die consciously are then consciously reborn into wisdom, truth, and the other attributes of the upper astral of the fourth dimension. It does not mean that they will chose lives of spiritual greatness (as the ego might measure greatness) for many will have ordinary, but conscious lives. It does not mean they will not have consciousness work to do, because life will happen to them regardless. They will likely be in advanced training in the school of life – not necessarily an easy assignment. When the initial portal to spiritual awakening appears, their conscious passage through it may thrust them urgently and intensely into the fourth dimensional work.

Ascension implies expanded consciousness. In truth, higher frequency energies are descending into human form, anchoring more of

Awakening Memory

the Divine on earth. In some ways we can see enlightenment as a "descension" of spirit into matter. On this path we are both ascending and descending. The Star of David symbolizes that union between heaven and earth. One of the equilateral triangles represents the energies of expansion and ascension and the other represents the anchoring of the descending Divine Light. Together they represent heaven on earth.

When Jesus took leave of the earth, his mastery allowed him to elevate the frequency of his cellular structure to levels beyond the visible. He was not the only one to have left in the ancient way. In his ascension the levels of frequency elevation were well beyond the visible, but one could contemplate the elevation into a fourth dimensional frequency to begin with – the mastery level of the sorcerers. The sorcerer's are important to us because they pursue fourth dimensional mastery, and we must master fourth dimension to attain higher consciousness. It must be said that ascension is no less complete should one chose to leave the body behind in full ascension. For many, that is the most expedient way to complete the detachment from this world.

A good way to visualize ascension and frequency is through a well-known scientific fact. In our third dimensional world, physics has described the visible spectrum of light – from red to violet. The nerve receptors in our eyes receive frequencies within the visible spectrum, which are transmitted to the brain for imaging. We humans see in the colors of the spectrum. However, scientific instruments can detect infrared and ultraviolet frequencies existing beyond the visual capabilities of our eyes. We know these frequencies exist but we cannot physically see them.

In truth, infinite frequencies exist but on earth, in third dimension, we are limited in our vision to this small but dazzling spectrum. What happens when we attend to our spiritual work and begin incorporating more light into our field? At first the light will fill the vast spaces of our higher dimensional matrix, but, in time, it will begin to penetrate and shift the physical body with the soft, but noticeable, glow of awareness.

With mastery, frequency can easily be raised beyond the visible spectrum and lowered back again at will. Jesus, the mysterious Saint Germain, and the Immortal Himalayan Master Babaji are three examples worthy of investigation.[1,2,3] Though we must save the details of this work for mastery-level awareness, know that there are those who have

Awakening and Healing the Rainbow Body

witnessed the materialization of the Masters in many cultures around the world. The Ascended Masters do exist and reveal ascension to us. Every step we take along this path allows more light and frequency to enter. We are in a process of ascension.

Initiation

We may hear and read a lot about initiation. For obvious reasons, the initiatory journeys of the indigenous shamans do not translate well into our culture. Where there was no hierarchy, we create hierarchy. Many "shamans" have come to our culture marketing initiation to sincere spiritual seekers. Outwardly, our egos embrace this external assistance on our quest along with the "priestly" or "healer" identity that accompanies initiation. Inwardly however, the longing to know who we are in this very confusing and rarely affirming world is unresolved. Though energetic support is the principle gift of the Elders in the Andes, let me share a bit of their spoken wisdom - their simplistic truth about initiation. Life is the great initiator, period. Life provides the opportunities for mastery and the opportunities to touch higher consciousness, if only for a precious moment. When we experience these moments, our lives are irreversibly changed – our reality shifts. That is initiation.

We can learn from the marketed "initiation" and may call that to us for important realizations. We can learn discernment for future encounters. We can learn to master jealousy when our friends are given a "higher" status than our own. We can learn detachment when we realize, in all honesty, that we have not suddenly become great healers, or visionaries, or whatever was promised to us. Life and its lessons persist. We still have our work. We chose these great gifts of self-awareness, which our soul draws to us in our life, in order to learn detachment without pain, projection, or self-pity. Silence and invisibility are amongst the powers of magic and mastery, to be approached in our future work. For now, we learn to exercise discernment.

How does life initiate us? If enlightenment is to be ours, specific initiatory gateways must be transited. On this path, these gateways are described by assigning them to the four earth elements, earth, water, wind and fire. Many smaller shifts in consciousness occur as we engage the fourth dimensional work of water and air, but the mastery of these two elements is coincident with self-realization. The gateways, however they might be described, are identical energetically on all spiritual paths.

We experience an invitational gateway when we are catapulted onto our spiritual paths. We must write or speak about the event. We must honor it in every way and all of the individuals who facilitated this greatest of initiations for us. Sometimes these wake-up calls are subtle shifts of consciousness but quite often they are rude awakenings with considerable sting. Styles do vary in the spiritual work.

Fortunately, hard styles can be softened as we change our reality. There is no need for suffering. If we have not yet shown our gratitude to those who assisted our awakening, it is never too late to lavish it upon them.

Water

Water is the element of emotion. Emotions and feelings are two very different things. A feeling is something organic occurring in the body at a cellular level. Feelings of fear, for example, are cold and sinking. Feelings of anger, conversely, are hot and rising. When feelings occur, they send signals through our multidimensional body to our unconscious (subconscious), where we have stored all of our past experience and relevant information. When the feeling meets the experiential archives, an emotion is formed as energy. Our emotional body expresses this energy as an emotional reaction, usually with verbal projections to reinforce it. Though we will explore this in depth in later chapters it is fundamental to understanding the water initiation, and so it is presented here as well.

What would happen if the past experiences, the energetic triggers of reaction, stored in the unconscious were suddenly to disappear? This would be similar to amnesia. We would not remember how to react, only how to feel. Each of our experiences would be akin to that of a newborn – pure, and in the glow of awareness. This is our journey together. The water initiation demands that we move out of emotion, out of reaction, and into our feelings, which are links to the Divine. Two chapters of this book are devoted to the water initiation. We will liberate our selves from our past, clear it from our unconscious, and regain the powerful awareness of our own energetic nature.

Awakening and Healing the Rainbow Body

Because we are not in this place of energetic awareness, dramas play out in our lives and energy is lost to this drama. When unaware, our emotional bodies are particularly easy targets for energy loss to fourth dimensional predators. These are the energetic thought forms, which can prey on our energy from the unconscious. Energy can be taken directly, most commonly through addiction, or indirectly, through emotional reaction. We will discuss predation extensively in further chapters but it is mentioned here to emphasize the importance of disengaging emotional reaction to conserve our precious energy.

In this work, we will find that our egos are consummately invested in controlling our lives. Our egos are great dramatists without conscious awareness of their acting. Engaging the ego in combat constitutes a poor tactical choice in this work. Instead, we will engage the ego in self-discovery, preoccupying it while the power of higher self begins to guide us. The result can be a successful disengagement from the emotional drama, good direction from higher self, and more opportunities to experience tranquility. With self-observation and self-correction, we can repair the leaks and distortions in our emotional field, and become conduits, like the bamboo, for the Christ Light to enter the earth without fourth dimensional interference.

Wind

Wind, or the air element, is associated with our brain's capacity to store and access information, our ability to process the information, and our ability to communicate it through language or action. Information storage and processing are most often unconscious – taken for granted or automatic. The wind initiation demands that we "lose our minds." How do we lose something so integral to survival, communication, and the human experience? We work with awareness – bringing what is unconscious into consciousness and deciding whether it is useful or not. We work with detachment from our need to be right, successful, validated, smarter than, and so forth. Naturally, the ego plays a big role in the mental field. Our work relies completely on self-observation and self-correction. The water initiation process helps to loosen some of the grip that the mind has on us. Our emotional work, well done, eliminates the need for much of the information we store. What we are left to deal with are the foundations of judgment, criticism and opinion and the mental internal dialogue.

Having honed the skills of self-observation during the emotional work we will turn our observer's eyes and ears to our thoughts. Spoken or not, thoughts have a power equal to or greater than emotional reactions because fourth dimension, both our own and the collective unconscious, is thought field. It acts as a conduit for thought through a medium astonishingly cluttered with our own experience or, in the case of the collective, with the collective experience of humanity. We will learn to dissociate from mythic, archetypal behavior patterns left over from the Greek and Roman period – the last time our culture had myth. We will, in subtle and meaningful ways, pull away from the predominant cultural imprinting to create a new reality based on positive thought. What we think *does* matter. Self-observation and self-correction will reveal our thoughts to us for responsible transformation.

Our goal is to arrive at the gate of fire, the eye of the needle, in good physical condition, without baggage, with a free mind, and a well-managed ego. As we will see, fitness at the physical and etheric body levels is also important since limitations of the body and its energy system can sabotage a perfectly good mission. How will we feel? The feeling is liberation, and it brings with it plentiful energy and strength, but also the stillness, the silence, and the serenity of self-realization.

Together, the water and air initiations represent our journey through the fourth dimension, our unconscious, to connect with our higher self. When we have succeeded in disengaging the emotions and mind, we experience a mini-ascension into the upper astral – our spiritual-mental field. Here, we will work on the final integration of personality (ego), completing the transition to higher self. There, we reap a harvest of previously obscure gifts encoded in our spiritual-mental body scaffolding. Here, we connect with our inner truth, wisdom and unlimited creativity. As higher self stands before the next gate, in that state of tranquility, we have come as far as linear thought, learning, and doing can take us.

Awakening and Healing the Rainbow Body
Fire

The fire gate is called the eye of the needle because we must be stripped clean of our former life to pass through it. This initiation is accompanied by a massive reality shift - the separation from time and space, the full firing of the "lightbody," and the opening of the heart. It is transformation of the highest order. Fire, as the great transformer, opens a whole new journey to us in the fifth dimensional landscape. In this landscape we will walk the path toward Christ Consciousness, the full embodiment of our light – in love.

Those who are familiar with Christian symbolism will recall that the Sacred Heart of Jesus is depicted with a flame reaching upward from the heart. The flame symbolizes the fire initiation and the transformative power of love. In the Andes, *munay* translates as the power or force of love. Most of us have never felt anything like it because *munay* has not been overtly present on the earth since "The Fall." That will change as more and more of us move through the gate of fire. We must believe that in humanity's future, there will be healers capable of realigning our rainbow bodies as Jesus did – through merely touching the hem of his robe with intent. Crowds followed him everywhere longing to be in the presence of his *munay* – the power of his love.

The Andean prophecies of the Elders have long predicted the present era as the end of time. It is the end of time as we have known it - the end of linear time. Fifth dimensional love has no limitations. It cannot be contained within "the box," which is defined by time and space. Space and time cannot hold the expansion that accompanies the heart opening. In fact, the heart expansion can be frightening when it is first felt. It can feel like a whirling vortex that might literally explode the heart. We can and will block the heart's opening if we have not embodied the attribute of fearlessness. Because there is a natural progression on this path, the heart's capacity to open will mirror our ability to release fear. When we do feel it opening prematurely (we are sometimes given glimpses of this power) the experience is easily controlled by our protective instinct to shut it down. When we no longer need to shut down the heart, it will open fully and fearlessly.

The gate of fire is just the beginning of another journey with different parameters and gifts. An entire world exists within the heart.

Awakening Memory

Our passage through the eye of the needle requires that we have embodied light ("lightbody"). Literally, our frequency must be that of the portal's frequency, which is fire/light. "Lightbody" is also a reference to self-realization and enlightenment. Being enlightened does not mean that we never revisit fourth and third dimension either. Nor does it mean that we stop growing for it is just the beginning of heart exploration in no-time/no-space. This path asks us to be inter-dimensional navigators; to create and sustain *munay* in a world dominated by fear. To be in our true power and light in a world manipulate by power abusers. How else will we be of service to others? The fire initiation is but one step on our journey back to God.

Earth

There remains one more initiation - the earth initiation. It is realized on many levels, for it is the path of service and service has many faces. The highest service we can be doing for the earth and humanity is achieving our own enlightenment – doing our work. As soon as we set foot upon this path, this initiation begins unfolding. It sounds simple, since we are already doing our own work, but looks can be deceiving.

If we are truly walking the earth initiation, it means that we cease to worry about whether or not our partners are in step with us, or how our girlfriends are doing with their ascension process. We no longer need to care-take the spiritual lives of others - none of that matters. All that matters is that we take care of ourselves - that we be responsible for our own ascension. Isn't that a handful anyway? Here again, anything else is a distraction. This first level of the earth initiation is self-service. Those who have been steeped in self-sacrifice may feel guilty taking care of their own enlightenment first. In such cases, it is important to recognize guilt as a limitation and move beyond it.

We must understand that our efforts at achieving enlightenment will not go unnoticed. Not that we want a write-up in the paper, but people will naturally be watching our transformation and will overtly or secretively be attracted to the path. Rather than forcing the path on those around us, we learn to walk in the light, sharing from the heart with those who show interest.

Awakening and Healing the Rainbow Body

This initiates a new form of service – being of service to others. This is the second level of earth initiation. We must be ready to walk our talk, to be impeccable on every level, and authentic to the core. We can see why it pays to mind the business of our own enlightenment first. This is high level service. We don't have to become world teachers, gurus or new age stars. We need to go to work, have lunch, play, watch the movies, and attend gatherings – all the time making the right choices, standing firmly in our truth, and bringing our dazzling light and love into the hearts of others.

At its highest level, this initiation brings forth the Bodhisattva – the service aspect of the Buddha. As the story goes, when Buddha reached enlightenment, he went right to the gates of heaven. There the guardians at the gates recognized his light and invited him to enter the kingdom of heaven. Buddha replied, "I will not pass through these gates until all those on earth have passed before me." He returned to serve. He returned to lead others through the eye of the needle.

This service is for the few, not the many. There are some Bodhisattvas amongst us. Part of their enlightenment process is the realization that they are not here to live their own lives, but to enlighten the lives of others. They might very well be world teachers – or simple servants of spirit. They have ascended before and will continue to ascend and return in this spirit of service.

There are further initiations to be discovered by those who move beyond the heart. They are all connecting steps to our God-presence – our Essence, that part of us that never left the heart of God.

The Dimensions

After numerous references to the dimensions, the time has come to define them. The dimensions are holographic energetic spaces within a larger hologram, whether it is our personal holographic field, the earth's, or that of the universe. It is the nature of a hologram that each fraction (our field) contains and is capable of reflecting the whole (the collective human field). This takes place on many levels with all fields ultimately being holographs of God (All That Is). If we believe this concept, we can no longer deny that We are God.

Awakening Memory

For each of the dimensions described below, it is important to remember that each exists within our own field but also on the level of the collective. We store our life experience in our own unconscious (fourth dimension) until we die, then it becomes part of the collective. Conversely, predatory energy exists in the collective fourth dimension and cannot enter an individual's fourth dimensional field unless by invitation through their own fourth dimension – usually unconscious.

Each layer of our field is anchored within our core while extending out to varying degrees around us. The layers communicate with each other energetically through the chakras, vortexes of energy associated with nerve plexuses in the body, but also through pathways within the field that connect one layer or body to the next above or below it in frequency.

As we move through the descriptions of the dimensions, we will see this journey as one of expanding our frequency and dimensional awareness. Each dimensional expansion (the expansion of our awareness to include the next dimension) raises our frequency. Sometimes, we touch the higher frequencies long before we attain them. These are fleeting experiences coming through our field from our higher self and beyond, to help us remember who we are. It is a mistake to attach significance to these occurrences because attachment to the phenomenon of them can limit us. We can gratefully acknowledge them as energies that will one day become anchored in our awareness, and move on with our work. Once anchored, they will become part of our everyday experience.

First Dimension

There is not much to say in describing the first dimension. It is the densest form of matter, akin to the core material of the earth. Its counterpart within our bodies are mineral elements, especially in bone and the skeletal structure it give us. It is difficult to penetrate; providing a strong foundational feature of our multidimensional bodies.

Second Dimension

The kingdom of crystals, lying within the earth's second dimensional consciousness, contributes to the meridian channels beneath the earth's surface. They are energetic transmitters and conduits of living energy. We also have this system of energy within our bodies – the electrical energy of Qi/prana that animates the physical body. The second dimension also includes the devic realms of plant and animal spirits, as well as the worlds of the fairies, gnomes, and elves.

Third Dimension

Third dimension, this reality, is all too familiar to us. It is "the box." It comes with the limitations of the physical world (time and space), and has been well described by science. These laws of the physical world deem that all things born will die, giving back to the earth what was taken from it for life. Within "the box" there is not a space for laws that contradict those of the physical world. For this reason, humanity is ever pursuing the mystery of what exists outside "the box." It becomes a quest for many, and their spiritual journey begins.

Though our presence in this third dimensional earth realm requires the combined physical, etheric and emotional aspects of our holographic field, it is primarily the stage for life's drama, associated with the emotional field. Managing that field, by becoming masters of the unconscious (the fourth dimension) is the work of this path presented in this text. This mastery requires significant attention to the physical (first dimensional) and etheric (second dimensional) bodies as well.

In the Andes, the third dimension, this reality, is called the *kaypacha*. In legend, it is remembered that Inkari, the son of the sun, a mythic, godlike figure who came to earth bringing civilization, created the *kaypacha* as a temporary school of third dimensional life for the soul. The *kaypacha* is the school of life, replete with its dramas, intellect and self-conscious ego. Any myth we chose to study will present this reality as being born in dualism. This reality seems about as far into separation as consciousness can go. How else could atrocities like war exist? They seem a steady and natural part of the third dimensional landscape. Moving beyond war requires that we live life in a frequency beyond third dimension, as well as the fourth dimensional thought field that creates this reality.

What becomes crucial to understanding the creation and sustaining of third dimensional reality is the universally held myth of loss and return. In Christian-based culture, the myth of separation is that of

Awakening Memory

the fallen angels. One (Michael) chose the path of light and the other (Lucifer) chose the path of darkness, both taking their legions with them. War began. The myth of Adam and Eve sustains the same sense of loss and a longing to rejoin what was once whole and joy-filled. These are reflections of "The Fall" – mythic stories that reflect a sudden loss of consciousness and fall from grace or a more gifted life in the higher dimensions.

We can find similar myth in cultures around the earth – for example the creation of the T'ai Chi (yin and yang) from the Wu Chi in Taoism. They all speak to the creation of a dualistic world of light (third dimension) and a world of darkness (fourth dimension). When we engage this work, we are stepping outside third dimension ("the box") to explore and master the unknown within the darkness – fourth dimension.

Fourth Dimension

Between this reality and "heaven" an enormously complex and vast world exists. It has been called the unconscious, the astral, the fourth dimension, and, in the Andes, the *ukhupacha* (the dark interior world of shadows). The Andean myth tells us that Inkari's coming, accompanied by the coming of light (the sun), into a primordial space, forced the creatures of the primordial space to make a decision. They were given the choice to embrace the light or to crawl between the crack and crevices into the interior world of darkness. Most chose the darkness. This myth reflects the creation of a distinct collective unconscious world and its predators at the time of "The Fall."

The sorcerer's description of the dark stream of awareness is likely another reference to that collective fourth dimension. Our own fourth dimensional space or body is connected to the collective by a selective channel – we can and do draw from the collective (living mythic archetypal behavior patterns) but the collective cannot take our energy, except by conscious or unconscious invitation, until the moment of death. Carl Jung spent a good deal of his life exploring our relationship with the fourth dimension. Joseph Campbell's[4] lifelong interest was the gold mine of myth contained within the collective unconscious and individual unconscious. Our modern mental health field was created to understand and heal this dimension but because it is academically based it must rely on third

Awakening and Healing the Rainbow Body

dimensional tools and parameters to do so. Unfortunately, for that reason it experiences some limitations of success in its efforts to heal all fourth dimensional illnesses.

Fourth dimension is a thought-form landscape. It is the mental blueprint responsible for creating and sustaining the reality of third dimension. It is a realm of instant manifestation. With true understanding of this landscape comes an opportunity to create realities that support rather than obstruct enlightenment. On the collective level, there is a staggering amount of human experience and thought (primarily, but not completely, negative) cluttering the fourth dimension that has been generated since "The Fall." It is a complex and fascinating dimension. Since it is a major part of the work presented herein, we will look in depth at fourth dimension.

When the sorcerers speak of the dark sea of awareness sucking us into itself at the time of death, they are speaking of the collective unconscious. All of our life experience and our life force will go with us when we journey there in death, if we have not become self-realized. It is added to the collective "garbage" of humanity, which propels us back onto the earth in another incarnation from the lower realms of the fourth dimension – the lower astral. That human collective "garbage" hovers around the earth and causes humanity to keep repeating itself. The same thing happens on an individual basis if we have not resolved experiences in our life before death. Beyond resolution, there is detachment and transformation of the experiences. The experiences of our life could be pre-deposited in the collective fourth dimension as harmless or even helpful energies if we will own them, learn from them, and release them.

We have our own fourth dimensional holograms, which exist within the collective fourth dimensional hologram. Within each of these holograms, fourth dimension can be divided into three layers, in keeping with its relationship to the mental body, which has three layers, the emotional, the intellectual and the spiritual. In Hindu philosophy, the first two layers represent the lower astral and the spiritual layer represents the higher astral. There is a distinct difference both in content and vibration between these layers. Let's approach each of these layers separately, looking both at our personal and the collective hologram.

Awakening Memory

The Emotional-Mental Body

The emotional layer of the fourth dimension is our entry point into the unconscious. In this work we initiate our ascension process by accessing memory of emotionally charged events in our lives. In doing so, we are reaching into this emotional layer of the fourth dimension from the cognitive space of "the box" - this reality. Our process is one of clearing this layer of life experience memory by taking responsibility for it. We can then give it to the collective unconscious in a responsible way that does not add to the collective garbage. If the vibration of our intent is very high, this giveaway may even help to transform the collective unconscious. Holding onto painful memories and the third dimensional emotion accompanying them can cause serious problems in the physical body. We can release them now to avoid that consequence. If this work is to be complete, we will also release the joyful memories to the collective and, in so doing, send joy into the fourth dimension and free our selves to greater joy. There is no need to covet joyful memory or those associated with them. It is limiting and not in the present.

At the collective level, this layer of the astral or unconscious looks like the center of Hong Kong on a business day – all of it vying for our attention. If we could see into the collective fourth dimension at this level we would find a mirror of our world crowded to overflowing with disincarnate energies who live still attached to their earthly lives under the illusion that they are still in body. Soon they will be back in body. In the meantime, they can be troublesome to those in third dimension.

In addition to disincarnate spirits, we would find the predators, energetic beings who survive by directly, or indirectly, tapping into the energy of humans. Our energy may be resourced in numerous ways, most notably through drama, emotional and mental turmoil, addiction, and all unconscious activity, which can, if excessive, create portals between our hologram and that of the collective. The predators move in with every imaginable distraction to mask the theft of our energy – loud music, mental torment, anxiety and addictive bondage.

Some unfortunate humans become living conduits, energetically enslaved to the predators. These humans, many of them with great charisma, create turmoil, sensationalism, and addictive substances to harvest energy for the predators. They may or may not be conscious of

Awakening and Healing the Rainbow Body

their deleterious role in the unconscious. Energetic entities created from thought form can also reside or transit through this layer of the astral to harm life in the third dimension. This information is meant to provoke awareness, not paranoia. The only way to combat predatory energy loss is through awareness – expanded awareness. Becoming aware of such energies is a giant step towards self-sufficiency but also a necessary step towards mastery.

Collectively, the most entrenched energies in the emotional layers are the human dramas that have been playing out for ages. These create huge patterns and programs that are exceedingly difficult to break for they require enormous shifts in collective consciousness. Part of our longing for the second coming of the Christ or, for that matter, our fixation on earth changes and disaster, is our desire for a shift of that magnitude to occur and the knowing that it would take a great catalyst to make it happen. It is easier for us to look outside ourselves than to create that miracle within.

On the personal unconscious level we can encounter our hungry ghosts in the emotional layer of the fourth dimension. We can manifest our worst nightmares, and lose energy in every direction. Within this layer of the unconscious a communication system extends well into the next layer of the fourth dimension, the intellectual. Since the emotional layer of fourth dimension is the interface with third dimension, thought-based energies will find their way into our reality by way of the communication network within the fourth dimension.

The Intellectual-Mental Body

Here, and in chapter nine, the use of metaphor simplifies an otherwise complicated explanation of the intellectual layer of the unconscious. The similarities between this layer of the unconscious and a computer are hardly surprising since computers were designed to mimic our intellect. We will use this metaphor throughout the work to make intellect accessible for healing and transformation. The nervous system, especially the brain, is our physical body link to this layer of fourth dimension.

Stored within this mental layer of our personal fourth dimension, with access to some major communication pathways, are mental

Awakening Memory

constructs like programs, patterning, and all of the information we cannot readily remember but have stored on our hard drive. Many of these constructs are developed through the data gathered from life experience, and some are inherited. Regardless of their origin, they make information instantly available to us. The information is filtered through the emotional layer of our personal fourth dimension into this reality where it often provokes a full-blown, usually predictable, reaction from our emotional body. Our search engines will continue to resource information in this way until we consciously release some or all of it from our hard drive. This is part of the healing work in this layer of our rainbow body. If we can unload useless information, rewrite programs, and regularly upgrade our system, we can alter the outcome of our lives.

In addition to information gathered throughout our lives, we will find energetic entities that we have created through aberrant or obsessive thought. In chapter nine, we will discuss accountability for our thoughts, a critical, if tedious, part of the fourth dimensional work. Thought creates reality, though not always to our liking or in our best interest.

The mental collective layer of the fourth dimension, as we might guess, harbors the thoughts generated from the earth plane for ages. It is likely that there have been interventions to transmute the contents of the collective unconscious at pivotal moments in human history. For example, the great flood and the ice age were historical geological events, which turned the tide for humanity. Cataclysmic events may be the most effective way for earth to shake loose the yolk of human behavior. It has been a long time since anything like the flood has happened on earth.

Within this layer of the collective unconscious, traveling the airways to our reality, are the myths and their resulting archetypes and symbols that unconsciously steer societies, races, nations, and all human beings. Myth is begun and kept alive through communication and behavior - the living word. Western civilization is still operating from a mythic reality created to establish and anchor the patriarchy in the culture. In the preceding age, the myth had anchored the matriarchy. For a brilliant look at how some of the female archetypes survived the patriarchal takeover, read *The Asteroid Goddesses* by Demetra George.[5] She has tracked the goddesses of Greece and Rome through the astrological influences of our solar system's asteroids.

Awakening and Healing the Rainbow Body

Within these two lower astral layers of the collective unconscious, harmful energetic entities born of thought forms can be sent to harm people in this reality. This is called black magic. Many an innocent (unconscious) person is responsible for harming another in this way through obsessive thinking and mal-intent. Remember that we are out of "the box' here - the walls having collapsed along with the concept of space. These entities do not experience obstructions in the unconscious unless the recipient is an adept, both capable and aware. If they have enough power of intent, they may penetrate our personal fourth dimension and energetically attack us. We give our unconscious consent to invasive thought forms by living mindlessly. Most people would not be aware that someone was obsessing about them – or think to relate that to a sudden loss of energy, illness, or pain.

These little slipups of black magic are nothing compared to the real thing. Black magicians with power use their intent to energetically wage war with their enemies. Of course, they are not impeccable, but they are powerful. As we gain back the power lost to us at "The Fall," we will find that the edge of the sword we walk towards mastery continues to narrow as the frequency increases. In other words, the temptation to abuse power can be overwhelming. It is best to master the attributes of this path well before this power comes to us.

Like all levels of the unconscious, we affect the mental layer, and it affects us. It is a two-way street until we gain some mastery over the way in which we think, and discernment in the way we receive thought. This is one good reason to use discernment with channeling and channeled material. Though there have been impeccable people who have successfully brought useful fourth dimensional information to humanity, we need to exercise caution. Over time, the material brought through can lose focus and actually become extraordinarily negative and fear-based, or ego gratifying.

Within these two lower levels of the unconscious, so important to the work of the water and air initiations, floats an egg of luminous filaments. The filaments of this, our luminous body, are our core beliefs. These beliefs reflect our reality back to us from our fourth dimensional thought field template. These filaments form a bubble around us that contains the conscious and unconscious awareness of our particular state of

Awakening Memory

consciousness. It is this luminous body that mobilizes during the process of enlightenment. We call it the luminous body because it is made of light filaments.

In the collective there is distinct separation between the lower and upper astral. It is an ascension step to penetrate the boundary or membrane of this separation. When we die, we journey out into the collective at our level of awareness. If we have attained the frequency of the upper astral in our personal unconscious, we will journey into the upper astral in death. The luminous body and our consciousness make the journey into the astral or collective unconscious at death through the point of attachment that existed between the personal and collective in life. We will come to know this as the assemblage point in the next chapter. The journey through this point of attachment accounts for the life review present in the stories of many near-death experiences. Here the accountability that we will undertake in this work is forced on the soul. Christianity portrays this as judgment by God whereas, in reality, it is the individual who must take responsibility for his/her own actions.

Existing portals from the personal hologram of fourth dimension to the collective provide numerous opportunities for the transiting soul to be captured by the bardo of the unconscious as described in Tibetan Buddhism.[6] This would account for some less than pleasant accounts of near-death experiences. In death, the unconscious person can be helplessly lost in the bardo – the full force of the collective fourth dimension. While trapped in the unconscious cycles of karma, the soul is bonded to consciousness that is, essentially, recycled personal and collective fourth dimensional thought form energy. Could there be better motivation to attain mastery of this dimension than that?

Through its assemblage point, the luminous body will reflect an after-death experience in keeping with the persons previously held beliefs, until the illusion fades and the soul faces either the opportunities for growth in the fourth dimensional world or another incarnation. The luminous body exists in both the personal (in life) and collective (in death) hologram. Core beliefs, birthed through life experience and held in the unconscious, are our pivotal instruments of self-transformation. Changing core beliefs will be our constant exercise until, in mastery, we can change our reality, as needed, instantly.

Awakening and Healing the Rainbow Body
The Spiritual-Mental Body

After gaining some mastery over our core beliefs and making some space in our personal hologram through practices of the water and air initiation, we will begin to access the third layer of the unconscious through the expansion of the luminous body. Initially, our inroads into this layer will be threadlike paths of insight. The flow of energy is subtle but ever expanding as we continue to clear the lower layers of the unconscious. Our work in this layer of our rainbow body is, primarily, with ego and personality integration. As we detach from emotion and mind, ego frantically invests in the spiritual path. Since the investments are usually recent, the damage is not as extensive as that in the lower bodies of fourth dimension. However, the patterning may look like a familiar story. The ego's unwillingness to relinquish control makes this part of the path a challenge. Fortunately, we have insights and tools that will accelerate the work of awakening and healing the spiritual-mental body.

What awaits us in the spiritual layer of the fourth dimension as our luminous body of awareness gradually expands? A new life will be upon us where creativity, imagination, wisdom, truth, and "knowingness" (a marriage of wisdom and truth) reign. How does this make a difference in our lives? If we have done our work well, the programming, which had held us in repetitive patterns, has been replaced by autonomy. Discernment has been won through self-observation. Instead of doing things the same old way, we are inspired by imagination to create options of higher frequency with ease and grace. Instead of continually accessing the hard drive for information, our work of downloading the hard drive opens us to inspired wisdom – truly helpful, seemingly guided, insight. In fact, it is guided by our higher self, because higher self is operative in this higher layer of the fourth dimension. Our higher self becomes our guide.

Inner truth is a huge energy to access, beginning as ripples that pulse through the field and activate the body, and progressing to the day when we stand fully in our truth. This, combined with the inherent wisdom of higher self, give us that "knowingness" - an unerring connection to our purpose. At this stage of self-realization, the work becomes bridge building; expanding the pathways into the spiritual-mental field until the luminous body mobilizes, taking our consciousness completely into higher frequencies.

Awakening Memory

As that consciousness expands, further treasures come into our awareness in the fourth dimension. Again, the energy is subtle, understated, as we access these treasures. We cannot be looking for fireworks on this path. Fireworks can start grass fires of long-term distraction. What happens instead? We can expect to be surprised when we realize that we are using gifts we didn't realize we possessed. For example, one day we become aware that we are having a "mental" conversation with our dog or cat. It seems perfectly natural until we realize that we have never had a clue what our pet was thinking. The same might happen with people, especially children, but in the beginning pets are generally more open and willing to communicate telepathically with us. Our pets help us bridge to our gifts in many ways, not the least of which is being great mirrors for our behavior as well as reservoirs of unconditional love.

There are countless possibilities in the gift department of fourth dimension but we will discover and use that which our soul encoded into our rainbow body before incarnation. In our next chapter, we will explore these concepts in detail.

It should be said that a number of ways exist for someone to access gifts, like clairvoyance, without first clearing their lower fourth dimensional layers. Like channeling, it opens the recipient to a wealth of information, as well as hidden agendas, from the lower astral that may be from our, or their (the clairvoyant's) personal hologram. If we are seeking information from someone who has not already become self-realized, the risk we take is that open portals to the collective may exist in their field or ours through which controlling or manipulative energies can access our field.

At the appropriate level of consciousness expansion, the gifts we need to fulfill our mission on the earth will become part of our awareness. In the process of this expansion, we can come into a true appreciation of the yin (inward and hidden) energy that prevails in the unconscious. This energy is to be embraced rather than shunned. Would we take away the night because of our lust for light? Our power is found in the balance.

Using the metaphorical image of a department store for the fourth dimension, our self-motivated journey through these initiatory gateways of emotion and mind constitute many floors of the store, beginning with

Awakening and Healing the Rainbow Body

the subterranean storage area, clearly the interior world of our more deeply hidden shadow self. The floors extend up through the entire retail division of the building, which symbolized the remainder of the emotional-mental field. The second section of the department store complex includes the administrative floors, symbolic of our intellectual-mental field. These levels are separated from the higher floors of the department store where the air is clearer and the view better (higher astral) by a restricted security system (the limitation of our core beliefs/awareness). Expansion of that system into the higher floors of the department store makes us aware of the gifts, wisdom, truth and all of the higher qualities that were stored there all along. Ultimately, we find our higher selves seated comfortably in the penthouse, with a dynamic view of the unconscious and conscious.

Self-realization, the unerring and clear view of our conscious and unconscious lives, is ours at the culmination of the water and air initiation. With higher self as our guide, we have arrived at the eye of the needle. Whereas the emotional and mental layers of the unconscious held us captive in our patterns and programming until we healed them, the subsequent expansion of the luminous body into the upper astral has opened up a world of gifts and higher qualities that bespeak liberation.

Fifth Dimension

When Inkari, the son of the sun, created the *kaypacha*, he spoke of another world beyond the end of time called the *hanaqpacha*, higher consciousness. His descendants have told us that the end of time is upon us. Their prophecies tell us that the *kaypacha* (third dimensional reality) is collapsing as higher consciousness (fifth dimension) opens to us. It may be quite true that earth and humanity are facing this great leap in consciousness but whether true or false, we will each face this leap if we seek enlightenment. Just as space falls away in fourth dimension, time falls away in the fifth dimension, breaking linearity completely. Having walked our spiritual path in the manner of climbing a mountain (or the escalators in our department store), we are now unable to proceed because of this dimensional shift.

The fifth dimension cannot be accessed through mind or emotion - the old paradigm. Schools of knowledge don't exist in the *hanaqpacha*. This is the place of the heart – the circular, soft, joy-filled heart. Remember

Awakening Memory

the eye of the needle? To pass through that gate into fifth dimension, we must be free of fourth dimension - our baggage. We must become very still and tranquil to slip through the needle's eye. We must be outside time and space to free fall into the arms of love.

Inkari traveled on a ray of the sun with a rainbow as his shield. When we slip through the eye of the needle, we arrive in fifth dimension in our healed and awakened rainbow body. In that space of awareness we have full consciousness of our rainbow body, including our fifth dimensional field, though mastery of it is yet a dim flicker in the future. It is not, by any means, the end of the path, though, for many, to arrive in the hanaqpacha in one piece as an incarnate being is quite enough. This, after all, is full ascension.

In all honesty, most of us will find our niche somewhere in the comforts of the linear spiritual layer of fourth dimension, giving our gifts to the world with a true dedication to life on earth. Remember there is no hierarchy on this path, only purpose, and in fulfilling ours, life doesn't get any better.

Fifth dimension has a journey of its own – the journey of the heart and the fire initiation of transformation. It is the journey of the Christed Self. A whole new level of learning opens with vastly different parameters. Fifth dimension is "heaven" and we are asked to live it on earth. Christianity has led us to believe that heaven is up in the clouds, but in 1945, the Nag Hamadi Codices were found hidden away in earthen jars in the Egypt desert, and the truth began to be revealed. Within the Codices there were a number of Gnostic gospels written by those who were closest to Jesus.

In his gospel,[7] Thomas the Twin, the brother of Jesus, wrote that Jesus spoke of the kingdom of heaven as "being spread before us on the earth, but people do not see it." Many of the sayings of Jesus recorded in this gospel remind us to look within, for too often we make the mistake of searching outside our selves for truth, wisdom and guidance. Heaven is right here, when we live in our hearts. In fact that fits beautifully with the holographic nature of the universe. Higher consciousness is not a space or place - an in "the box" concept. It is a holographic state of consciousness just like the other dimensions.

Awakening and Healing the Rainbow Body

Sixth Dimension

As we complete our walk through fifth dimension, activating our rainbow body, we gradually incorporate the Christ Body. Our consciousness is expanding to encompass Christ Consciousness, the love-centered path of planetary ascension. Few people who walk the journey through the eye of the needle into the fifth dimension move beyond it. Opening the heart is a big project for humanity at this time. It is surely where the intent of all enlightened humans is focused. But there are those who will walk the path of energy mastery in the sixth dimension.

This is the path of the magician – the master of moving energy. Those walking this path will master their energy body – the etheric double. Most of our energy bodies are randomized, not part of our consciousness. It is a body of power, one capable of seeming miracles. In an instant, a mother, forgetting her limitations, lifts a car to save her child trapped beneath it. Her energy body has momentarily organized itself and entered mastery. In mastery, the magicians are able to control their energetic bodies through the right use of the will. There are many examples of this mastery in *The Brotherhood of the Magi*.[8]

Seventh Dimension

Seventh Dimension is cosmic - home to stargates, sacred geometry, and the path of the cosmic body. Being in cosmic body is an experience of oneness with all that surrounds us. The feelings are of bliss.

We will touch many of these dimensions again as we journey through the rainbow body. Then we will begin building our bridge from the third to the fourth dimension, as we become miracles in our everyday lives. We hope to find our dimension of mastery in this life. Within it we will find our bliss and fulfill the purpose of our soul.

---

[1] The Life and Teachings of the Masters of the Far East Volumes I-III, Baird Spalding, Devorss & Company, 1924.

[2] The Magic Presence and Unveiled Mysteries, Godfre Ray King, The Saint Germain Press Inc., 1935 & 1982 respectively.

[3] The Autobiography of a Yogi, Paramahansa Yogananda, The Self Realization Fellowship, 1998.

Awakening Memory

[4] Any of Joseph Campbell's books, audio tapes, and videos on myth.

[5] The Asteroid Goddesses, Demetra George, ACS Publications, 1986.

[6] The Tibetan Book of Living and Dying, Sogyal Rinpoche, Harper San Francisco, 1992.

[7] The Gospel of Thomas, The Hidden Sayings of Jesus, translated by Marvin Meyer, Harper San Francisco, 1992.

[8] The Brotherhood of the Magi, Jessie E. Ayani, Heart of the Sun, 2002.

NOTES

THE RAINBOW BODY

Enlightenment is expansion of consciousness (awareness) into our full body of light – "lightbody." As we have already discussed, this is a step-wise process for most of us. The path to "lightbody" begins in the realms of the linear, but must end before the eye of the needle outside of time and space. Thus, we cannot arrive at explanations and predictions about "lightbody" using our ingrained mental capabilities. Instead, it is a time when we rely on the gifts, which open as we walk the path. Because these gifts are not known or available to us without considerable self-realization work, we have many good reasons to live in the present rather than to project the future. Life in the moment represents the expressway to higher consciousness. All of our tried and true methods of avoidance had best fall away.

The concepts presented in this chapter, and to a lesser extent in the entire book, cannot be found in "the box." Outside "the box" nothing can be scientifically proven because the laws of physics do not apply there. We will remember our selves at levels of consciousness where we are light rather than form. The beliefs of shamans and sorcerers, as well as visions and experiences from my own journey will be used to describe

Awakening and Healing the Rainbow Body

that which is unknown in ordinary reality. These ideas will be grounded into the physical world through medicine, both western and oriental, and through scientific concepts. For this chapter, I must relate part of my own spiritual journey. My intent is that this sharing will activate your own imagination, vision, and wisdom throughout your work with this material, and that it will be expansive as well as fun for you. Remember to take what is yours, and leave the rest behind.

Filaments of Light

When I first encountered the shamans in the Andes, I was told that we had a luminous body – a body of light filaments. My familiarity with biochemistry, quantum mechanical theory, and their curious bedfellows, Chinese medicine and martial arts, allowed me to accept this information without question. I had already made a mental link between the transfer of electrons in metabolism with the body of Qi, or life force, which animates the physical. I understood that our parents gift prenatal Qi to us when we are conceived, because metabolism present in the egg and sperm continues uninterrupted in the fertilized ego – the embryo. Replenished by food and oxygen, the electrons available to us through physical and energetic metabolism animate the physical body until death. It was no surprise to hear the shamans talking about the rivers of light (meridians) visible to them within our physical bodies but it became obvious to me that the luminous body they were describing was different than the etheric body of Qi.

They spoke of this luminous body as an egg of light, the *wiracocha*, within which each of us exists. This was a stretch and, to be honest, I was initially forced to take it on faith. Understand that, in the high Andes, such gems of information were rarely given, hugely important, and necessarily augmented by vast reservoirs of imagination. In retrospect, I believe that they actually awakened a greater capacity for imagination in my own fourth dimension, expanding my consciousness in the process. Holding this concept within, I returned to my everyday life.

Then, one day, while bookstore browsing, I came across *Sacred Mirrors*[1] by Alex Grey. Near the end of the plates of Grey's *Sacred Mirrors* series of life-size paintings, there were three plates portraying the energetic systems that interface with the physical body. These three paintings

The Rainbow Body

provided a stunning visual activation for me. The first, entitled *Psychic Energy System*, depicts the body of Qi (etheric body), which animates the physical and acts as a principal conduit of the higher energies with our nervous system. In that painting, Grey illustrates the chakras - vortexes of energy that connect the emotional body and higher bodies with the physical through the etheric body. The painting is unquestionably electric. The emotional body is depicted as a glowing electric aura surrounding the body.

On the following page of *Sacred Mirrors*, the painting, entitled *The Spiritual Energy System*, shifted my reality. It seemed to portray the *wiracocha*, the filamentous egg of light talked about in the Andes. Since first seeing this picture, I have come to regard the egg of light as the luminous filaments of our beliefs, fixed somewhere within the fourth dimensional mental body. This luminous body defines the field or expanse of our awareness with its limitations.

The third "light" painting, called the *Universal Mind Lattice*, depicts the luminous body within a more complex matrix of light. In workshops, I use this picture to help explain the fourth dimension. Though part of something vastly more complex and magnificent, Grey's *Universal Mind Lattice* can be thought of as an aspect of God. In it we see a complex organized network of light filaments within which is the human *Spiritual Energy System*. It is a beautiful depiction of our place within a greater reality. God is "All that Is." "All that Is" is Light/Energy. I recommend that you see the plates of these paintings and experience their visual impact. This was my second out of "the box" encounter with the filaments of light.

Not long after seeing Grey's art, and all the while continuing my journeys to the Andes, I finally felt a strong compulsion to read Carlos Casteneda. Perhaps thirty years prior to that time I had picked up his first book, read to the point of taking the mind-altering mushrooms, and put it down. I knew that it was not how I would walk my path of conscious awakening. Twenty years later Carlos and I were both in different places. I picked up *The Power of Silence*,[2] his second-last book, and began to read. The book provoked a number of activating realizations.

Firstly, I realized that Casteneda had a wealth of knowledge surrounding the filaments of light that had particular appeal to me in his

Awakening and Healing the Rainbow Body

later books. Secondly, it became clear to me that sorcery was not my calling. Which was why I could not pursue the books earlier in my life. Now anchored in my true calling, I could access the deep truths held within sorcery and used them for self-realization.

The stories in Casteneda's books became my third encounter with the filaments of light and my first understanding of the assemblage point, which I will write about next. Since reading these books I have arrived at my own concept of these truths but always recommend that students read Casteneda's later books, which are referenced at chapter's end.

The Assemblage Point

One beautiful story in *The Power of Silence* provided me with a pivotal understanding of reality. Casteneda's mentor, Don Juan, took him a long way out into the desert to some distant mountains. Wearing him down getting there helped to provide an out-of-mind opening for his experience. In the mountains, he led him to a cave, which had the power to provoke surreal experiences. It was within that cave that Carlos first saw the filaments of light. Everything, including himself and Don Juan, appeared to be made of light filaments, many of them bundled into streams of filaments. Before long, the vision faded and Don Juan explained that the cave had facilitated a shift of his assemblage point. Previous stories had presented the assemblage point as a magical place where our view of reality was anchored.

The unconscious person's assemblage point rarely moves – they live their lives and die without radically changing their view of reality. The sorcerers relentlessly pursue the shifting of the assemblage point until reality can be shifted at will. This is mastery. Later on, it occurred to me that when his vision faded, Casteneda's assemblage point did not return to its previous place because he had changed his relationship with the filaments. In so doing, his reality shifted and he truly believed in the filaments of light. What we believe is what we get. We do create our reality though most people are not conscious of that power. The deeply held beliefs that shape our reality are called core beliefs.

While thinking about that Casteneda story, Alex Grey's paintings flashed before my eyes. In that moment, I touched a deep truth within me. The filaments of light (our core beliefs), composing the luminous body in our astral field, define the limit of our awareness. The flexibility and mobility of the luminous body is dependent upon our ability to change those core beliefs and, in the process, to become fluid – possibly expanding the luminous body into the higher astral of fourth dimension where our gifts and higher self await us. The assemblage point, therefore, is a fourth dimensional phenomenon when we initially engage our spiritual work. Having some mastery of the assemblage point is essential to complete liberation.

In *The Active Side of Infinity*,[3] Casteneda speaks of the assemblage point's attachment to the dark sea of awareness – what I interpret to be the collective fourth dimension or the collective unconscious. It is through the assemblage point that the dark sea of awareness sucks our life force and experience at the moment of death. This explains the experience of journeying through a tunnel towards the light (the light filaments of the collective fourth dimension) reported by those who have had near-death experiences. Herein lies the realization that our own fourth dimensional hologram is linked via the assemblage point to the collective fourth dimensional hologram. Within the tunnel, as we leave this reality in death, we encounter our personal bardo as we transit through the collection of experiences that was our life.

Our assemblage point is fixed securely, except in sleep (and certain mental disorders) where "other reality" dreams manifest through the sliding of the assemblage point along the streams of filaments comprising our attachment to the fourth dimension. In our work we will consciously move the assemblage point by altering its composition and frequency as we change our core beliefs.

Don Juan also refers to the filaments of light as intent – the prevailing force in the universe. This definition fits well with the concept of the universal Matrix of Light filaments. Our own filaments of light originate from within the Matrix of Light to form our Luminous Body, In fact, everything in the universe originates in the Matrix of Light and is God. Through mastery of our own consciousness we are able to manifest from that matrix into this or any reality. Intent is the power of the magician.

From the energetic view, what occurs in self-realization and, ultimately, in God realization? We are pushing the luminous body out to expand our reality – our awareness – in this process of enlightenment.

Awakening and Healing the Rainbow Body

We are moving our assemblage point (reality) through the holograms of consciousness with each frequency shift in our attainment. When we walk through the eye of the needle, we cannot take our fourth dimensional luminous body with us. A fifth dimensional luminous body is formed; its filaments gathered from the light matrix of the fifth dimension. It is my belief that the luminous body collapses in that ascension – a small but certain death – then is reformed from the fifth dimensional filaments of light – core beliefs of a higher realm of consciousness. Its (our) frequency is then that of a fifth dimensional consciousness and the luminous body has become infinitely more luminous and fluid.

Our core beliefs, because they are thought forms, originate in the fourth dimensional aspect of the Matrix of Light we call God. If God is all there is, then God makes everything available to us. We have choices about reality, and that is power. Each filament of light in our assemblage point/luminous body represents a core belief held at a specific level of consciousness and frequency. For example, a core belief that "no one loves me" does not have a very high vibration. As long as it remains in our field, we will manifest the lack of love in our life. Likewise, a core belief that "there is not enough" will manifest a life of poverty consciousness until it, and all of the core beliefs that have sprung from it, have been changed.

I offer the suggestion that talk therapy has limitations because it uses the cognitive process to access memory from the subconscious then, through insight, expects that the assemblage point will permanently shift. The assemblage point is not in third dimension ("the box") but, in the unenlightened person, exists in the dimension where the memory was held (fourth). If the therapist were to guide the client into that space and have them shift the assemblage point by changing core beliefs within the fourth dimension, reality would shift instantly. That is why the journey to change core beliefs on our *Pachamama's Child*[4] CD takes the participant to the fourth dimension to change the core beliefs. Upon completion of the essential cognitive work, clients could be taken on such a journey if and when they were ready to change and sustain their new reality.

Our most deeply held core beliefs come from childhood. We have all gradually or radically altered many of the family-held core beliefs demonstrating some innate talent at assemblage point shifting. It was hard work, but well worth it. We can search out the remaining beliefs held by our child and move into other areas of life. For now, we can begin observing what beliefs we do hold.

Assemblage points are not limited to individuals but are created in other bodies of consciousness as well. Families have an assemblage point, which holds them together in a certain belief system. Once we begin to observe assemblage points, we will find them in all organizations, government, churches, corporations and so forth. If, for example, we are in conflict with the dogma of a certain church, we are better off changing churches than to waste time and energy trying to change something as rigid as dogma. If something used to fit, but now causes discomfort, our assemblage point is ready to shift, and we are now faced with a choice to stay or leave. This does not mean that we are powerless to change institutional assemblage points. If a democratic process is present within it, the institution can shift through group effort. Likewise, inspired leaders can shift the assemblage point of more hierarchical organizations. Witness the protestant churches that now accept women as ministers. Progressive movements exist within many institutions that are dedicated to shifting organizational assemblage points.

Relationships could have assemblage points but most often are a quagmire of enmeshed filaments. In our culture, we regularly give our power to others without consciously realizing that the filaments of our emotional body have been bartered to meet our needs. This is called co-dependency and it is more common than not. If we have a conscious partner, we might want to begin reconstructing our reality together in a relationship assemblage point. This leaves each partner to have an autonomous existence within the relationship. We will work extensively with entangled filaments and autonomy in chapters 7 and 8.

By far, the most interesting assemblage point about which to speculate is that of the psychotic. In clinical psychosis, however brief or lengthy, it appears that the assemblage point (reality) collapses and any reference point between the individual hologram (who I am) and the collective hologram (the collective experience) is lost – a truly frightening prospect for the unconscious individual. A master of the fourth dimension might do this deliberately to explore fourth dimension. When we talk about the rainbow body, we will discuss what may be happening in the holograms on the energetic level in psychosis.

Awakening and Healing the Rainbow Body

In spiritual psychosis, or spiritual emergence, a similar event occurs, but the dissolution need not be permanent. The assemblage point can destabilize when an event, realization, or spiritual trauma causes a radical shift in beliefs. The assemblage point is literally torn apart and the reference point for reality is lost, either temporarily or permanently, depending on the kind of care given to these people. Within this context are stories we may have heard about the dark night of the soul and re-emergence into higher consciousness. Eckart Tolle's[5] story of emergence contains this feature.

One interesting example of spiritual emergence is that of author Margaret Starbird. In her book entitled *The Goddess in the Gospel*,[6] Starbird writes of her experience as a charismatic Catholic while researching the life of Mary Magdalen. The results of this research can be found in her first book, *The Woman with the Alabaster Jar*.[7] Her research was prompted by a strong disbelief in the information presented in *Holy Blood, Holy Grail*,[8] the first book to be published suggesting that Jesus and Mary Magdalen were married partners with a family, whose lineage has continued to this day.

By her own accounting, Starbird spent a few days in a mental ward because her world fell apart. She lost her reference point when her research overwhelmingly confirmed the work published in *Holy Blood, Holy Grail*. Her assemblage point shifted radically, and likely destabilized, because so many long-standing beliefs were broken at once. She momentarily lost her reality. She came through the experience into a new reality where her beliefs had come into alignment with her research. I applaud both Starbird and Tolle for their willingness to share their intimate spiritual experiences, and I highly recommend their books.

It is my belief that if we have died with our consciousness in the upper astral (our luminous body having advanced into the higher astral of fourth dimension) we return with an assemblage point in the spiritual-mental body (the upper astral) - born in truth, wisdom, creativity and imagination. It seems plausible that we might also have joyfully jumped of the wheel of karma upon entering the higher astral to be more closely aligned with our soul's purpose, and a more collective notion of self. Could this not be a simple explanation for the so-called crystal children being born now who seem aligned with truth and wisdom rather than the cultural? They seem, at least to me, to be old souls upon the earth who have had some success in navigating the path to enlightenment.

One important point to remember is that once shifted, the assemblage point must remain fluid and ready to shift again in our quest for self-realization. Too often we get comfortable in a certain place and spiritual growth becomes limited. This is especially true when we begin manifesting a better life and don't want to risk surrendering it. If we are truly intent upon enlightenment, life will push us past our comfort zones to continued growth. Will it be with ease and grace, or pain and suffering?

The Rainbow Body

More than a year prior to this writing I was given a vision. Though brief, the vision had a profound effect on my own assemblage point. Increasing clarity has come to me since that life-altering glimpse beyond "the box." In the vision, I saw a series of filamentous geometric scaffolds. The scaffolds were stacked one beyond another in the colors of the rainbow (Illustration One at chapter's end depicts a similar geometric stacking). At the front of the stack the scaffold was red, and the most distant scaffold was blue-violet or indigo. Familiar with the holographic nature of the many bodies incorporated into our field, I assumed that the rainbow of scaffolds was related to those holographic bodies – perhaps a cross-section.

During the year following that vision, a series of life experiences propelled me into expanded heart awareness – a major liberation from mind. As a result vision has continued to unfold. What I am about to share of the rainbow body does not energetically conflict with the esoteric traditions I have studied in the past. Yet, it is completely different from anything I have previously learned, or that I have been able to conceptualize. The presentation of this vision necessarily enters the abstract because its inter-dimensional nature causes third dimensional language to falter. This vision is surely shared by others on this planet who have expanded their awareness in similar ways, and who have used their specific life experience to arrive at their unique interpretations. It is what it is - my vision and truth - and I offer it for what it might be worth to your spiritual growth.

Awakening and Healing the Rainbow Body

Geometry of Light

The Matrix of Light that is God, All that Is, is the principal hologram. Like all of the holograms it contains, the Matrix is geometric in its energetic form – the Source of sacred geometry. It is depicted as white light because all colors can be separated from it with a cosmic prism. However, we need to understand that the cosmos does not exist within our visible spectrum alone. The visible spectrum defines the limit of our physical perception through the eyes, and that is hugely limited. The cosmic spectrum is infinite. Each level of expanded awareness we encounter through life or death broadens our perception of light.

Everything in existence is a microcosm of the principal hologram – the God Matrix. For example, galaxies, solar systems, and planets are microcosms of the God Matrix. Our original holographic field is a microcosm of the earth's and our cells are microcosms of our holographic field, and all are microcosms of the God Matrix. Nothing contained within the God Matrix, which is All that Is, is separate from that Matrix.

The geometry of each hologram of light in existence is unique and yet reflective of the Matrix. The macrocosm of our holographic body template (our Original Birth Template) is reflected in each layer of our scaffolding. We will see how this works as the description of our holographic field unfolds. A great deal of compression is required to manifest in the physical – to hold light as form. On occasions of consciousness expansion, the true restriction of this compression can be felt, metaphorically, as "layers of an onion" falling away. The core of the onion is our Essence, that part of us that cannot be touched by the world. It remains, always, in Oneness. We can regard Essence as our Original Divine Template brought from the Heart of God as part of the soul's journey of exploration and growth. Let us explore these concepts within the human holographic field.

The Soul's Journey

God, All that Is, is all Consciousness. We can think of creation as a great out-breath of God, the Light Matrix. It is a concept in keeping with a big bang, an experience of the physical universe no doubt driven by this out-breath. Energetically, we can imagine that this Infinite Light Matrix willed something like an internal explosion, so that, within Itself, It created

The Rainbow Body

holograms of Itself, which began a journey to the very edges of the Matrix. It would not be possible for microcosmic holograms of the Matrix to journey beyond it. The original holograms were huge variations on the Matrix, which, in keeping with the momentum of the out-breath, spawned their own microcosmic variations. This process went on until the infinitely varied holographic consciousnesses of Essence were born. The process continues within our own holograms at the level of Essence, as we are, in that consciousness, able to manifest our selves as God (I AM). God-realization occurs when awareness has expanded to the level of Essence, the twelfth dimension - our journey home.

These Essential Consciousnesses were complete unto themselves (in Essence) as microcosms of the Light Matrix. The scaffold of their hologram (Original Divine Template) was in harmonious resonance. The first through eleventh dimensions did not exist for Essence, nor did the luminous body, which now dwells in our fourth dimension. Essence learned to lower frequency to experience dimensions beneath the twelfth. In this experience, new holograms and their templates were created to facilitate this experience (Illustration Two depicts such a template or scaffold). Each hologram provided new experience for Essence and new ways to gather light in anticipation of the next inbreath of the God Matrix when greater light would be brought to the Heart of God for the enrichment of all.

Because levels of consciousness came into being for each dimensional hologram, egos emerged as guidance systems within the dimensions. Gradually, as consciousness gained strength in dimensional awareness along the spectrum of lowering frequency, the ego guidance systems lost touch with Essence. This did not change Essence, which remains today as it was created. When consciousness began to explore the third dimension, ego remained a powerful guidance system for manifestation in this reality where fourth dimensional thought forms become reality. Many egos began to explore control and manipulation, bone-fide aspects of God – "All that Is."

Death did not exist. Death became part of the earthly experience and the fourth dimensional luminous body with its limitations came into being through the circumstances related to "The Fall" of mankind. The veil dropped suddenly when egos exploring control and power managed to trap egos exploring third dimension on earth. It could also have happened on other planets and in other solar systems. For those trapped in third dimension, the result was our mythic banishment from paradise. At this time, the existing individual consciousness became what we call soul. Soul holds a degree of memory of Essence. Soul consciousness fashioned that memory into the Original Soul Template of light geometry to hold that pre-"Fall" memory. Each of our souls began a quest to regain the immediate post-"Fall" awareness through earthly incarnation. Pre-"Fall" awareness was not Essence but the level of conscious awareness held by ego prior to "The Fall." At the time of "The Fall," the collective unconscious of humanity began forming from the fourth dimensional thought form matrix. The collective unconscious is a model for our individual fourth dimensional mental body.

The soul consciousness modifies its fourth dimensional luminous body, drawing light filaments from the fourth dimensional matrix to provide a thought field for manifestation in third dimension. This thought field, upon each incarnation, reflects the awareness of the soul, but it is mutated by incarnate life. Over many incarnations the luminous body became rigidly bound to the fourth dimensional matrix causing the earth and her incarnate humans to fill the collective unconscious with the repeated experiences of lost and searching souls. Little by little, the soul's template lost the memory of Essence and began to reflect more and more of the fifth dimensional awareness instead (the limitation we call heaven). Reality became limited and "the box" (third dimensional reality), which cannot see beyond third dimension, was created. The lower collective fourth dimension (lower astral), from which "the box" is projected, holds humanity and earth in bondage.

Egos that had fallen into the low vibrations of control and manipulation developed the fourth dimension's capacity to create predatory thought form manifestations that continue to tap into and drain the energy of humanity. How this bondage occurred is not as important as the recognition that it did occur, and our release from it through awareness. One truth is unequivocal. From the perspective of "the box" we have no vision of the larger picture and intent of God. We don't even understand the motivation behind the intent of those who want to control us. It may actually be the predator's way of increasing God's Light. It may be valid for their soul experience. They have lost consciousness as well. It may be the Divine Plan unfolding. What is important is that we have a choice about how our energy is used and we can learn to exercise that choice on our own return to the Heart of God.

How does the soul begin its long journey home to Essence and the Heart of God? In awakening, we begin to loosen the rigid attachment of the luminous body to the unconscious and shift the assemblage point within it. Remember that the luminous body, linked at birth to soul consciousness, consists of core beliefs, both collective and personal. In the unconscious state, it rides on an interface with the filaments of the collective in the lower astral. We can call the unconscious state bondage to the astral in cycles of karma and reincarnation.

In death, when the luminous body collapses or enfolds, it and our fourth dimensional thought-patterned consciousness containing all the life experience it acquired, is siphoned into the astral (the collective unconscious) through the assemblage point. An unconscious life will produce a reality in fourth dimension much like that on earth using the luminous body with an assemblage point somewhat modified to accommodate the dimensional shift and the mental body scaffolds of the rainbow body. If we are to believe the sorcerers, the life force accompanies the life experience into the fourth dimension at the death of an unconscious person as signaled by the cessation of respiration and animation within the body. It is possible that their reference to the life force is more accurately thought of as awareness or soul consciousness, or it may be that death is the ultimate energy source for the predatory awareness in fourth dimension. Quite possibly, it is both.

Where is the Essence in all of this process? The Essence is never touched by the events of any lifetime. It remains always the Original Divine Template of the hologram as a reflection of God. We may not be conscious of our Essence, but it is conscious of us – faithfully holding space for our liberation.

We can think of consciousness as the substance of awareness within the All that Is. Consciousness permeates all realities and has numerous phases or appearances. When in body, we are consciously aware of third dimension, and yet we may be aware that the unconscious and superconscious exist as well. There are levels of consciousness associated with each holographic dimension. Each level of consciousness has frequency and limitation. As a hologram, each consciousness is part of the God Matrix. The soul is conscious at the level of its growth and maintains that level in spite of the limited consciousness of third dimension. Our journey here on earth may prompt us to reconnect to that soul awareness as part of our spiritual journey through fourth dimension and beyond.

It is the soul consciousness that instigates reincarnation, encoding into the fourth dimensional scaffolding of our rainbow body the intent for growth through life's challenges and gifts. The soul consciousness must have originated as a template guidance system at "The Fall" when the lights went out. It is modeled as a remnant of the Essence, which previously had no need for a definition of our third and fourth dimensional awareness. Essence is the I AM consciousness template that has not forgotten that It is God. Soul consciousness is a small part of our total consciousness representing the part of us that fell into fear and helplessness during the events of "The Fall." Essence cannot abandon that part of itself nor can it be integrated into our consciousness in the present state of distortion of our original geometry and light. If Essence is the light geometry of our I AM presence or Divine Self (True Ego), then soul consciousness can be thought of as a distortion of that True Ego (I AM), which holds a dim, fragmented memory of that True Ego.

There also exists a lower ego, which is very much attached to earth reality through wants, needs and desires. In our work, the lower ego must give way to higher self (higher ego and soul consciousness), which can guide Essence towards it to, in God-realization, merge our soul consciousness with our Original Divine Self (I AM) as templated by Essence. On our journey back to the Heart of God, we will incorporate the frequencies of the higher dimensions into our working (soul) consciousness.

One of the most important events for the soul is the advancement of the incarnate consciousness to the higher astral through the shifting of the assemblage point. When that occurs, the soul consciousness and the consciousness of the incarnate being merge, and when the incarnate transitions in death, it is to the higher astral. This is a conscious death and freedom from the limitations of the lower astral and its wheel of karma.

The Rainbow Body

The key to liberation from the wheel of karma, is to become a master of the luminous body and its assemblage point, thus liberating the soul. Mastery of the luminous body, and the reality it templates, allows us to control the placement of the portal – the interface with the collective.

While bound to the cycles of karma, we leave this earth in death and return in birth bearing a luminous body consistent with our level of awareness. It guides our experience in the after-death realm where further growth is not only possible but may be easier than on earth. Each time we incarnate, the soul gathers filaments to form the rainbow body scaffolding around the luminous body. The first geometric scaffold of light to be put in place is the layer of the fourth dimension where the assemblage point will be anchored – and so it is.

Using this fourth dimensional scaffold as the template, the remaining templates of the rainbow body are created, stepping down to the etheric body and up through the intellectual-mental body. The physical body template originates from the parental DNA, conforming as a best fit with higher body templates put in place by the soul. The soul is using a higher body DNA activated to the level of our awareness.

Expansion

Our first ascension step brings the assemblage point fully into the spiritual-mental body hologram, which was templated in the image of the soul. As we will see, this geometry will have suffered minor distortion in the living of life, and some work will be necessary to realign it to the Original Birth Template of the soul. Once this is accomplished, the templates of the remainder of the rainbow body, which have been cleared of distortion through this work, can be realigned with soul using the power of intent. This restores the Original Birth Template, the soul's blueprint of the rainbow body, present at birth. At that point, we are self-realized, masters of our assemblage point, and, as Casteneda has written, in the glow of awareness. The restoration of this glow of awareness is the healing and awakening of the rainbow body presented in this book.

With expansion beyond the lower ego consciousness, we are able to conceive of our selves as a group consciousness where individual needs and desires pale somewhat before the group mission. Monadic consciousness expands our awareness further - to that of a large group of souls working on an equally large consciousness project. So begins the expansion to the Heart of God where ego and separation do not exist. The holograms expand and incorporate the microcosms as part of the great cosmic in-breath of God.

In considering our own level of awareness within our hologram, we must not overlook the fact that each of our holographic bodies can communicate with a collective version of those holographic dimensional bodies. Ordinarily there is little communication between the collective and the individual - with the obvious exception of the fourth dimension where the assemblage point links the two. Likewise if the luminous body collapses in ascension to the fifth dimension it would be reformed with fifth dimensional light filaments - its assemblage point anchored to, and communicating with, a collective fifth dimension.

Spirit

Let us explore the multiple phases of consciousness. An excellent metaphor is that of the three phases of water – solid (ice), liquid, and gas (steam). We have the self-consciousness of the human intellect and emotions when we are incarnate; we have soul consciousness linked to our multi-dimensional hologram of infinite potential; and we have something called Spirit.

Spirit is a phase of consciousness that interacts with other Spirit. Through the interface between any of our dimensions and their collective counterparts, we might experience a visitation of Spirit. For example, disincarnate beings are able to visit us "in Spirit" (our Spirit meets their Spirit) through the fourth dimensional interface. This is not intended predation but it can feel quite invasive when we do not understand it. Sometimes the disincarnate person's Spirit is reaching out for help, and, if it is our calling, we may have occasion to magnetize this sort of energy to our own Spirit to help release heavy emotions that the disincarnate Spirit is carrying. Perhaps heavy emotions are restricting the disincarnate's acceptance of their new fourth dimensional environment because they are binding them strongly to third dimension. If the heavy energy can be cleared, their souls are freed of the emotional bondage.

In such a case, it would be good to be involved in the mastery of energy to avoid taking on their heavy emotion – or at the very least to be

The Rainbow Body

aware of what is happening. If we are unaware, the heavy emotion can sap our energy. Those with the gift of clairaudience could communicated with the Spirits as a medium and help them let go in that way.

On another level, it is through a fifth dimensional interface (our Spirit in our fifth dimension interfaces with the collective fifth dimensional Spirit) that the Spirit of Christ might engage our Spirit. At the level of the seventh dimension, the cosmic, we, as Spirit, could receive the Angelic Presence. It is something to be aware of and nothing to fear. Spirit is a phase of consciousness, like steam, that is able to permeate the interdimensional interfaces if we are receptive to it. Surely Spirit is the phase by which some people are able to see and communicate with the Spirits of nature in the second dimension, just as mediums are able to speak to disincarnate Spirits in the fourth dimension. It is, perhaps, the phase of consciousness that brings us Bliss and Ecstasy, when Spirit is in union with higher realms. This is in stark opposition to the heavy energy of the fourth dimension.

Incarnation

The portal through which a soul enters the earth realm is positioned on the collective fourth dimension interface relative to the current level of soul awareness. That soul consciousness, which journeyed through the fourth dimension searching and growing, much as it did in third dimensional life, attaches to the collective filaments at what will become the new assemblage point. The scaffolding of that layer of the fourth dimension will be projected around the luminous body as the architecture of the first rainbow body hologram. It will be used to guide the creation of the lower scaffolds.

Once both of the lower astral fourth dimensional scaffolds stabilize, the personal thought field comes into being – the mirror of what will develop in "the box." Essentially, a hard drive with a working system is put in place to support "the box." Within the fourth dimensional light scaffold geometry are encrypted the parameters of the soul's new journey. These encoded programs can be thought of as the genes of crystalline DNA at fourth dimensional frequency. In the state of death, when all of the experience of life becomes collective, the soul has clarity about its growth and karma. The geometric filaments of these scaffolds support the soul's life plan – The Divine Plan – and reflect this state of clarity. They are usually directed towards increased awareness of the higher self.

The ambitious soul has every opportunity to encode the life circumstances that will provoke growth and healing in grand and difficult ways. Energetically, these encodements bear weight in the scaffold, distorting it slightly from the soul's native geometry. In the spiritual-mental scaffold of our fourth dimension, the DNA crystals encode the gifts and qualities of the higher astral which are drawn into the scaffold with the selected filaments. Higher self, a function of the higher astral, is a consciousness related to soul, which is created to guide the placement of this scaffold and the selection of filaments.

When the process of constructing the fourth dimensional thought form portion of the hologram is complete, the soul, guided by the karma and growth goals that have influenced the fourth dimensional scaffold, uses the collective thought field to search the earth plane for potential parents. The soul will try to find a good match for the Divine Plan held in the geometry of the scaffold. When the parents have been chosen, the soul begins to gather the lower scaffolds using the fourth dimensional scaffolding as the template.

An emotional scaffold is put in place from the filaments of the earth's emotional body. We tend to associate the emotional body with life's drama and emotion because it does engage the school of life, but it begins simply, as an energetic vehicle for two-way communication between the lower bodies and the first scaffold of the astral (emotional-mental) field. In life, we store emotion in this field, which can cause imbalance in the field. Though it begins as pure light geometry, it quickly becomes an integral part of our in "the box" reality.

The etheric template is drawn from etheric filaments of nature - the pranic force field inherent in nature. Remember we are talking about the template and not the Qi itself. These five scaffolds of the hologram invisibly hold space for the moment of conception. The assignment of the rainbow body scaffolding is to maintain order within the hologram. Though the combined physical, etheric and emotional template exist in the third dimension, it is only the physical template that is in form and therefore subject to the laws of the physical world.

The Rainbow Body

The DNA of the parents, which encodes the body's genetics, determines the physical body and its scaffold. However, the guidance system for fetal development is not the parental DNA but the soul-directed DNA of the etheric template. It is, for example, this etheric guidance system that instigates the development of a liver from a single chosen cell when all cells have that potential. Though it is a marvel of molecular complexity, the physical body has no innate capabilities of indefinitely maintaining order. Order is contrary to the laws of the physical world where all of nature tends towards disorder (one of the laws of thermodynamics).

Along with the random combining of their DNA (meiosis), the parents gift a portion of their own Qi (prenatal Qi) to the embryo at conception. This little pot of prenatal Qi then grows and strengthens through the metabolism of the mother as the fetus develops. This gift of Qi comes in two forms - the energetic form of electron transfer reactions that are already taking place in the egg and sperm prior to the event of conception, and as a liquid phase present in the cellular fluid. These reactions continue as cell numbers increase, and as the mother furnishes oxygen and nutrients through the umbilical cord. These reactions continue until the individual's life ends.

At some point during the maturation of the fetal nervous system, the etheric template makes an energetic connection to the physical by laying down endings, contacts called nadis, along the trunks of the nerves. Prior to nerve development, the primitive nervous system is likely the point of direct contact with the etheric template, while the light geometry of the template guides development and growth. With the mature connection, the developing fetus comes into full contact with its holographic template, which provides an independent system of energy meridians (Illustration Three depicts the holographic rainbow body).

At that time of contact, the first stress is placed on the hologram at the point of its lowest frequency, the physical. The genetics of the developing fetus and its physical template are imposed on the templates of geometric light scaffolding designed by the soul. Because it can never be a perfect geometric match, the result is a little torque or distortion in the multidimensional body. The second stress comes at birth, when the soul draws cosmic energies into the hologram that influence the geometry.

Awakening and Healing the Rainbow Body

These energies are received, and stored by our fourth dimensional templates.

These cosmic energies are determined by the position of the stars in the heavens and the architecture of our solar system at the moment of birth. The birth process is initiated by the soul to provide the best possible influence for the soul's purpose. However, these energies can slightly distort the template while encoding energies of destiny into the astral field that have a celestial timing. In addition to these influences, the hologram and its templates must compress into the final alignment to provide a functional field of light energy, the rainbow body, which stabilizes the process of incarnation in the physical body.

The chakras - vortices of energy that interface all layers of the field in alignment with nerve plexuses in the body – provide an inflow and outflow system for the energies of life on earth. We can call this the indirect communication system of the hologram while the actual template-to-template interfaces are the direct connections.

We are born with near perfect alignment of our scaffolds in a rainbow light spectrum in spite of the slight distortions. Independent of the soul's level of growth, the aligned geometry of the scaffolds creates, in the newborn, a bridge to the spiritual-mental body and higher self. We will call it the bamboo – a conduit of higher consciousness. We are born in complete consciousness of our hologram and its potential. We are born in conscious awareness of our soul and the Divine Plan it has put in place for us. Casteneda has referred to this as the glow of awareness. How do we so quickly lose that consciousness and its glow of awareness?

Life Happens

In my workshops, many participants have been able to track the loss of their glow of awareness through the memory provoked by their childhood pictures. Often, the difference in the pictures is observable, remarkable, and sad. If the glow of awareness has not completely diminished by school age, a remarkable loss occurs at that time. I have heard many stories of childhood relationships with fairies, elves, nature spirits and friends from other dimensions – possibly guides from second dimension and the upper astral of fourth dimension. I have also heard many memories of intrusive energies, scary beings and nightmares unprovoked by external sources that were likely lower astral contacts.

In addition to the minor influences of familial physical DNA and astrological influences, it is the amnesia itself, the bondage to death and reincarnation, that creates the setting for the loss of consciousness. A baby is helpless to express the clarity and consciousness that accompanies him/her into the world. When newborn, the infant uses sleep time to reconnect with soul consciousness, but as awake time increases the baby comes more and more under the influence of the reality around him/her - a reality created by parents, siblings, family relatives and friends, and the culture. We can make an enormous contribution to maintaining the infant's soul connection through the positive reinforcement of their divinity, exemplary living, and unconditional love.

Frustrations cannot be communicated when infants are confronted with realities in opposition to their own assemblage points and luminous bodies. In time, through observation and experience, as well as direct commands from those around the child, the assemblage point shifts to insure survival in the prevailing reality – the original core beliefs set in place by the soul are changed. Additionally, patterns are sometimes carried within the blood lineage encoded in parental DNA, which influence the entire hologram through its communication network. If the child inherited such blood codes, these patterns begin to creep into the child's field as well, with sufficient reinforcement from the family behavior. If a child does not carry the blood codes, core beliefs surrounding these patterns in the family's behavior will likely be integrated into their assemblage point, but without the strong reinforcement of the blood codes.

When engaged in the healing work, the core beliefs are easier to change when the blood codes are not present. An example of this concept, might be criticism. A child is born into a critical family and much of childhood is filled with family opinions about everything and everyone. It is easy for a child to integrate these core beliefs and become critical of others or prejudiced. If they are not carrying the familial blood codes of criticism and judgment, they are more likely to become conscious of the fact that something is wrong with the family picture. Their life experience will not be as steeped in judgment and criticism as others in the family, and they will find more appealing life experiences instead. Like everyone, they have the option to break the family held beliefs and may wonder, at a very young age, why their family is so critical.

If the blood codes were present in a child's hologram, they would have inherited a lineage of criticism and would likely take up the family pattern with gusto. In this scenario, it might take a number of blows to the ego to shift the assemblage point, as in critical attacks directed at them. When tired of these lessons, the consciousness might be gained to shift the assemblage point away from that of the family. It is difficult, indeed, to grow up outside the family reality, but rebels abound who seemed to be connected to an inner truth far different from their family's patterning.

It used to be that the beginning of our educational life at around five years of age was the turning point for the glow of awareness. It marked the point when large amounts of information began entering our awareness and we began assimilating the core beliefs of teachers and culture – children are like sponges when absorbing information. We could call it the booting up of the hard drive. From that point on, life is all about information and knowledge, mostly to better our chances of survival. The mental field distorts and swells along with the issues of self-identity.

Presently, this happens well before school age due to media and computer technology, preschool emphasis on learning skills, and the need to keep up with peers while still very young. Awareness is dissipating at an alarming rate in children exposed to the above distraction, and they exhibit no ability or desire to be without external stimulation where soul consciousness might be contacted.

However the loss of soul consciousness happens for us, from that point on we are off and running in the illusion of "the box." The clarity of the soul consciousness is replaced by an ever-expanding lower ego. What begins as a simple need to define oneself turns into a potentially lifelong journey of self-absorption led by the fulfillment of wants, needs and desires. In later chapters, we will work specifically on these issues. For now, it is important to know what is happening to the rainbow body.

As the assemblage point changes, the luminous body changes, distorting and masking the original intent of the soul for the incarnation. With the data expansion of the hard drive, the intellectual astral scaffold becomes weighty and its geometry distorts. With the accumulation of life experience, our emotional-mental bodies fill with the "stuff" of our personal unconscious, expanding the scaffold and distorting the geometry with the filamentous networks or webbing of repetitive behavior and thought (Illustration Four). Communication between the scaffolds begins to break down and disintegrate altogether, except for the filamentous network of repetitive behavior pathways that dominate the lower astral bodies. All of this affects the scaffoldings' ability to support the third dimension, bringing destabilization of the body. As we move through the levels of rainbow body healing, we will discuss this in detail.

This beautiful rainbow body – a hologram of resonance, integrity, and awareness – gives way to a set of distorted holographic scaffolds, which have no ability to communicate with each other consciously. The bamboo, once a flowing conduit of awareness, has been squeezed and twisted to just a trickle of energy trying to find its way between heaven and earth. Pools of that energy stagnate in the bodies templated by the scaffolds, and, naturally, the bodies themselves begin to lose integrity.

In the holograms of many individuals, the geometry of one or more scaffolds actually mutates as the DNA of each scaffold succumbs to the pressure of life. This is no longer a rainbow body, but a randomized network of filaments that somehow is able to sustain life in the illusion because it is a reflection of that illusion. The original hologram, along with its resonance, is lost, and the soul's consciousness takes a beating. In this demoralized state, we become weakened to resist the seduction by the astral predators who can slip their own filaments through portals created by geometric distortion in the lower astral scaffolds (Illustration Five) and subsets of beliefs (sub-assemblage points) that serve desire. That is how invasive energies can hook into our field taking away our power.

How does this look in "the box?" We become dependent on the projections of predatory energy in this reality, like drugs, alcohol, cigarettes, pornography, gambling, heavy drama, mental obsession, and all manner of addiction. What begins innocently can lead us to this place of vulnerability and energy loss. Addictive behavior (dependence on something outside our selves) becomes an easy, but imperfect, substitute for the manifestation of joy and love in our lives that can only come from within.

Awakening and Healing the Rainbow Body

The knowledge of predatory energy is not meant to cause paranoia, but to awaken us to the true reality of life. We need to look beyond "the box" to find our power and reclaim it. Life will shift accordingly. Regardless of our level of awareness, the encoded soul growth and karmic lessons will appear as the innate timing dictates. Our buttons will be pushed. Life will happen. Our soul will give us the opportunity to restore our selves completely to the rainbow body of light.

What binds our world so tightly to the illusion? Fear is the binding agent. Fear is the prevailing energy of humanity. It has been since "The Fall." All negativity springs from fear because fear is the absence of love. Fear is the power of those who sap the energy of humanity from the unconscious. How do we become fearless and capable of love? Discipline is the key to awareness. Discipline mobilizes the assemblage point and awakens soul consciousness. I am not speaking of self-torture and self-punishment. I am speaking of self-observation and self-correction – the Master's path.

---

[1] Sacred Mirrors, The Visionary Art of Alex Grey, Alex Grey, Inner Traditions International, 1990.
[2] The Power of Silence, Carlos Casteneda, Washington Square, 1987.
[3] The Active Side of Infinity, Carlos Casteneda, Harper Perennial, 1998.
[4] Deep Trance Shamanic Journeys, Volume I, Pachamama's Child, Jessie E. Ayani, Heart of the Sun, 2002.
[5] The Power of Now, Eckhart Tolle, New World Library, 1999.
[6] The Goddess in the Gospel, Margaret Starbird, Bear and Company, 1998
[7] The Woman with the Alabaster Jar, Margaret Starbird, Bear and Company, 1993
[8] Holy Blood, Holy Grail, Michael Baigent, Richard Leigh, and Henry Lincoln, Delacorte Press, 1982.

The Rainbow Body

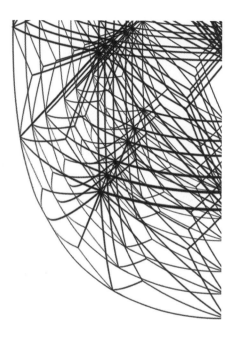

Illustration One

Awakening and Healing the Rainbow Body

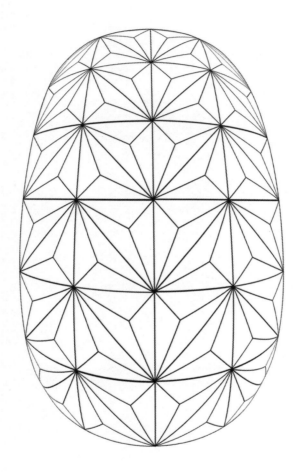

Illustration Two

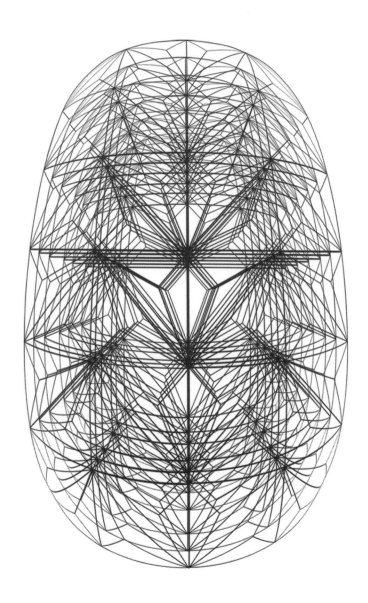

Illustration Three

Awakening and Healing the Rainbow Body

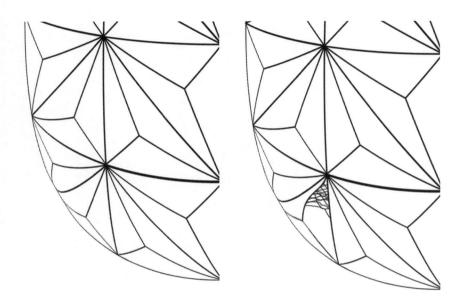

Illustration Four

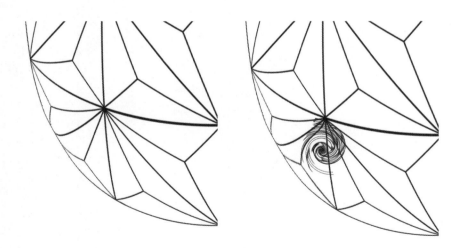

Illustration Five

THE ART OF MOVING ENERGY

The best way to approach entry-level energy mastery is to pay attention to the filaments. If we can begin seeing life in terms of energy and light, a powerful world will open to us. Be mindful that few have the ability to see the filaments of light, though it is not difficult to see a glow of pranic energy surrounding nature, especially at twilight. We can work with our personal orientation, which may be subtler than visualization – for example, a feeling of energy presence. We can allow our selves to find our own connection to energy without comparison or judgment.

As we proceed through this work of changing our lives (we are the miracle), we will learn to use intent, the prevailing force in the universe (filaments), to shift our reality into more conscious states of awareness. That awareness is more in keeping with our soul's intent than with the purpose we imagined for our selves in "the box." It is an easy progression but one that requires self-discipline. We may lose some friends in the process of self-correction, but new friends who support our new frequency will manifest in our lives – as will new button pushers for higher levels of the work. Let's remember that our soul had it all programmed into the scaffolding - and that included the discovery of this book.

Awakening and Healing the Rainbow Body

Moving energy is not just a phenomenon of the higher dimensions, but applies to our lives right down to the cellular level of the physical. If we forget any layer of our holographic body we will have geometry that restricts the flow of energy through the bamboo we are creating. Our objective is to become an inter-dimensional navigator. What does that mean? It means that our consciousness is mobile within our hologram and able to navigate the spectrum of light that we are. Our comfort zone may be the higher layer of the astral dimension where higher self is accessed, but we still need to be able to function in "the box," especially in service. Energy mastery's first step is self-awareness or self-realization – knowing our selves as light filaments and being able to use that knowledge to manifest different realities.

If we know the energies of each holographic layer and its interfacing collective consciousness, we have power over our presence in those dimensions – a very different picture from amnesia. To make sure that we have a visual picture of our own hologram interfacing with the collective consciousness hologram, let's visualize in fourth dimension. We have already discussed the concept of the assemblage point being anchored on a multitude of fourth dimensional filaments. The assemblage point is the interface and anchor between our fourth dimension and the collective unconscious (fourth dimension). Each dimension has bundles of filaments interfacing with our own field. It is in the art of shifting the assemblage point to a new anchoring point that allows us to access those realities.

For example, if we could shift our assemblage point and anchor it in second dimension, the world of devas, plant spirits, elves, and more, would open to us. There are those who are more comfortable in that dimension than this one. They may have an assemblage point that transits back and forth between the two dimensions to fulfill their mission. I am convinced that this is the plant's potential when a person uses a plant medicine like *ayahuasca*, the visionary plant of death in South America.[1] Many people write or speak of being confronted by a great serpent, who is the spirit of *ayahuasca*. The *ayahuasceros*, the medicine men who really know this plant, have journeyed countless times into these realms and know how the plant spirit can help to heal and awaken. And so it is with all of the plants; each has a gift to give us.

The Art of Moving Energy

The downside of many an *ayahuasca* journey, what may seem a hell to the participant, occurs when a person's assemblage point has no ability to move from its fourth dimensional anchor. The only way for the plant spirit to access the consciousness of the person is through that often hellish lower astral – a confrontation with the person's past. Some people use the ayahuasca to access this dark internal dimension to provoke their own awakening. Again, it is always our choice to go the route of pain and suffering, or ease and grace. If we intend to open our selves to energy mastery, a fascinating and powerful journey awaits us.

Essence

Another clear picture we want to have is that of our Essence – the original consciousness blueprint that maintains God-presence. Essence holds the geometry of the true ego – the I AM presence. The I AM consciousness, or Divine Self, is connected to Essence but is free to navigate within all realms of consciousness.

Likewise, our soul-consciousness (higher ego self or higher self) is connected to the blueprint of our hologram's scaffolding which it manifested in incarnation. Its realms of navigation are limited by its self-awareness. It is a remnant of the I AM presence, which is a manifestation of Essence. It holds the geometry of a higher ego, which is engaged in a search for its true ego self, a search that began with "The Fall." Lower ego, again, is a creation of third dimensional limitation.

There is a veil drawn first between our holographic presence and our soul consciousness or higher ego. The veil is life – everything we hope to clear as we walk this path. On the level of energy, we can think of this veil as randomized energy patterns created by our wants, needs, and desires. We connect more and more with higher consciousness as we release drama, clear our mental field, let go of our past, and tame our ego.

The second veil in our awareness is drawn between soul consciousness and the path that will take us to Essence, with its cosmic spectrum of light geometry. Essence expands in an immense twelfth dimensional hologram. Remnants of consciousness associated with the fifth through the eleventh dimensions are associated with luminescent geometric scaffolding that maps our eventual return to God.

Awakening and Healing the Rainbow Body

So, between our hologram of present consciousness and our ability to contact our soul lies the experience of this life – the baggage we are carrying in our unconscious and conscious states. That baggage includes conditions within our own bodies, all of the filamentous attachments to others, as well as the filamentous ties to energies held in the collective from our soul lineage, bloodlines, and unresolved thought forms, emotions, and so forth.

As our work progresses, the lower ego loses power to the higher ego, as soul or self-awareness grows. Higher self becomes the guidance system for the hologram from its place in the higher astral, close to the eye of the needle. The clearing of the scaffolds occurs as the work proceeds, allowing us to reinstate the flow of energy within the bamboo when soul alignment occurs. Soul alignment allows the full use of the chakra communication system with the outside world. Our hologram becomes fully functional and our higher self-consciousness, through discipline, is able to accelerate the lifting of the veil to the higher dimensions, drawing the cosmic hologram of Essence and Divine Presence towards us. Though the latter expansion is, usually, well beyond incarnations on earth, we can start the work right now.

How do we accomplish this? Part of the discipline is making choices about what enters and leaves our field. We are able to draw in, through the back of our chakras, all available energies as tools for our guidance system. Like most people, we might previously have been drawing in fear-related energies from the collective consciousness. These energies enter our hologram and influence the reactive emotional energies leaving our field from the front chakras – energies like anger, or hatred, or self-pity.

When we ask higher self to take the helm, we can consciously choose the energies entering our field, and the most beneficial energies are virtues – like kindness, acceptance, patience and gratitude. If we can bring these energies in, the energies leaving our field will look more like compassion, joy and love. Exercises like these begin before we fully connect with higher self. In fact today is a good day to begin with the simple observation of what we do take in and release. Even as our body is a living organism with many functions, so too is the energetic body we tend to ignore.

The Art of Moving Energy

One day, higher self, using guidance tools incorporating all the attributes outlined in chapter one, will help to guide us through the eye of the needle – a journey taken without the baggage of the past or preconceptions of the future. In self-realization and passage through the needle's eye into the heart-centered realms of the fifth dimension, our Christ Self is the focus of attainment, drawing Essence even closer. Actual geometric shifts will begin to occur within our scaffolding to align it to our consciousness memory before "The Fall."

Healing the Rainbow Body

Our healing work will begin with the **physical body** and, ultimately, it will end with the physical body. This is the body encoded with the genes of our bloodlines. Throughout our upbringing, the scaffolding of the physical body can shift the geometry in the lower scaffolds causing distortion. The work we will be doing with core beliefs, drama, and the mind, in the fourth dimension, will begin to lessen the hold that this body's geometry has on us. This will ease the tension between the physical and etheric, allowing the etheric template to more authentically hold the physical form.

As our work progresses it is necessary to return to the physical body. For example, the price paid for overdoing physical clearing is usually a setback illness caused by released toxins. If we have not been detoxifying our bodies, we will want to be gentle in the beginning. If we have not been exercising or working with our breath, we will put our bodies in an uncomfortable state of toxic release by over doing it.

Our body is the temple – the vehicle of ascension in the earthly dimensions. If we are to integrate a body of light into our earthly life, the body must be able to hold it. Remember we are bringing the Divine right down to the base chakra – embodying heaven on earth. Additionally, for some of us, the unfolding Mission of Christ Consciousness and Planetary Ascension will require mastery over the physical form. That is not a Mission for the faint of heart, or for those lacking discipline and self-awareness.

In energetic mastery, there is the need to change the bloodline DNA to better support the journey towards Essence and the new scaffolding that accompanies that journey into the higher dimensions.

Awakening and Healing the Rainbow Body

We will continue to prepare the physical body for possible shifts in this direction. In the process, we will begin to enjoy the benefits of good health that consciousness bring us. We can consider the material in this book to represent the ascending triangle in the Star of David – a pyramid of health beginning in the physical and ending at the eye of the needle – the gateway of fire and portal to the body of light.

The **etheric body** interfaces on the nerve trunks with the physical body. It is the template that guided formation of the physical body and the source of energy that animates and energizes it. Conversely, it is the physical body, through proper metabolism and respiration that provides our richest source of electrons for the etheric body. We could call it a symbiotic energy relationship. Healing of the etheric body is aimed at increasing energy flow, reducing stagnation, and correcting aberrant geometry. Healing at this level has immediate benefits for the physical body as well as the interfacing emotional body.

Because the genetics of the etheric body differ somewhat from the bloodline genetics, the etheric body, being more flexible, will stretch itself to conform and to hold an etheric form when bloodline genetic flaws do not. When the individual is young this is easy to accomplish though it does ask the higher scaffolds to shift as well. However, as the individual ages and the energies of life affect the field, the job of holding form becomes challenging for the etheric template. We will look in depth at the healing of the etheric body.

Our **emotional body** is an energetic bridge between the physical world and the fourth dimensional or astral world. It sends messages through the etheric to the physical, which release the chemicals of feeling into our bloodstream. In this way, we can feel joy, anger, fear, and so forth, in the physical body. Unfortunately, this body's interface with the mental (astral) field creates a steady flow of information from the computer system of the unconscious that misguides the pure feelings of the body, turning them into preprogrammed reactions. We will work to distinguish between the two, and consciously isolate the feeling when healing the emotional body.

The holographic emotional field is fully within the physical and etheric fields but extends beyond them, creating part of the aura. This body is our emotional bridge to others – a field in which reactions are given and received. Everyone knows what if feels like to get too close to an angry person. How often do we think about how our reactions are affecting others? Healing in this body will entail the clearing out of stuck emotions from the past, allowing energy to flow unobstructed. Such stagnation in the emotional body distorts its geometry and can affect the etheric body's ability to hold form in the physical body. The result is disease.

Most people do not have command of the emotional body. In fact, for many, the filaments of this body have been directed to lodge in the emotional bodies of others. This thought-directed, boundary-less invasion of another's space is driven from the lower astral for the purpose of fulfilling wants, needs, and desires. It amounts to the giving and taking of power. In this realm, we mistakenly call some of this love. A big part of our healing work is retrieving the filaments of our emotional field and removing those present in our field that do not belong to us. Our power in the world of energy (intent) is greatly diminished unless all of our filaments are returned to our field.

The physical body, etheric body, and emotional body combine to give us our third dimensional awareness – an awareness of our selves in body on Mother Earth. Healing in third dimension should be geared to acknowledge the role that all three bodies play in our health on this plane. The bloodline DNA directly affects the physical scaffold, and influences all of the other bodies through the imposition of energies it encodes, for example, a genetic mutation. A genetic disorder, which inhibits the smooth flow of electrons, would directly affect the etheric body. A disorder of the myelin sheath of the nerves would surely affect the way in which energy is circulated and felt in the body. A disorder involving brain chemicals would greatly distort the ability of the emotional body to have clear communication with the physical.

DNA encoding the etheric and emotional templates, and all templates of the higher bodies, can mutate just as our physical DNA can mutate – for good or for ill. As we age, the toxins of life present within our cellular fluid begin to fray the ends of our physical body DNA, compromising the integrity of DNA replication and protein production. Important structural proteins and levels of enzymes reduce with age and the body loses its efficiency and resiliency. The same thing happens with the DNA of our higher bodies. There are causes of mutation on the energetic levels similar to those on the physical. We are capable of clearing the toxicity at all levels, correcting the scaffolding to its original geometry, and repairing or, if necessary, "mutating" the DNA to accept the body of light.

Our work with the lower astral bodies, the **emotional-mental** and the **intellectual-mental**, will begin to restore our energetic power system as the original soul-consciousness templates are cleared. This is the work of conscious dying as previously discussed. It spans the two great initiations of water and wind. It is all about self-awareness gained through self-observation and self-correction. Healing of the lower astral opens the higher astral and the **spiritual-mental body,** and its gifts, to us.

Our objective, in entering the unconscious, is mastery of the assemblage point – mastery of our reality. To do this, we must understand the unconscious as a thought-form field as closely interfaced with its collective counterpart as are our lower bodies are with theirs. For example, our etheric bodies draw Qi from the collective etheric body of nature through food and air. Once we have established some power in the unconscious through clearing, and regaining any energy lost to predators, we will be able to mobilize our assemblage point and begin gaining control over it. Then, the art of moving energy with intent truly begins.

Every exercise described in this book is a form of moving energy. It is important to be solid, systematic, and patient in our work. We must respect our own timing in this work and in all that we do. We must use caution when considering anything that offers a quick fix, magic bullet, or immediate access to the higher realms. We must be disciplined to avoid the sources of predatory energy in this reality. Our journey into energy will begin with the art of discernment and the discipline of self-observation and self-correction.

Marketers of the New Age would lead us to believe that we have no power to heal without their products, that our DNA has no capability of activating itself without their help, or that we too can learn to channel the masters, thus becoming a guru to others. The list is endless – a supermarket of illusion. If we regard it as such, we may be able to have some fun shopping. If we take it too seriously, we will lose our power in the supermarket. Time may prove the New Age to be a short-term exercise

The Art of Moving Energy

in discernment. Enlightenment has been around throughout the ages. There are no certificates or diplomas of self-realization. They wouldn't fit through the eye of the needle.

Restoration of the Glow

Having been born into the world with our glow of awareness offers some hope that we can restore it. No one else can do this for us. Our life experiences and thought forms reflect the loss of awareness. We alone have the ability to access the memory of those experiences and thought forms and, through discipline and the acquisition of the attributes of the path, mobilize our geometry, returning it to its original form. In that form, energy flows through our bamboo, higher self is our new guidance system and the original intent of the soul for this lifetime, aligned with our Original Birth Template, is fully restored. Once this intent is realized, we are free to pass through the eye of the needle into fifth dimension.

Critical to the restoration of awareness is the smooth flow of energy in the holographic body. The luminous body, made of core beliefs, is no longer a rigid barrier obscuring our gifts but a flexible, mutable energy of intent, lightly anchored with new bundles of filaments anchoring our consciousness in the upper astral. All holes where energy was previously leaking are repaired during our healing journey. Any portals in the lower astral, where predatory energies had previous access to the field, are protected.

When the field is in energetic balance, we enjoy smooth communication from scaffold to scaffold through their interfaces. In addition, we have smooth communication with the outside world through the back and front chakra vortices. As our work progresses, the energetic resources with which we inform our field shift from the wants, needs, and desires of the lower ego to the virtues of the higher self. All of this contributes to the flow of energy through the bamboo. We are grounded on the earth but are communicating with the heavens – and the communications are clear.

The most important quality to embody with respect to the restoration of our glow of awareness, is discipline. There is no place for weakness once we begin to walk on this path. Weakness does happen, even with consciousness, but it will cost us valuable time and energy to regain our power. Mindfulness – attentiveness – is required, and that takes discipline. That is why we will begin with some physical disciplines to awaken the warrior nature needed to walk this path in power.

It might be a good time to insert a word or two about balance. Part of our journey is the integration of masculine and feminine energy within us – bringing the yang and the yin into harmony. This begins in the physical body and continues through the healing of the holographic field. If Essence, our Original Divine Template, originated when we separated from God, its yang and yin will be equally balanced because that original consciousness (I AM) is androgenous. Balancing yin and yang will become part of our work as we move though the healing of each layer of our field. In the study of T'ai Chi, for example, they speak of becoming iron wrapped in cotton – the soft, pliable exterior characteristic of the spiritual warrior. It is all about energy.

This is an invitation to engage the art of moving energy – to become the master of our reality. This path will lead us to the eye of the needle, the passageway leading beyond time and space. In self-realization, we can transit through the needle experiencing the implosion or collapse of our previous holographic awareness and its rebirth in our body of light. The tranquil space before the needle's eye lies within the still landscape of the awakening heart.

---

[1] Wizard of the Upper Amazon, Bruce Lamb, Atheneum, 1971.

NOTES

PART TWO

Healing the Rainbow Body

PHYSICAL FITNESS

Ascension begins and ends in our physical body. Acknowledging that simple truth and incorporating it into our assemblage points can make all of the difference when it comes to discipline and motivation. The body is affected by, and affects all of the scaffold geometry in the hologram. If we cannot maintain health at this level, our journey on earth will revolve around the dis-ease in the physical body instead of our missions. In this chapter we will learn about the complexity of the physical body and the simplicity of preventative medicine. In further chapters, influences of the etheric, emotional and mental fields will be added. Because we are multidimensional, no field can be ignored in complete health.

If we have ever chanced to study anatomy, physiology, and the biochemistry of metabolism, we have an appreciation for the work of mastery that is the body. The intricacies of a well-functioning body are as mind-boggling as are the aberrations that lead to its dysfunction. A serious dysfunction spawns a cascade of debilitating events that can soon lead to the demise of the physical body. And yet we have amazing resilience, and inherent powers to heal our selves.

Awakening and Healing the Rainbow Body

Unfortunately our culture has traded wisdom for knowledge and in so doing has lost the balance that is health. Knowledge limits us to third dimensional reality – this physical world. In that world the approach to medicine is mechanistic and based on the laws of physical science. In frustration, and often desperation, an alarming number of people have turned to alternative medicine, paying out of pocket for these medical expenses. An ever-growing number of Americans are opting out of health insurance altogether – most because of escalating costs, but a substantial percent due to conflicting ideologies. Western medical clinics are incorporating alternative practitioners into their partnerships to avoid loss of revenues to alternative medicine but also because medical students and patients have generated a genuine interest in complementary medicine. The assemblage point of western medicine may be shifting, slowly but surely.

There are now ample opportunities to find medical doctors who have personally been opened to alternative ideas and energy, and who have incorporated those concepts and training into their own practices as well as their own lifestyles. If seriously ill, and under medical care, it is most important to continue with prescribed therapy as we begin to expand awareness as to other options. In no way is the material presented herein a substitute for ongoing medical care or medical counseling.

In *Molecules of Emotion*,[1] a lay-oriented book about the science of feeling, noted researcher, Dr. Candace Pert, makes the observation that almost all cancers are caused by our environment. She is not talking about the pure lakes and mountains of the high country. She is talking about environmental pollutants in the air we breathe, the water we drink, the depleted and chemically manipulated soil in which we grow our food, the toxins sprayed on our food to control the insects attracted to weak crops, and those we apply to our skin. To the list of toxins, a growing number of health conscious people would add the vaccines we inject into our own and our children's bodies and the antibiotics and other pharmaceuticals, which we take "to cure" dis-ease. Though they are able to assist us, they are toxic loads to the body. We can also add the food additives and preservatives, the leaching of estrogen-mimicking molecules from the plastics we use to store and market food and drink, and the chemicals of stimulation and relaxation that we have come to depend upon. These are

Physical Fitness

found in coffee, tea, chocolate, sugar, alcohol, and recreational drugs. Monitoring toxins in our environment requires awareness and vigilance. If we can master the art of moderation, these chemicals can be used at appropriate moments to assist the body rather than to create a dependency or addiction that can harm it.

Science has, on one hand, opened the door to true molecular understanding of our physical world with a physical medicine beyond the imagining of early scientists. On the other hand, science has also created the poisons that have come to harm us. It doesn't take much to upset the balance within our bodies – or our planet. Like all of our institutions, western medicine is fear-based and curative rather than love-based and preventative. It seems we are always picking up the pieces and trying to right the wrongs in our world – a sure sign that we lack the foresight that comes with intuition. We readily give our power away to that which we fear, or to that which mystifies or overwhelms us - and medicine is no exception. Though there exists within the system some appreciation of the cause of disease, the extent of dis-ease now present in our culture will continue to overwhelm and exhaust the medical establishment and all of our resources until something radical happens to shift consciousness.

To walk this path, we must learn to take care of our selves – to be responsible not just for our emotional and mental life, but for our physical bodies as well. If, as we read this, we feel resistance welling up within us and find our selves mentally quoting some recent study about the benefits of chocolate or wine, let's try to separate our selves from the marketing. If we become sensitive to our bodies by learning to turn off our minds and listen within, we will be aware when we are putting them at risk. If we chose to have a glass of wine with dinner, we must be aware that we are taking in a toxin, which will put our liver under some stress. If we are in good health and aware, we can drink the glass of wine with the assurance that our liver will metabolize it for us. If we are compromised metabolically, we may damage cellular integrity throughout the body. In other words, we can drink the glass of wine consciously – and, if we take in toxins moderately but frequently, we can, and should, cleanse our livers regularly. If we are truly addicted, guidance should be sought to manage our journey to wellness. If we are willing to make some lifestyle changes, our bodies can be detoxified and revitalized as the temples they were meant to be.

Awakening and Healing the Rainbow Body

Medicine as War

People will argue that cancer has always existed. This may be true but one hundred years ago people didn't run out of fingers counting the number of their friends who had cancer - and in the prime of their lives. Cancer is epidemic in our culture. Historically, the enemies of health have been the infectious plagues spurred on by poor hygiene, contaminated water supplies, and inadequate sewage disposal – that and just plain working the body to exhaustion. Through modern medicine, we have prolonged life but, simultaneously, our science has compromised the quality of that life. An ever-increasing number of people are dying with morphine dripping into their veins, rather than with their boots on - vibrantly living life.

Western medicine is continually looking for new strategies to combat disease when it is the assemblage point of the institution itself that must shift. We need only change the fear-based beliefs that support medicine as a metaphorical defense department. Observe the language used to describe medical treatment - strategies, prognoses, advertising, and research. Microbes are enemies. We are fighting cancer, waging war on AIDS, battling dis-ease, and on and on. As long as we regard our selves as separate from the rest of life we will never know peace – not in our bodies and not in the world. Our medicine is a reflection of our politics and religion because the same adversarial (fear-based) belief systems are fundamental to each. Are we not part of this landscape - Mother Earth?

At the same time Louis Pasteur used bright field microscopy to put forth the germ theory about microbes that established medicine as a curing profession engaged in the art of war, another man, Antoine Béchamp put forth a very different theory. Through dark field microscopy, live (rather than fixed/dead) blood analysis, Béchamp discovered that microbes, or their potential, are always with us. In the blood he discovered microzymas, which held the potential to become different microbes, depending on the environment present. Microbes are everywhere, including within our bodies. They are not always invaders bent on harming us, though occasionally we ingest contaminated food or water and inhale a good dose of airborne microbes that do overwhelm our systems from without.

Physical Fitness

We also share microbes with others through intimate contact, blood transfusion or contamination, and respiration. These can be harbored in the body for a long time before the milieu becomes toxic enough for proliferation. We accept the role of friendly bacteria in the gut, but we have a hard time seeing the goodness in a streptococcus in our respiratory system. Like all of life on earth, we are interwoven in a grand scheme of balance. As long as that balance is maintained, all of nature is healthy, and flourishes. As soon the balance falters, the weaving loses its integrity.

On his deathbed Pasteur is said to have admitted that Béchamp's theory was correct and his own was not. It was too late. The germ theory was already embedded in allopathic medicine – and remains so today. It is time we adopted Béchamp's theory, which supports a holistic approach to microbial beings of all sorts. It is time to regain our immunity, which can maintain our systems in a state of balance. Microbes - yeast, viruses, parasites, bacteria, and more - flourish in toxicity. If we are toxic, we can expect to be sick. If we take poisons to suppress an uprising we are adding to our toxicity. We may succeed in suppressing the uprising but we have seeded the next foray by driving the "enemy" deeper into the body.

Suppressing microbes (or any manifestation of dis-ease) can cause them to go deeper into the body to survive. When disease processes are suppressed within the body, the body must find another way to express the dis-ease – often resulting in a more sinister manifestation of the disease than previously expressed. As we engage the clearing of the body those microbes will be drawn out and the infection will be reexperienced until we regain the balance. We can find some reading material on live blood findings and have an analysis to see what is happening in our own blood. We can become aware of the risk factors for drugs we contemplate taking, and read the growing body of literature about the risks of vaccination and the use of antibiotics. Of the vast number of books written about holistic medicine where we can research our physical bodies and beyond, two highly recommended books are *Radical Healing*,[2] and *Vibrational Medicine*.[3]

Radical Healing is a beautiful synthesis of the world's medicine and healing wisdom, rich with the information we need to take care of our selves in the toxic environment we have created. Dr. Ballentine has compiled an easy to read medical bible, which incorporates allopathic medicine and alternative medicine with many examples from his own health experience. He has included the story of Pasteur and Béchamp in this book. In *Vibrational Medicine*, Dr. Gerber offers a similar though less personal perspective, including interesting scientific data validating energy medicine. The medical doctors who wrote these books help challenge our thinking about many aspects of healing, and expand our awareness of the body.

How, then, do we turn medicine into the landscape of love? Once again, the place to begin is within. We can love and respect our own bodies. In educating and taking care of our selves we can face medical problems rationally and without fear. We can find ways to shift our consciousness away from the old assemblage point's adversarial foundation to one of co-creation. When enough of us shift our assemblage points, medicine will change as well. It is already changing on a small scale to accommodate those who enter the system for assistance with their own healing, without giving away their power for a quick fix. Beyond the initial shock of such patients, doctors have to love them for their willingness to take responsibility for their own lives. Participation has more impact than knowledge alone. We are part of the landscape, and can be active in building the new one.

Where does the adversarial backdrop originate in our culture? The collective unconscious influences us through myth and the actual history of events on earth. Our collective thought patterning is very much about war, empire building and the abuse of power that accompanies these patterns. Our cultural systems are based on war. Is it any wonder we have such violence and mindlessness all around us? Even war protestors take a militant stand in their actions. The collective is a yolk we can and will shake off. The pulse of liberation is already beating in the hearts of many.

Amidst all of the violent history of mankind, the mystics held a space of peace, and their legacy and legends endure. Can we be in this world without being of it? Can we hold a space of peace and love where there is violence and fear? Of course we can. We are not volunteering for the firing squad by turning our backs on fear. We can actively hold love and peace in our hearts as energy, not as action. This is the feminine way. Peace begins within.

Physical Fitness

Healing the Body

There are two essential paths we walk while healing the physical body. We would like to regain our health and then maintain health within the concept of balance. The first path is corrective and the second is preventative. In addition to each path, there are two sides to the path. We must find the balance between the yang, doing side of the path, and the yin side of the path, with its energies of nourishment and non-doing. Regaining health can appear complex and overwhelming whereas prevention is simple but requires discipline.

We will still be healing and clearing the physical body when we reach the eye of the needle. It is an ongoing process because we do not live in a bubble. Life continues to happen, the environment is polluted, and we are part of it. It is good to begin a program for the physical work now that will continue and expand as we progress through the rainbow body healing. Supportive physical programs are built gradually but persistently. Beginners will want to avoid overdoing physical exercise that could lead to serious detoxification. We will build up to our ideal workout one step at a time. If the bottom falls out of our initiative through a toxic reaction, like a cold or flu, it can set back our entire effort.

In addition to our personal regeneration program it is recommended that for the cleansing efforts, organ and systemic health monitoring, and, if necessary, the nutrition, we seek the guidance of one or more trusted alternative health care practitioners. An initial evaluation using kinesiology, meridian diagnosis, iridology, or computer-generated energy analysis, would provide a great base reading for our program. We can do this without giving our power away to anyone. There is no one person with all of the answers. We must use discernment to make our medical choices. If we are informed, we can take an enlightened and powerful stance against western medicine's predilection for conducting human experiments. It is a research model that has worked well for investigative medicine but we don't have to participate in it.

For example, hormone replacement therapy has its advantages but now, after millions of women have used it, we know that it dramatically increases the risk of breast cancer. The live polio vaccine was developed to set up a living culture of the polio virus in the small intestines, but now we know that the virus wandered in many people and may be partly responsible for fibromyalgia, and possibly an array of post-polio-like symptoms. We can become researchers on behalf of our own health, then go out and get what we want for support. We can use our inner guidance system to fit the pieces together. Keep in mind that alternative practitioners can be equally mired in the "fix me" assemblage point of western medical doctors.

It is not a bad idea to develop some skill in self-diagnosis as well. Dr. Ballentine's *Radical Healing* will certainly help to guide us, but we can also ask that some kind of connection (a guidance system) be established between the body and higher self. As our spiritual work progresses into the higher astral, our internal guidance system will kick in fully, but we can begin working with it now. We can use our external support system to verify our results. We can explore muscle testing, pendulums and divining rods for starters. The hardest part of making the inquiry is keeping our thought processes out of the inquiry. We can practice removing our preconceived ideas from the test and let the innate knowledge of the body resource the data bank for us.

On a personal note, I came to know my body's message system through my support person, whose use of muscle testing/kinesiology opened the door for his own clear medical intuition to enter. After many years of recommendations with good results, my body began sending messages to me through an internal voice – sometimes yelling out the name of a supplement to get my attention – "grapefruit seed extract now!" I would get right on it, then check with my practitioner for verification. In time I learned to trust the voice, and to know that it was the same voice he was listening to when he tested me – my higher self.

The process of dis-ease is complex, reaching from the physical body right up through the astral. Any dis-ease that might be present in our bodies could have many components from our higher bodies. Here, the intent is to heighten awareness not to diagnose. Some important avenues of pursuit will be presented for our research with referenced books at this chapter's end. As a generalization, the following might be considered as the most common causes of imbalance in the human body in our culture:

Physical Fitness

1. <u>Inadequate Nutrition</u> - due more to poor choices in diet rather than to lack of food, but also due to the general lack of nutrients in our soils, producing food without life-sustaining nutrients.
2. <u>Food and Chemical Poisoning</u> – due to additives, preservatives, sugar, processing and overconsumption of foods that are highly allergenic and that cause glandular dysfunction.
3. <u>Drug Poisoning</u> – prescription, over the counter, recreational, and all consumption addiction.
4. <u>Heavy Metal Poisoning</u> – due to inhaled and ingested pesticide and fertilizer residues, chemical industry products, and the heavy metals in vehicle exhaust, dental amalgams, and vaccines, to name a few.
5. <u>Lack of Exercise</u> – aerobic, stretching, and strengthening.
6. <u>pH Imbalance</u> – due to all of the above. This can combine with the stored toxins and food residues to provide the toxic environment for proliferation of the symbiotic microbes.
7. <u>Poor Immune Function</u> – due to all of the above. When not overwhelmed, the immune system plays a major role in maintaining a healthy, balanced body.
8. <u>Abuse/Overuse of the Body</u> – including untreated injuries, sports related strains and injuries, work related physical abuse like repetitive motion injury, general stress and neglect.
9. <u>Our Emotions and Our Intellect</u> – the subject of chapters seven through nine.

These imbalances cause toxicity. The toxicity allows our ever-present symbiotic microbes to proliferate causing pain, lethargy, immobilization, obesity and malnutrition, arthritis, tumors and the list goes on. We are the sum of our parts with a body in need of holistic attention. *The pH Miracle*[4], an eye-opening book about health recovery is outstanding. We can make it our bible of health recovery. Countless people have used Dr. Young's dietary program to turn their health around, restore energy and strength, and reach their ideal weight without counting a calorie. However, it requires the discipline of lifestyle change – no problem for warriors on this path. It is shown that we will most often respond favorably to an alkaline diet and no longer crave the foods that are responsible for acidity and the most common debilitating dis-eases of the body. In fact, we begin

Awakening and Healing the Rainbow Body

to crave the foods we need to balance pH. Dr. Young's is a microbiologist whose approach to healing is empowering and scientifically accurate.

Here are a few suggestions about cleansing that circulate by word of mouth but never seem to get written down in one place. A good support person will likely mention them as well. When contemplating a liver cleanse understand that cleansing the liver will download tremendous toxicity into the intestines. If the colon has not been cleansed, do that first. If the colon is reasonably clean, start a colon cleanse three of four days prior to the liver cleanse to assure that released toxins will not accumulate in the colon. Continue the colon cleanse through the liver flush (Heroic) or for the first week of an herbal liver cleanse. We can give our body a refreshing alkaline boost upon waking each day by drinking fresh lemon juice tea (an ancient Chinese practice). It is recommended that you cleanse, especially the liver/gall bladder, with support person supervision.

We will find that much of the self-correction work before us will release restrictions placed on the physical body by the emotional and emotional-mental bodies. If we are not walking this path in a body free of pain, excess weight, stiffness, lethargy, and mental clarity, we may want to get with the program. Healthy remedies and good guidance should not be expensive. We can learn to recognize the red flags of practitioners who are actually the purveyors of supplements. We can find someone who is really interested in our health. We can find people in our community who have true health, and ask them who has helped them achieve that balance.

Formula for Health

Here are some simple but important suggestions for good health. Implementation of these suggestions is not difficult. Intelligent support abounds, especially in the books referenced in this chapter. Simplicity and intelligent support are equal in their importance. Balance and health depend upon the full integration of each into our lifestyles. In the next chapter, we will be adding to this list by making recommendations for the etheric body. We can call this the twelve-step program for physical body en-lighten-ment.

Physical Fitness

1. Aerobic Exercise.
2. Whole Body Stretching.
3. Strengthening Exercise.
4. Breathing Exercise.
5. Detoxification.
6. Eating Live, Fresh, Organic Food in pH Balance.
7. Supplementing Deficiency.
8. Drinking Pure, Living Water.
9. Sunshine, Fresh Clean Air, and Sufficient Rest.
10. Avoidance of All Toxic Substances.
11. Stress Reduction – Quiet the Intellect.
12. Love and Joy Replace Fear and Suffering.

Aerobic Exercise

Sustaining an elevated heart rate, appropriate for our age, for at least twenty minutes, constitutes aerobic exercise. The benefits far outweigh the effort, though getting going in a practice can be difficult, if not painful. The heart muscle and the lungs are exercised, at the same time more oxygen is delivered to the body. More oxygen means more energy. Energy begets energy, and produces "feel good" results in the body and temperament. It is win-win all the way. Obviously, the side benefits are fat burning, weight loss, muscle toning, and some strengthening. As we age, muscles lose their resiliency and can become flaccid in no time at all.

A good program of aerobic exercise should be performed three to four times a week. If we are not already engaged in aerobic activity, we had best take it easy in the beginning, slowing our pace and the number of workouts per week until our bodies adapt. This is one exercise system that will start downloading toxins into the muscle and blood because a lot of toxicity is in the fluid and tissue surrounding cells. Strong exercise will also release toxins from within the cells (especially fat cells), but we can expect an immediate release from muscle tissue and interstitium (tissue that holds us together). Drinking a lot of pure water, especially during and after exercising, will help to flush the toxins.

Initially, it is not uncommon to experience an uprising of microbes with cold or flu symptoms. If symptoms are insignificant, we can slow our

Awakening and Healing the Rainbow Body

workout but continue to workout lightly to keep the energy flowing. Drinking extra pure water will help flush the system. The workouts should cease temporarily if we don't feel good, and, obviously, if we should become more seriously ill or bed ridden.

If time permits, as a warm-up to aerobics, or perhaps on the other days of the week if time is short, we can make sure that the lymph system is exercised. The lymph system takes up cellular waste from the fluids surrounding tissue and deposits it in the blood stream via ducts in the upper thoracic area. Muscles must pump the lymph upwards. Walking is essential to good lymph drainage and gentle bouncing on a good (very springy) rebounder[5] is excellent. It is called the health bounce. If serious problems with swelling in the lower extremities exist (tested by pressing the thumb into the flesh around the ankle area and monitoring the depth of indentation as well as the time it takes for the ankle to look normal again), moving the lymph is important. Lymphatic massage can be especially helpful. Those with desk jobs, where there is little motivation for movement during the workday, would be wise to get up and walk around often. During free time, a stimulating walk could mean the difference between health and dis-ease. We can find tasks to break our relaxation time or we can use the rebounder occasionally during the day. The lymphatic system is largely responsible for removing toxins from the body and should be in good working order.

Everyone's preference for aerobic exercise will differ. Swimmers will need to adjust their workout time to achieve the desired heart rate. Swimming is a great way for us to exercise while taking it easy on our joints. Those of us who are group motivated can join a club or a martial arts studio and take advantage of good instructors, trainers and equipment. For those who prefer to work alone, there are many opportunities for exercise at home with videos, or we can pursue the many outdoor activities where we live. We do need to work up a good sweat for true aerobic fitness, this has an added bonus because sweating is an excellent form of detoxification.

Whole Body Stretching

To balance the aerobics and keep the body supple, whole body stretching is essential. This is not the same as the ten-minute cool-down

Physical Fitness

after aerobic exercise. I am referring to a complete yoga workout, or some other stretching system. Yoga is excellent because it works with the intellect as well as the breath. If there is time, this exercise is most beneficial when it follows the aerobic workout since the muscles are warmed up and easy to stretch. However, it may work better for our schedules to do yoga or stretching on alternate days. The important thing is that we stretch out thoroughly.

There are many forms of yoga to choose from, and certain kinds of yoga could fill the aerobic and/or strengthening requirements for a healthy body as well. One well-grounded and well-rounded yoga practice (and a good reference regardless), is that taught by Swami Satyananda Saraswati.[6] We can chose what appeals to us. Almost every town has a yoga center for good instruction and group participation. Even if we prefer to work out at home, an occasional appraisal of our postures is very helpful and helps us avoid injury or imbalance. For yoga at home, there are many videos available for every kind of yoga. It is best to wear loose, comfortable clothing.

Strengthening Exercise

Many aerobic forms of exercise, as well as serious yoga and martial arts, do strengthen the body. However, most aerobic dance forms do not strengthen it and, moreover, many aerobic forms put stress on the body that stretching alone will not neutralize. For example, cycling can traumatize the neck and the wrists, and many forms of aerobic exercise strain the lower back if the critical muscles involved are not strong. When our bodies are young and naturally supple, these forms of exercise tend not to strain the body, but when we begin to age, the opportunities for injury increase.

There are many forms of strengthening exercise, the most common being the use of free weights or machines with weights. These are recommend under the supervision of a trainer, at least in the beginning. Pilates is superb. Again, it is highly recommended to get at least weekly instruction at a minimum with Pilates since strengthening exercise with incorrect position of the body can eventually result in injury. Pilates develops core strength by working the internal muscles of the body. It corrects poor posture, strengthens typically weak muscles, and gives the body overall muscle strength and tone. Testimonials for Pilates abound from many people who have recovered from serious back injuries using it. Strengthening our core muscles takes the low back strain out of aerobic exercise. Combining Pilates with deep tissue bodywork could profoundly correct serious posture problems. A combination of weight training and Pilates is ideal and can take less than an hour and a half, three to four times a week.

Attending to the yin side of exercise, it is important to have regular massage and chiropractic or osteopathic care. Even if it is once a month, bodywork and bone alignment are essential to releasing toxins, reducing injury, and overall good health. If our structural alignment is deemed in good shape, we can trade the chiropractic or osteopathic for a second form of bodywork. If we are receiving deep tissue work, we can counter that with something subtle, like cranial sacral therapy. When we are in the mood for a different kind of massage, there are many other modalities to explore. If fate should find us in a spa offering aix massage or hot stone therapy, we can leave our body behind and fly.

Breathing Exercise

Though breathing will be addressed in the etheric body chapter, it is good to mention it here as well. Aerobic exercise has to do with breath, but it is not conscious breath exercise. The lungs do get an incredible workout, but they can be doing that without being fully utilized. If we follow the breath component of Pilates, designed to expand and strengthen the lung, we will be getting a more complete lung workout. However, there are breathing practices ages old that can help restore the body, detoxify volatile toxins, and add to our energy stores.

Most of our breath-training regimes come from Asia. Some of them spring from yogic traditional while others are anchored in martial arts systems. There are also examples of indigenous systems that have come out of shamanic practice - for example, the fire breath. Breath has importance in every esoteric tradition. We can find the system that appeals to us and begin training. We might find it beneficial to experience as many forms as possible to see and feel the benefits of each. This could become a fitness research project, especially since it is a requirement of energy

Physical Fitness

mastery. It goes without saying that breath work is only beneficial when the air is relatively free of pollutants.

Detoxification

Consider detoxification as the cleaning and maintenance of the temple. The frequency of cleaning depends on the amount and depth of accumulated waste and the exposure to toxicity present in the environment on a daily basis. As we continue our work together, detoxification will be necessary to truly let go of many deeply held issues. Though our memories are retrieved from the astral, for example, we hold all that has happened to us in our complete rainbow of bodies.

Initially, a thorough, well supervised, colon cleansing is imperative. If we seriously detoxify into a plaque-filled and sluggish colon we are asking for trouble. Once the colon is clear, we can detoxify the major organs, beginning with the liver, our body's detoxifying center. Liver cleansing will likely be perpetual as long we live in a polluted world, but how often depends on our toxic intake. Gall bladder health has much to do with fat intake and the genetic capabilities of the gall bladder.

When the liver is humming, we can turn our attention to the kidneys, respiratory system, blood, circulation and heart, and our immune systems. Exercising will help clear the lymphatic system, and attending to food allergies and parasitic/fungal infection will begin to heal our irritated and often leaky small intestines. The stomach will be soothed when we balance food intake, but many herbal cleanses exist to get things in order when they are not.

One of our largest organs, the skin, is an excretory organ as well as an absorbent organ. We can release toxicity through the skin, especially in thermal baths, steam rooms, saunas, and sweat lodges. We can, conversely, take in toxins that are topically applied – cosmetics, chemically-laden sunscreens, insect repellant, perfume, and so forth. We can learn to read ingredients, buy wisely, and avoid toxins when at all possible. Guidance from our chiropractor, homeopath or naturopath in our cleansing process is essential until we are able to manage it our selves. In the beginning, the best approach is to avoid overwhelming our systems, as we could begin to feel ill. After all, we can take into account the years of toxic buildup and give our selves a reasonable time to reverse it.

Awakening and Healing the Rainbow Body

If we read the references well, we can find a person whom we can trust to give us a whole body evaluation, then follow their recommendations about where to begin. Homeopathic and flower essence therapies can be an enormous help throughout this process, but herbs will be key to cleansing the physical body. As our detoxification efforts continue, we will want to keep good notes. It is a wonderful way to get to know the miracles that are our bodies.

Eat Live, Fresh and Organic Food in pH Balance

This sound like a tall order, and it is. Sound nutrition is the biggest challenge in our culture today. It is a sorry state of affairs when we have to hunt for real food. In the typical supermarket, ninety percent of the food is processed, and of the other ten percent, the meat (dead, of course) is contaminated with hormones, antibiotics, fear and suffering, and the produce is chemically laden and, if inorganic, dead. People who eat the Standard American Diet (SAD) are eating degeneration and death. Restaurant food has an additional bonus – eating the cooks' attitude. Naturally, that applies at home too, but it is easier to control in our own kitchen. Imagine the mindlessness leaving the kitchen of a fast food restaurant.

In America and Australia nowadays, most every community has a store with organically grown or produced food. We must sometimes pay a higher price for food with life, but the consequences of eating dead food should make this the highest priority in our health plan. In time, as we create a greater market for organic produce, it will become plentiful and inexpensive. The day will come when we put the chemically dependent agri-business out of business and turn the land back over to organic farmers. There is no other way to regain our strength as a people and to restore Mother Earth's depletion. In rural Europe, the ubiquitous markets supply beautiful in-season organic produce, as do the markets in countries too poor to use modern agricultural techniques. Reading at least one of the many books written about the perils of the modern agri-business would contribute greatly to our awareness and motivation. We do need to be informed so that we can make informed choices for our health.

The very best of all worlds is to grow our own food. If for no other reason, we will realize what fresh produce is supposed to taste like. If we

Physical Fitness

don't garden, we can look into the many community farms that bring organic produce to our door once a week throughout the season, or we can shop our local farmer's market, scouting the organic growers. They will be there. Most big cities have community supported farms as well as organic farms that sell to local groceries or have roadside stands. One thing that occurs to few people is the seasonal and geographic nature of food. In our stores, we have produce available year round from all over the country, and the world. Even though it may be organic, it will throw us out of balance because we are not eating in season. Eating tropical fruit when we live in a temperate climate is also hard on the body. Since it is truly hard to resist indulging out of season or out of our growing region, it is recommend that such indulgences constitute a minimal part of our daily diet.

Another important point to make is the amount of processed food on the shelves of organic grocery stores. It is still processed food. It is still dead even though it began with organic products. It is wise to minimize these items in our diet. Our greatest toxicity comes from the food we ingest. We are literally being food-poisoned in our culture. In addition to chemical additives, pollutants in fish, and pesticide residues, we have to consider foods that are toxic in, and of, themselves. The most common food allergens are wheat and other glutinous grains, corn, processed soy, dairy products (especially cow), sulfites in wine, and eggs. Commonly ingested, but outright toxic foods include pork, sugar, alcohol, coffee, MSG, aspartame and other chemical sugar substitutes.

When we are allergic to a food – often from having overconsumed it earlier in life – it acts as an allergen setting up an immune response in the small intestine not unlike an autoimmune dis-ease. Resulting inflammation blocks the normal absorption job of the small intestine leading to malnutrition. Eventually, we may end up with leaky-gut syndrome or another malfunction of the digestive system.

Sometimes food causes the release of toxins or harmful mineral deposition because of a reaction peculiar to an individual's body. A lot of these peculiarities come through the bloodlines. For example, many people with osteoarthritis are simply allergic to the nightshade family of plants. This is so common we can find warnings about the deadly nightshades in folk medicine, macrobiotics, and so forth. The family

Awakening and Healing the Rainbow Body

members, tomatoes, potatoes, eggplant and peppers (caspicums), produce or release an acid in the body which causes calcium to deposit in joints. Eliminating these much loved foods when symptoms appear will greatly reduce the arthritis if not eliminate it. If we come from a family where osteoarthritis is prevalent, we may want to have our support person muscle test us for this familial biochemical reaction. Discipline is required to maintain a diet free of allergens (just as one free of toxicity) but the rewards far outweigh the effort. The regaining of energy, freedom from pain and suffering, a happier outlook on life, and a trimmer body are compelling outcomes. Once we are cleared of allergy though abstinence, an occasional indulgence will not hurt us.

There is always the question about the need for vegetarianism as we walk the spiritual path. There are many reasons to support vegetarianism, both political and spiritual, but the choice, in awakened consciousness, is up to our bodies. If our body is craving meat, we can eat organic lamb, free-range chicken, or turkey, the only three reasonably safe meats. If meat-eating is deep within our bloodlines – meaning that our body would naturally expect it – we must take our time withdrawing from it if we are becoming vegetarian. Deep-sea fish provides another good source of protein. Again, we can trust the presentation in *The pH Miracle* for a vegetarian diet that supports an alkaline pH.

Many long term vegetarians have permanently lost muscle mass from protein starvation. How does that serve the body? In protein deficiency, after muscles mass is metabolized (destroyed) by the body to sustain organs, the precious enzymes of metabolism are destroyed, and, finally, the organs themselves will be lost. If we are going to be a vegetarian, we can make sure that we have adequate protein. Most vegetarians rely on soy for protein, which can be problematic if we are allergic to soy. There are ways of combining food to make sure we do get enough protein and there are plenty of vegetables rich in protein (see *The pH Miracle* book for charts of protein content).

For those who have cleansed and are eating good organic food but still crave meat, why not be attentive to our bodies? It is possible that your body accesses that form of protein more efficiently than plant based forms of protein. Like any food or drink with heavy energy, when our body no longer needs meat or fish, eating them will make us sick – like an

Physical Fitness

allergy. Learning to trust that our body knows its needs is the key, and then we can eliminate that which is toxic. This will naturally happen as our frequency raises.

Eating the right food in moderate portions (less and less as we age) will take all unnecessary weight from our body - naturally. It takes time for a lifestyle change to correct body weight and shape, but if the new lifestyle stays in place, the weight will not return. Lean bodies (not starved) are more likely to be healthy bodies for all of our years, while overweight bodies are more likely to attract degeneration and dis-ease. The stagnation and toxicity accompanying obesity will, ultimately, obstruct efforts to master the physical body.

We would have to be fairly oblivious or in a lot of denial to be uninformed about the danger of sugar. Every book on health will warn of the mood swings, the damage to the pancreas, and the diabetic future in store for sugar lovers. If we have Candida (a common systemic yeast infection), eating sugar or anything with sugar in it, including most fruit will inflame our problem. Why? Sugar produces acid in our bodies, and yeast proliferate in the acid. At the same time yeast consume the sugar to survive (this is the biology that makes bread rise). It is good to research Candida now, especially if we have any symptoms of Candida. As a result of our acid-forming, sugar-laden, dietary habits, Candida is epidemic in our culture. We can have pain, lethargy and bloating from the yeast and their by-products, which take the joy out of life. If we do have Candida (another thing for our support person to test), there are good diets to follow (*The pH Miracle*, for example), lots of information available, and some supplements that help reduce the yeast population. Even if we do not have an uncontrolled Candida population, it is best to avoid sugar as a proven potent toxin.

Candida brings up the issue of pH, another topic we will find in every good health book now. We should be in relative pH balance metabolically – blood pH 7.365. Those with Candida, and most people on the standard American diet, are decidedly acidic, while a minority of people tend towards alkalinity. A small roll of litmus paper used to test saliva and urine upon waking is a good way to track pH, though the most accurate way is a blood test. We can use the opposite food groups to shift our pH over time to neutrality, then maintain a balanced diet. The foods we love to love - baked goodies, candies, chocolate, coffee, alcohol, meats, and vinegar and/or sugar containing condiments - are all acid producing. We can learn to love vegetables, especially those in the dark, leafy green category.

Supplementing Deficiency

Our support people should be able to guide us to supplements needed by the body for proper function. We live in a less than perfect world. Our soil is depleted of the nutrients needed by the plants that used to provide a wide array of vitamins and minerals necessary to sustain health. A trip to the health food store can be overwhelming these days as the vitamins and minerals take up a fraction of the space allotted to other supplements. Many of the products available are metabolites, plant and animal components or extracts, herbs – both western and eastern – and formulas. The pendulum swings between taking nothing at all, to thinking we will have ill health without all of it.

This is another area where self-education pays off. Some of that education will come through our support people, but most of it will be through written material. Again Dr. Ballentine's book contains a wealth of information about herbs, homeopathic medicines, tissue salts, flower remedies, and how to use them. He also has an excellent nutrition section. It helps to know why vitamins and minerals are needed in the body. Antioxidants are highly recommended by most alternative health practitioners and mainstream doctors. Not only are they dis-ease preventatives, they work against aging and degeneration in general.

With the right guidance for our support people, we women can breeze through menopause without hormone replacement, and without hot flashing and mood swings. This time of life can be managed smoothly with supplements like progesterone creams (wild yam) and omega 3-6-9 oils. The array of supplements available to us at this time is unprecedented. We are fortunate to have this support, but must learn to choose them knowledgeably with guided support. We are all unique in our needs.

Herbal medicine has been around longer than any medical resource. Anyone who is knowledgeable about herbs can grow most of their medicine in their back yard or wild craft it. For example, there is more bio-available calcium in a nettle leaf infusion than in a calcium tablet made from chalk (calcium carbonate). Herbs are food holding the nutrients in a natural balance, while supplements are generally derived through some processing steps. Though there is plenty of good herbal information on the bookshelves, it is easy to get into overwhelm searching for answers. It is best to read the work of a herbalist who has come to know the plants personally than to browse through an herbal pharmacopoeia. For some starter remedies in any easy to read format, try Dian Dincin Buchman's *Herbal Medicine*[7] book. Dr. Ballentine begins his book with a good section on herbs as well.

On the practical side, to get sufficient antioxidants to live in top condition in our polluted world, we would have to eat piles of the food rich in them. That is the power behind supplementation – it is a concentrated isolate. However, research into foods that are rich in what our body needs is not a waste of time. In China, most families had (and still have), amongst their many servants, a cook who knew food as medicine. If the family came from the lower class, the women of the household would be well versed in cooking themselves. The menus would shift through the year as the cook provided foods to temper the elements, strengthen against the spring wind, cool the heat of summer and so forth. When someone became ill, the cook was the first person to offer support. It is quite fascinating to research Chinese cooking in this way. Books can be found in the alternative medicine bookshelves where Traditional Chinese Medicine is located or at Chinese herbal stores or schools. Look for books about food as medicine. This, along with good herbal lore and homegrown food, was the way our ancestors stayed healthy.

One of the universally depleted minerals in soil and therefore in food production is magnesium. It is also one of the most needed minerals in the body. Muscles depend on magnesium every day, all day long. Trying to find bio-available magnesium calls for the assistance of our support people. Many supplements on the market contain magnesium and calcium that will never be absorbed or utilized by the body. We should ask our support people to recommend a good multivitamin, and a good multi-mineral supplement with trace minerals for starters. Once that routine is established, we can branch out to fill other needs.

Those who are interested in rejuvenation and quality of life, but also freedom from the pain of inflammation and fibrin deposition in tissue, may be interested in systemic enzymes. For some interesting research information try the web at *http://www.drwong.info*, and for good products and the latest developments by one of the scientists who formulated the systemic enzymes, search the web for the brand name *Generation+*.

Drinking Pure Living Water

Pure water is the fluid of life. Because most of our body is water, being sufficiently hydrated is a top priority. Recommendations are for a minimum of two quarts or liters of water a day for the average weight person in normal weather. When we are working hard, sweating, or are in a hot climate, the intake should rise. Tea, coffee, sodas and juice are not a substitute for water. In fact some of our favorite drinks promote dehydration. To find out more about the bodies reactions to dehydration, *Our Body's Many Cries for Water: You Are Not Sick, You Are Thirsty*[8] is a real eye opener. Our bodies were designed to drink water.

Unfortunately, the water provided for us by our cities and smaller communities has been contaminated by efforts at decontamination. City tap water is toxic. Quite by accident, I once took the water from the tap in the city where I used to live, and boiled it down to a nearly dry pan. What was left in the pan was a gel, not water. It was a gel of all the chemical additives used to "purify" the water – not including the volatile components like chlorine that had boiled off. After that experience, I cringed at the very thought of drinking it, making soup or boiling food in it, or, for that matter, bathing in it. To be safe, we need to find out what is in our public water, then buy an appropriate filtration unit capable of removing the contaminants. We may have to turn to delivered spring water, reverse osmosis, or distillation to provide safe drinking and cooking water for ourselves, and our families. Well water can and should be tested regularly for contamination and may require filtration too. It should be noted that boiling chemically treated water may remove gaseous substances like chlorine, but the other chemicals remain.

To have a fresh running spring nearby, where we can collect the water in glass or polycarbonate containers, is the best of all worlds. Water that is gushing forth from the earth is living water. Water brought through pipes with pumps, including well water, is dead. Drinking out of plastic containers (or storing food in them) increases our risk of hormonal imbalance, due to the leaching of estrogen-like compounds from the plastic into the stored liquid or food. Hard plastic polycarbonate is the only non-leaching plastic. The colored Nalgene brand bottles sold in outdoor recreation stores are made of polycarbonate. We can find polycarbonate containers in two and three-gallon sizes at some organic grocery stores also. Look for a "7" in the recycling symbol on the bottom.

In lieu of living water, we can do our best to drink pure water in glass or polycarb containers. There are devices available that can change our home water supply into living water through reversing the flow of the water as it enters the house or exits our water tap. Some astounding research is being done about the nature of water, surface tension and molecular structure – all linked to rejuvenation and renewal. Those who are interested in researching water can turn to the web or any good bookstore for information.

Many people are searching out places to live where fresh, pure water is available. Though it is a good way to protect our selves, it is not always feasible, and we must consider the environmental impact on the future of those pure places. Perhaps the better plan is to correct the water where we live through the many systems now available for in-house water purification. We can also support those who have environmentally friendly ways to improve our water supplies.

Sunshine, Clean Fresh Air, and Sufficient Rest

Who would argue that sunshine, fresh clean air and sufficient rest are critical to good health? Yet our lifestyles and living environments often deprive us of all three. Sunshine activates vitamin D within our skin. Though we do not want to burn the skin, a certain amount of skin exposure to the sun each day, if it is shining, will assure us of adequate vitamin D activation.

In the following chapter, we will discuss air as a source of energy. In our culture it is also the source of airborne pollutants. Like pure water, fresh clean air is in high demand these days. If we all move out to the wilderness to have clean air, we will pollute what is there and likely come face to face with some intense survival issues. Perhaps the balance is to visit nature as often as possible and to include a lot of plant life in our surroundings to provide us with oxygen.

Awakening and Healing the Rainbow Body

Given that technology has been in place for years to produce nonpolluting automobiles as well as inexpensive power, we need, as a people, to begin demanding accountability from our leaders and the corporations that pull their strings. This will not happen if we do not demand it. The discipline, in this case, is to rise above complacency and demand conscious leadership. The genius is here to create a healthy future for all those on earth, not just a wealthy future for the few who control the resources of the world.

When I think of adequate rest, my memory stirs up a story read in one of James Herriot's books (the *All Creatures Great and Small* series). A country vet in England, Dr. Herriot was called upon to put down a dying sheep. The ewe's health had deteriorated beyond repair. Dr. Herriot injected a lethal dose of anesthetic medicine as is generally done to put an animal down. His dosage was incorrect, and rather than dying, the ewe went into a deep sleep. The sleep went on for a long time, until, one day, she awoke in perfect health. I will always remember this story because it validates the body's innate capacity to heal itself – if we would just get life out of the way. Our sleep at night is replenishing and healing, but only if it is deep. Everyone knows what if feels like to get up from a deep sleep like one reborn.

We should have that kind of sleep every night - sleep without aches and pains, disturbing dreams, and mental irritability. This is something worth working towards, because the body does know how to heal itself. People resort to drugs or herbs to induce sleep, but that sleep is not replenishing – it is desperate. The answer lies in our multifaceted healing process, for what we hold in our bodies are the products of our entire field. If we are dedicated to our healing path, deep sleep, with its inherent power to heal, will be one of our ultimate rewards.

Avoidance of All Toxic Substances

If eating living organic food and supplementing as needed is the yang or doing side of good health, avoiding toxins is the yin or non-doing side. Both sides require vigilance and discipline. Since toxins have already been discussed and good references have been provided, little more need be said.

Physical Fitness

Stress Management – Quiet the Intellect

Managing stress can be a full time job depending on our lifestyle and personality. The work we are beginning here will help in many ways to calm the intellect, resolve emotional issues, and create a space within our lives for peace. Those of us who must resort to scheduling for time alone, or time to be with friends, might want to take a closer look at our lifestyles. Many of today's illnesses are stress-related. Lifestyle changes as well as internal healing are required to restore health. Treatment of those suffering from stress-related dis-ease has at least three components – elimination of the stress source, organ/gland/system healing, and relaxation therapy.

Elimination of the source of stress may mean quitting our present job or changing our line of work entirely. Scaling life down to a reasonable financial commitment takes courage but rewards us with peace of mind – and often opens the door to a more profitable use of our talents. Those who have successfully reprioritized their lives feel strongly about protecting the peace they have found. Many people are working from their homes now. There is nothing wrong with a simple life. There is also nothing wrong with having things as long as they don't have us.

Assessing the damage to our bodies is another good reason to see a health professional. We can let our support people guide the restoration of our health, while we do the work of restoring it. Stress depletes the kidneys and adrenal glands very quickly and consistently. The kidneys, which hold the fire that warms our pot of Qi (next chapter), should be protected first and foremost. If our fire dims, our bodies will not serve us. Kidney depletion used to be found exclusively in the elderly. Now it is present in people of all ages who are living toxically and beyond their energetic capacity. The other system to suffer is the central nervous system (CNS). As the vital link to our Qi, the CNS should not be compromised, and yet we do it every day. Toxicity in the body stresses the CNS, as does over-stimulation by life's many distractions and addictions. Stress acidifies the body, promoting toxicity from within.

The CNS is a difficult system to restore though some of the techniques in this book will help in the healing. Becoming dependent on alcohol or even herbal relaxants is not the answer either. We must eliminate the source of stress in body, intellect, and spirit.

Awakening and Healing the Rainbow Body

The world of relaxation therapy has become a part of life in our culture – no, let's make that a basic survival need. Whether it be yoga, meditation in its many forms, hot tubs and jacuzzis, retreats in nature or an isolation tank, relaxation is being used by those who want to keep up their frenzied lifestyles, and do something for their bodies. Can we think about the concept of a lifestyle that is a meditation? Too often, it is a serious illness that makes such a lifestyle necessary. It may be something we want to write into our future – or our present.

Joy and Love Replace Fear and Suffering

The twelfth step in our program is a natural occurrence of enlightenment. If we have the discipline to stay with this work, love and joy will be ours, and fear and suffering will be dim memories of third dimension.

---

[1] Molecules of Emotion, Candace B. Pert Ph.D., Touchstone, 1997.

[2] Radical Healing, Rudolph Ballentine, M.D., Harmony Books, 1999.

[3] Vibrational Medicine, Richard Gerber, Bear and Company, 2001.

[4] The pH Miracle, Balance Your Diet, Reclaim Your Health, Robert O. Young, Ph.D. and Shelley Redford Young, Warner Books, 2002.

[5] Needak Manufacturing, 1-800-232-5762.

[6] Asana, Pranayama, Mudra, Bandha, Swami Satyananda Saraswati, International Yoga Fellowship - available in USA at www.atmacenter.com/books.

[7] Herbal Medicine, Dian Dincin Buchman, David Mackay Company, 1979.

[8] Our Body's Many Cries for Water: You Are Not Sick, You Are Thirsty, F. Batmanghelidj, M.D., Global Health Solutions, 1995.

ETHERIC FITNESS

      To understand the etheric body, we shall immerse our selves in the world of Traditional Chinese Medicine (TCM) – a medical system based on energy rather than mechanics. The Chinese see the body as a condensation of Qi, vital energy - activated and nourished by refined forms of Qi. Were it not for advances in quantum physics, the door to the east might never have opened because western thought is so anchored in form. In spite of that opening, it is a leap for most western-trained physicians to integrate eastern thought into their medical model. The marriage of these two seemingly disparate forms of medicine is one hope for the future of medical care, though the concept of prevention has been slow to take hold in the west. In China people pay the doctor to keep them healthy – and they don't pay him for treatment if they get sick. In the west the money is made from illness.

      At conception, in addition to the prenatal Qi, we are given a second gift called essence (different from Essence as we have already described it). In TCM essence is fluid whereas Qi is energetic. Translated roughly into western terminology, Qi is the gift of energy already moving in the sperm and egg – the electron reactions of cellular life. Essence, on the other hand is the ground substance of the sperm and egg, including the DNA and the inherent strength of the cells. The DNA combines to give us a unique combination of genes that encode our physical body. The ground substance, in addition to DNA, contains the milieu of cellular components, essential enzymes, and nutrients, which allow the Qi to flow. This aspect of essence, along with our genetics, determines our constitution.

If our parents were healthy and strong – their own reserve of Qi and essence being plentiful - we likely inherited a strong constitution and good health through this gift of essence. If our parents were depleted of Qi and essence, we likely inherited a weak constitution and the ill health that accompanies it. In the latter case, health becomes an issue early in life. How do parents deplete their Qi? There are many ways to squander our Qi. The Chinese feel that women become depleted if they birth too many children. Each birth depletes the stores of Qi in the kidney and the work that goes with child rearing can make it difficult to replenish. For men, the Qi depletes through excess sexual activity – specifically through excess ejaculation. Considering that a man's ejaculation contains the Qi and essence that is the gift of life in the released sperm, this makes perfect sense. That is why systems of tantric sex were developed: to reserve the Qi and essence for longevity and spiritual growth.

In our culture, parents can become depleted through stress, overwork, addiction, poor nutrition, illness, and toxicity. Should we be considering having children, the most important gift we can give them is to be in an optimal state of health and strength at conception. The pregnant woman must maintain that state of health throughout the pregnancy and lactation. One day there will be children born to parents who have completed this work we are doing together. These children will be able to retain much more of their glow of awareness into adulthood. There could be no greater gift for the planet and humanity.

The organ that suffers from these depletions is the kidney, because the kidney fire keeps the essence warm, allowing the Qi to rise and flow through the etheric body. Those who become depleted suffer general loss of Qi (energy). Normally, the essence stays in the cauldron and the Qi is generated and sent out. Essence is very difficult to build up or restore, whereas Qi can easily be replenished. Restoration of the essence, in China,

Etheric Fitness

comes through mastery of such practices as Chi Kung and/or T'ai Chi – what we will refer to as mastery of energy. With that mastery comes the ability to alter our birthright and overcome the weaknesses of our parents, as well as the genetics we inherited.

Sources of Qi

After birth, the vitally important prenatal Qi is continually replenished through food (including liquids) and air in the processes of digestion and respiration. In western terms we would say that respiration is bringing in the oxygen essential to the generation of energy within the body and that the metabolites within the food are providing molecules needed to build and repair the body, and to keep those electron transfer reactions going. If the air, food, and water are alive, having their own healthy etheric fields, the gift of Qi within them is profound. Thus, we can see the benefits of organic food, living water, and fresh, clean air in our health regime.

There are two times of day, one half hour before and after sunrise and sunset, when the air is rich in Qi. This is the ideal time to initiate a breathing practice – especially out in nature. These magic hours are called the hours of power. At these times, it is possible to see the glow of energy surrounding trees and plants which are releasing vast amounts of Qi in the form of oxygen. This amplified glow is an etheric field just like our own etheric field, which emanates from and surrounds our bodies. Organically grown fruits and vegetables and living water have been found to have an etheric field. Conventionally grown produce and tap water have no etheric field, meaning that we can get fiber, carbohydrates, protein, fat, vitamins and minerals from the food, and hydration from the water, but it is not a rich source of Qi.

Long-term diets of dead food have given us the current landscape of degenerative dis-ease associated with aging. This has opened a whole new market of anti-aging drugs and supplements containing isolates of metabolites needed to stimulate certain glandular responses, or to provide higher enzyme levels for some task within the body. The shocking, and continually escalating, price of anti-aging supplements puts the higher cost of organic produce in perspective. It is the poor farming practices of the corporate agribusiness that have spawned the creation of a new anti-aging industry. Given that most city children, and a good many adults, have no idea where food comes from (aside from the grocery store), it is not surprising that people feel disconnected from the earth.

In addition to the traditional sources of Qi in Chinese medicine, we can include the sun. The eyes are able to absorb a golden light from the sun and transform it into Qi within the body. To protect our retinas, we never look at the sun when it is not setting or rising. In the beginning, we can limit our practice to fifteen minutes prior to sunset. If, when we gaze elsewhere, afterimages of the sun appear, the sun is still too strong. We can hold our hands together, palms spread to the sun and create a small triangle to gaze through. This will protect our eyes while they become more tolerant of the sun. If we limit our gazing to the actual sunset and/or sunrise our eyes should not be harmed. Those with eye disorders should consult their doctor before gazing at the sun. When looking at the sun, we should use a relaxed gaze without glasses. In time, we will be able to see the solar radiation entering the eyes. Our eyes are part of our nervous system, which is the physical interface with our etheric body. With the awareness of Qi, this will feel like a direct feeding of Qi.

Kinds of Qi

Qi acquired from air and nutrients combine together, with the help of the lungs, to form Gathering Qi - a form of Qi related to the heart and lung function, the strength of the voice, and circulation to the extremities. A more refined Qi than that extracted from food and air, Gathering Qi is catalyzed by Original Qi, the rising Qi from the kidney cauldron, to produce True Qi. True Qi has two forms of manifestation. Nutritive Qi nourishes the organs and runs in the meridian channels, and Wei or Defensive Qi flows to the outer layers of the body forming a defense against invasion.

It is a misconception that Qi is limited to the meridians and acupuncture points. Qi is flowing everywhere through tiny energetic filaments. When cold invades, the Defensive Qi protects against it. If we are deficient in Defensive Qi, herbs that move the Qi outward, such as ginger and cayenne, are helpful as are treatment methods like hot ginger baths, saunas, and steam rooms. When an etheric body is in good health, Qi is unobstructed in its flow, which is even in body, and tempered in

Etheric Fitness

strength. Any imbalance in the flow, size and strength of the Qi is cause for concern. A Chinese doctor would diagnose these subtle imbalances using pulse diagnosis, then prescribe an herbal remedy to shift the energy.

From the western perception, the flow of Qi correlates with the transfer of electrons from one molecule to another driven by oxygen dependent energy reactions. It is the biochemical song of life within, going on in every cell of our bodies, in the matrix of our structure and all of the fluids flowing within us. These reactions involve enzymes, the catalysts of metabolism. Loss of enzyme function correlates with degeneration and aging. Sometimes we wear out the enzyme system through over use (abuse). For example, alcoholics prematurely age their genetic ability to produce alcohol dehydrogenase, an enzyme essential for the detoxification of the alcohol molecule. Wearing out the system occurs when liver cells can no longer produce adequate amounts of the enzyme and the pressure placed on the genetic machinery to produce the protein debilitates the process. What might have taken one hundred years to malfunction destroys the liver (cirrhosis) through abuse.

In truth, these systems need never malfunction. The cell is an immortal entity. Given proper nutrition (a supply of Qi) without toxicity or mutation, it will live forever. This truth puts into perspective the concepts of our twelve-step program presented in Physical Fitness. We have enormous potential to improve our quality of life as well as its length.

Within the meridian theory of TCM, the Nutritive Qi cycles through the twelve meridians and their related organs in two-hour intervals throughout the day. Pathologies related to the Qi in a particular organ would be felt more intensely during those times or when the energy is transiting from one meridian to another. Many women awaken at three in the morning – sometimes every night. In the peri-menopausal years, they might find themselves, and the bed, soaked in sweat. At three in the morning, the Qi is moving from the liver meridian and its organ system to that of the lung. The liver, which governs the volume of our blood, regulates menstruation and menopause.

Qi and Dis-ease

When diagnosing dis-ease from the standpoint of Qi, Chinese medicine defines four patterns of pathology. The first is a deficiency of Qi

– not enough energy in the meridians. This is expressed as weakness in the organs, especially the lungs and spleen. The second is sinking Qi, an aspect of Qi deficiency that expresses as fatigue, sinking, organ prolapse, and depression. The third, stagnant Qi, appears symptomatically as bloating, migrating pain, irritability, and mood swings. The liver is prone to stagnation of Qi – PMS being one example. Lastly, rebellious Qi is Qi running the wrong direction – out of control, so to speak. Though the manifestations are different for each organ, this pathology would include insomnia, belching, vomiting and diarrhea.

These patterns of Qi are coupled with patterns in the other bodily fluids, including the blood, to arrive at a diagnosis. TCM is more interested in the flow of energy than molecular metabolic disorders. That is the difference between the etheric and the physical foundations of the eastern and western medical philosophies. At the etheric level of consciousness - the blueprint - the most important factor is the smooth flow of adequate Qi. Treatments are designed to correct the imbalances – for example, to urge the Qi to rise if it is sinking or to flow if it is stagnant.

Another way pathology is diagnosed in TCM is through eight principles of opposites: interior-exterior; full-empty; hot-cold; and yin-yang. Add to that the observations of pulse, face, tongue, disposition, carriage, bodily fluids, and so forth, and we have a complete picture of the energies within a patient's body. The picture must be complete before energy can be moved in beneficial ways. Though technical equipment has been developed in China to "see" the Qi, most practitioners of TCM rely on the ages-old systems of diagnosis to help their patients. It would appear that TCM, in many ways, more closely achieves the "do no harm" ethics of western medicine than does the western model.

What occurs in the pathological conditions of energy affects the matrix of the etheric scaffold, our second scaffold in the rainbow body. This scaffold holds the blueprint of the physical body – guides its formation from conception – and maintains the integrity of form in the physical throughout life. When Qi stagnates, for example, the scaffold geometry distorts. If stagnation is long term, it can damage and destroy the geometry of the etheric scaffold, which loses its ability to hold form. Without the scaffolds blueprint, the physical body succumbs to the laws of physics – degeneration and eventual death.

Etheric Fitness

From the standpoint of western pathology, the loss of form is most evident in cancer tissue, which is disorganized, nonfunctional, greedy for nutrients, and dominant, rather than co-creative. All of the energy gets channeled into this focal point of confused cellular growth to the detriment of other organs in the body. How did the Qi lose its smooth flow and come to stagnate in the first place? Generally, these things do not originate in the etheric body. If our Qi is diminished, we can look to the sources of Qi in our life and increase it. This Qi comes from the physical body to the etheric.

Likewise, if Qi becomes stagnant in the etheric body, look to the physical or emotional body as the instigator. There will be some form of toxicity present in the physical body, most commonly from a microbial overgrowth or a pollutant that is mutating normal cell function. Something as simple as chronically contracted muscles (those frozen shoulders) can constrict Qi, and the healing matrix around wounds can cause Qi to reroute itself. Unexpressed emotion can stagnate the Qi from the emotional body.

Let us turn to a few examples. If we are excessive consumers of sugar, it is quite likely that we are feeding fungal organisms, such as Candida Albicans. In addition to the typical abdominal bloating from small intestine inflammation, a common place of infection in women is the outer breast tissue closest to the lymph glands. As the yeast population grows, the tissue swells slightly and becomes tender. Yeast multiply - spurred on by the level of sugar in our bloodstream and interstitial fluid. As they eat, reproduce, and die, the yeast organisms leave a lot of debris in the infected tissue, which taxes the lymphatic system. Qi begins to loiter as the infection begins, and is in full stagnation when the tissue becomes tender to the touch. The energy in the etheric scaffold is being compromised and cysts or tumors could begin to form around the debris-laden infection.

This is one theory of tumor-genesis being proposed by holistic medicine. If we eliminate sugar from our diets, the swelling and tenderness disappears – almost immediately. However, it remains vulnerable tissue. It could take years of a sugar-free diet to truly eradicate the Candida as an out-of-control pathogen in the body. If we begin eating sugar again, the previously infected areas seem to preferentially re-infect.

For another example, we will take a smoker who has been exposing his lung tissue to the toxins in processed tobacco for many years. The deposits of tar in the lungs compromise the function of the lung tissue – respiration. Respiration is one of our critical pathways in sustaining Qi, which means that he has both systemic and localized dysfunction. In addition, chemical additives and nicotine have the ability to mutate the cells directly, which also causes disruption of Qi flow. Unfortunately, our smoker works in a pathology laboratory fixing tissue with volatile chemicals, like acetone (a volatile and toxic component commonly found in nail polish removers). The combination of tobacco and inhaled, and topically absorbed, solvents (he was unable to do a good job while wearing gloves) caused lung lesions, and compromised breathing to occur in his early forties.

    The scaffold of his etheric body stagnated around the chemical mutation in the lung tissue – another case of form distorting the blueprint. In time, the scaffold was damaged and tumors appeared. He quit smoking, and eventually had to quit his job because of debilitation. This bought him a little time. He eventually died of lung cancer coupled with metastatic colon cancer. Once the etheric body is severely damaged, the pathways of degeneration open throughout the body since the blueprint has lost its integrity. He did nothing to assist the etheric body because he and his doctors didn't know it existed.

    These examples are extreme, but they both began with simple self-imposed toxicity. In the first example a painful, and invasive, diagnostic breast cancer biopsy (widely supported because fear levels are so high) might be avoided through strategic and immediate dietary change. In our second example, immediate cessation of both smoking and inhalation of toxins could have been coupled with radical detoxification, etheric blueprint restoration, and the cancer therapy. Alternative medicines can compliment conventional therapy improving the outcome, attitudes, and quality of life.

Moving Qi

    TCM offers an array of treatments, which are often used to compliment each other. Acupuncture is the most widely used treatment in eastern medicine, as it is practiced in the west. Acupuncture moves nutritive Qi in the meridians to the organs governed by the meridians and the flow of Qi in general. Each defined acupuncture point influences

Etheric Fitness

Qi somewhere in the body – often at a distant site. The way in which the needle is inserted governs how the Qi is being influenced; for example, to calm rebellious Qi or to move stagnant Qi. The desired outcome of acupuncture is harmony – the balance of all opposites within the body. Needles are often inserted at two sites along a meridian to move energy within it. The patient can easily feel this energy circuit connect and circulate. There is no denying its electrical nature.

For those who don't care for needles, Qi can be moved through meridian massage. Tui Na, a traditional Chinese massage, awakens Qi in the meridians through a pleasant circular motion. Chinese meridian massage follows the meridians with deep pressure in the direction of meridian flow. Acupressure and its Japanese counterpart, Shiatsu, stimulate the acupuncture points manually.

The herb, mugwort, is made into large incense sticks called moxa. A burning moxa stick (moxibustion) can be used to move Qi through its proximity to an acupuncture point or region of stagnant Qi. The closer it gets to the body, the more Qi moves, though the heat can sometimes be intense, especially with tender-skinned areas of the body. Mugwort has special properties conducive to moving Qi and the recipient feels this movement as a warm flush of energy running through the meridian. Visualizing the energy movement makes the treatment even more effective.

Sometimes, a vacuum is created in glass cups, which are place on regions of stagnant Qi. This treatment, called cupping, effectively draws stagnation from deeper areas of the tissue up to the skin for release. When stagnation is severe, bruising will occur.

The last two major therapies available to the TCM practitioner are herbs and food. Of course, herbs are food, so we are really talking about nutrition therapy in both cases. However, the pharmacopoeia of China contains little if anything we would want to have for dinner – deer antler, for example. In the west, we generally take these herbs in pill form but, traditionally, they are cooked in prescribed mixtures and taken as a tea. In China, all traditional hospitals have an odiferous herbal medicine kitchen somewhere within their bowels. Those who venture to cook Chinese herbs in their own home, risk a major evacuation of their families, and close neighbors. In the traditional hospitals of China the herbs are prepared and brought to the patients instead of drugs. It is an interesting experience to visit a Chinese pharmacy (often part of Chinese grocery stores), where a true herbalist is on hand. In addition to being able to see the herbs, the herbalist will often provide a free pulse diagnosis.

As previously mentioned the cooks of China move the Qi with their cooking. Menus are based on seasonal needs (cooling food in summer and warming food in winter) as well as the immediate needs of, say, a child with the sniffles or a grandma with pain in her joints. Those recovering from illness or those who are unable to chew, like, the elderly, invariably receive a bowl of congee at mealtime – flavorful rice gruel. We can sometimes find shrimp or chicken congee on authentic Chinese menus – usually served late at night for its ease of digestion.

We can find out more about Traditional Chinese Medicine, in the basic book, *A Web That Has No Weaver*.[1] It is a good layman's guide but also a standard text in most acupuncture schools. From the viewpoint of Chinese Medicine practiced in the west, look into *Between Heaven and Earth: A Guide to Chinese Medicine*.[2] Both of these books present the five-element theory of medicine as well. This is another school of Chinese thought based on the flow of Qi and organ relationships. It incorporates the macrocosm/microcosm approach to understanding our relationship with the earth, her elements and energies. Most often, the five-element theory of medicine makes more sense of imbalances in the body than any other kind of medicine.

Restoring and Nurturing Qi

Now we enter the realms of prevention and self-cure – what we can do to heal and maintain our own etheric body. Some of these systems and techniques should be added to our physical body regimen to complete the marriage of energy and form in our bodies. In addition to health prevention and cure, the martial arts provide a number of pathways towards energy mastery. Each has its own gift, so we must not be surprised if our etheric bodies urge us to include several areas of interest in our energetic health regime.

In the martial arts, secrets of energy were kept within families or in monastic settings where the art of moving energy was practiced to mastery. There are still masters in China today who are able to project their Qi at a distance, bouncing their willing (or not) victims off the wall without touching them. These stories are part of the magic of China. It was not that long ago that basic martial practices became public.

First and foremost of the Chinese martial arts is T'ai Chi Ch'uan. Though T'ai Chi is taught as a slow-moving form composed of a series of movements, it is, in fact, a martial art. Any of the movements in the T'ai Chi form can be accelerated in self-defense. However, the most important T'ai Chi principle is to yield – nonaggression. As already mentioned, it embodies the concept of becoming steel wrapped in cotton. It is that kind of soft strength that permits yielding. Sometimes these are hard concepts for us to grasp because our culturally held beliefs urge us to muscle our way to victory. In China, if one can out run the opponent, they run.

The practice of T'ai Chi Ch'uan is a wonderful way to restore and move Qi. In the beginning, learning the dance form calls for memory, balance, body coordination and the discipline to practice. Eventually, the form becomes a fluid exercise to relax the body and engage the spiritual. With the appropriate breathing, which is usually taught when the form comes more naturally, T'ai Chi becomes an all-in-one physical/etheric body workout for limbering and strength. Ordinarily, it does not constitute aerobic exercise, though it could be practice at that pace. In China many of the older people are in the park every morning practicing T'ai Chi to stay young and avoid illness.

When I learned the Yang family form of T'ai Chi, I was told that I would feel the Qi with ten years of practice. My immediate reaction was to suggest that more diligent practice would shorten the time (good old Yankee logic). I was told that my plan would not work though more practice would surely help my form. Ten years is the apprenticeship in T'ai Chi and it has nothing to do with the whims of the master. It has to do with the time necessary for the etheric and physical bodies to become consciously integrated. Although I felt the Qi from time to time, it was ten years of practice later - almost to the day – that the apprenticeship was complete, and Qi has been part of my conscious reality ever since. An experience like this gives us an appreciation of apprenticeship that is not usually part of our upbringing.

There are many forms of T'ai Chi to choose from, some of them more demanding of strength and flexibility than others. Studios abound

Awakening and Healing the Rainbow Body

in most cities and towns where we can begin to learn T'ai Chi. If our path becomes mastery, the right teacher will undoubtedly appear. I can recommend two books about the Yang form; *T'ai Chi Ch'uan for Health and Self-Defense*[3] written by my teacher's teacher, T.T. Liang, and *Yang Family Secret Transmission*.[4] There is a wealth of information about our potential relationship with energy in both of these books.

The other Chinese form of restoring and building energy is Chi Kung (or Chi Gong). Chi Kung builds internal strength, bolsters immunity, and increases energy through a series of held postures. Breath is the key to building and circulating the energy in a posture that might otherwise seem depleting – as most strengthening exercises are. The practice becomes, like T'ai Chi, a meditation. Chi Kung is gaining world recognition for its power to heal and protect the body. Simple to learn, but difficult to master, the Chi Kung postures can be integrated into just about anyone's lifestyle. The practice is very centering, calming, and at the same time, energizing.

The hard-style martial arts, like Northern and Southern Shaolin (kung fu) in China, Karate in Japan and Tai Kwan Do in Korea, are aerobic forms of exercise that martial amazing energy and power in the body. If we are so inclined, a combination of hard and soft-style with Chi Kung plus stretching would certainly fulfill the criteria for the first four steps in our twelve step program, as well as number eight - stress reduction. I can recommend one book about Chi Kung[5] though I am certain there are many books and videos with good instruction if we cannot learn from an experienced teacher.

In Japan, Aikido is a high martial art, which incorporates the strengths of both hard and soft styles of self-defense and mind-body integration. It does involve mat work, so may be limiting for some people. Aikido is a highly regarded martial form. In addition to these systems of energy, there are many I have not mentioned, all with value to the etheric body. It is best that we go where we are drawn and sample several before committing to one. Community centers will often offer short, affordable courses that provide easy introductions to the systems available. If we are headed for energy mastery, some energetic discipline involving apprenticeship looms in our future, as the etheric body will need to be mastered.

Etheric Fitness

Chi machines have appeared on the market of late. They do move Qi in the body though they would have to be combined with some breath work to actually generate more Qi. Though they are a poor substitute for actual exercise, they might be very helpful in rehabilitation, getting energy to circulate in the elderly, and as a precursor to massage. I have also experienced a light bed that delivers electrons through the meridian system. The inventor calls it an electron donor. The experience not only ups the energy of the etheric body, it must help to clear the rainbow body scaffolding because there are significant reports of diseases being cured with a series of light bed treatments. Still experimental, these beds are being installed in hospitals where they will be used in trials for cancer patients. If successful, they could become standard treatment procedure for many hospital patients, and do make an appealing addition to health spas.

That brings us to the conclusion of our discussion of Qi and the physical-etheric dynamic. Next, we will begin moving energy in the emotional body, our third dimensional holographic layer of the rainbow body. Our practice routines of physical and etheric fitness will help to support us through the emotional body work, and then into the fourth dimension.

---

[1] The Web That Has No Weaver, Ted J. Kaptchuk O.M.D., Congdon & Weed, 1983.
[2] Between Heaven and Earth: A Guide to Chinese Medicine, Harriet Beinfield L.Ac. and Efrem Korngold, O.M.D., Ballantine Books, 1991.
[3] T'ai Chi Ch'uan for Health and Self-Defense, T.T. Liang, Vintage Books, 1977.
[4] T'ai-chi Touchstones: Yang Family Secret Transmissions, Compiled and translated by Douglas Wile, Sweet Ch'i Press, 1983.
[5] The Way of Energy, Master Lam Kam Chuen, Simon & Schuster Fireside Book, 1991.

NOTES

EMOTIONAL FITNESS

The third scaffold of the rainbow body is that of the emotional body. This body serves as a bridge, both to the outer world through its interface with the etheric body, and between the third and fourth dimension through its interface with the emotional-mental body. We meet and interact with other people through the emotional body. We could think of it as the stage upon which life's dramas occur. We will see how those interactions with others may have compromised our autonomy while they were creating the experiences of life that have lodged in our fourth dimension.

The emotional field is also the body that translates feeling into emotion through the integration of the body's molecular response with the mental field's memory bank – information from the hard drive. The result is reaction. We will learn how to isolate and appreciate the pure feeling as a body signal – a red flag for pending reaction, and its accompanied energy loss.

Our emotional body has the ability to act as the intermediary, keeping the world of thought and our third dimensional experience in focus. Within this focus, an equilibrium can be maintained, which opens the energetic pathways for inter-dimensional navigation.

Soul Retrieval

A brief preface is in order, before we launch into the emotional body work. As we proceed with this work, it is necessary to be cognizant of the predatory energy. Fourth dimensional thought-form predators are somehow able to sustain themselves on the energies of our emotional dramas. Though all emotional reaction contributes to their sustenance, there are some amongst us who are unconscious of the way in which they serve these energies by creating and sustaining drama and emotional turmoil. In our present culture, this turmoil can be seen, on a frightening scale, in film, music, written material, pornography, television, video games, drug traffic, corporate and civil crime, terrorism, counter-terrorism, and on and on. It is everywhere, and it reflects a disregard for human rights, morality, and dignity.

Remember that third dimension is a manifestation of fourth dimensional thought form. Humanity has been unconsciously "guided" into a world of violence and emotional reaction; perhaps it is to control and maintain us as an energy source. The path of liberation requires vigilance to recognize the negative energies around us, awareness of the truth behind them, and the courage to disengage them. The reward is liberation from controlling unconscious energy. There is no reason to fear predatory energy. Conscious awareness alone provides sufficient protection for us to walk this path with the blessings of harmony and grace.

The unfortunate energetic aftermath of having lived our lives unconsciously is a loss of power. Our emotional body scaffolding does not look like a brilliant network of light filaments forming a golden-yellow layered web around us, but rather a web of disorganized filaments connected to other people and possessions. To be sure, we have not given our selves away entirely, but the experiences of life have taken their toll. Before we can take complete command of our emotional body, it is necessary to retrieve filaments we have attached to the rainbow bodies of others, and to remove the filaments others have attached to our rainbow bodies. Since these filamentous exchanges were guided by beliefs, a big

Emotional Fitness

part of retrieving our filaments and returning those of others will be changing the core beliefs in our luminous body that support dependency and attachment.

In indigenous cultures, the shaman is able to enter a trance state to journey back into the life of his client to retrieve lost parts of their soul. Though these reports have a romantic attraction fed directly by our "fix me" beliefs, they do not serve those of us who have autonomy. In our culture especially, we might be best served if we have profound reservations about turning the care and retrieval of our soul over to anyone else. The work we begin in this chapter, accessing and clearing the fourth dimension, *is* soul retrieval. We will become our own shaman, as we access the unconscious and change our lives. We will learn to love all that we have experienced in this life as the path our soul intended. Then, with ease and grace, we will be able to detach from those experiences as if they were part of past-lives, and step into the now moment.

The obvious place to begin regaining our autonomy by accessing the fourth dimension is through the filaments that keep us in energetic bondage to others. We use one of the sorcerers' techniques called recapitulation. There are a number of levels to recapitulation with some of them reserved for energy mastery. In our present work, recapitulation is the art of remembering the past, re-experiencing and owning the energy loss and gain, and then consciously releasing the experience to the collective. We will be mindful to recapitulate by taking responsibility for each experience. In this way, we transform the energies as memory associated with each experience and contribute positive energy to the collective. Other descriptions of recapitulation, which do not incorporate this level of self-correction, will release the experience intact to contribute to the collective experience in fourth dimension. Some will not connect with fourth dimension at all. To walk this path in integrity, we must complete all three aspects of recapitulation.

Another way to look at the filaments exchanged with others is as hungry ghosts. We cannot be free of the memories they carry until we have made restitution with them. This is about taking responsibility for our lives. There are no victims in this work – meaning that filamentous exchange is never one-way. Even those abused as children must take responsibility for having called their childhood to them as part of life's learning experience.

When we engage in drama, we mismanage the filaments of our emotional rainbow body scaffolding. Usually, it has to do with how we get our needs met. If we want something from someone, we may throw a little hook (a sticky filament of our emotional body) into their field – literally extending one of our filaments into one of their chakras. When this happens, the person can feel "hooked" or caught by someone else. It feels invasive. Likewise, when someone wants something from us, they extend their filaments into our chakras. Without consciousness of our energy field and these possibilities, we leave our selves wide open to this interaction, and can become doormats to these invaders.

Usually the sacral or solar plexus chakras will be the target of filamentous extension, though the heart can also be involved. We make bargains with people; "You do this for me, and I will do that for you." We use these extended filaments to control or pull the strings; "If you don't do this for me, well, forget ever having sex again." Generally speaking, those of us who succeed at getting our needs met in life are either consummately industrious or masters of manipulation – or the not uncommon combination of both.

These are the dramas of life. We have just never thought of them energetically. When we die, these scenes will be played again, as our life review, while our consciousness moves through the portal of our assemblage point into the collective fourth dimension. As part of healing the emotional body our job is to replay the scenes now, retrieve our filaments, give back the filaments hooked in us, transform the scene, and practice vigilance that it doesn't happen again. Having done this work, death will open entirely different doors for us. Ours will be a conscious death. It is also necessary to recapitulate our attached relationships with things – possessiveness with objects.

It is important to understand how and why this exercise works. The dramas, which provoke the exchange of filaments, take place in the third dimension through the emotional body. However, the thought forms driving the urge to extend the emotional body's filaments into the lower bodies of another person's rainbow body originate in our fourth dimension – our unconscious. This invasiveness can never be entirely unconscious because the emotional body has played a conscious role in the drama. This third dimensional component makes it easier to observe our selves in drama and change our behavior to retain the integrity of our own rainbow body, and to restore the filaments of others.

Our hungry ghosts tend to be right at hand as conscious memory, whereas the vast reservoir of past memories are packed away in our fourth dimension because they are painfully difficult to own, or simply happened a long time ago. We have direct pathways from the emotional body to the emotional-mental body in the fourth dimension. Their scaffolds are directly connected. Knowing what it feels like to harbor an unpleasant memory, we can more readily make the link between the extension of our filaments into another and the invitation we extend to the hungry ghosts to lodge the memory within our emotional or emotional-mental field. It is as if we had video recorded the scene. Now we will ask that it be replayed.

We will get some command over the dramas later in this chapter, but our first course of action must be the retrieval of our own filamentous field and the removal of extraneous filaments caught in our chakras using recapitulation. This work is done by accessing memory and replaying the scenes of our life to see exactly where we have lost our power, or taken that of others. By taking responsibility, we not only retrieve our power, we consequently set other people free to their own ascension. Furthermore, as previously stated, when we take responsibility for the events of our life, then recapitulate to return filaments, the experiences we are recapitulating will not contribute more negativity to the collective consciousness – and we will be free of them. Responsibility is the key, therefore we must be certain that the ego is not in anyway still attached to blaming others or winning an argument.

Recapitulation is a powerful example of how self-service serves others. It is the first step to gain power over the fourth dimension. Once we have begun to access memory, starting with those hungry ghosts that will not leave us alone, the doors to the unconscious will open and memories will flood into our consciousness. We need only intend healing with a willing spirit, and our entire field will engage the process. The only opposition we might encounter will come from our lower ego, and the futile protests of those who had previously hooked us.

Awakening and Healing the Rainbow Body

We have all been in long-term relationships where the invasive filaments can be so plentiful that they wrap themselves in bundles, called cords. This is quite common in parent-child relationships and intimate relationships that are either very intense or that have years of drama and dependency. For example, it is part of our cultural urge to protect and nurture our children, and in doing so, to cord with them. We only want the best for our children. Right? Then why can't we let go of them? When a child is born in the Andes, the baby is offered to *Tayta Inti* (Father Sun), and *Pachamama* (Mother Earth), who are believed to be the true parents of the child. This places the child in right relationship with nature and the cosmos. The biological parents agree to watch over the child, with enormous love, and to release the grown child to his/her own path in life. This takes the hierarchy out of parenting from the moment of birth.

How many doctors would have rather been artists? How many people have followed in their parent's footsteps because no other way was available to them? How many of us are desperately looking for our purpose in life in our fifties and later? These misfortunes are the result of cording. Parents do not believe that their children are capable of knowing their calling. Because we advise our children from their early years, steering them into lucrative fields, their true calling can elude them until much later in life, when dissatisfaction becomes intolerable. By that time, the level of our control and manipulation has caused so many filaments to enter their field that they are bundled in cords. Likewise, their mounting resentment at being controlled has likely contributed to a two-way exchange of emotional body filaments.

Allowing a child to unfold is nerve-wracking but rewarding. We are rewarded with the future observations of their happy, fulfilled lives. Many times the child is more spiritually advanced than that of the parent. In such a situation, steering a child towards an intellectually consuming career could stifle their spiritual growth – even create enormous karma between parents and child. Obviously much of what we do call in is karmic, and for our greater growth and light. On the other hand, when future societies live in a more enlightened state, one difference will be the elimination of the parent-child cording.

At any age we can release our children to their soul's path. It doesn't mean we don't love them. It doesn't mean we don't want them to succeed. It means we want them to be free. In so doing, we will gain our own freedom - freedom from the manipulation that cording fosters, and freedom from guilt when they make human errors. This parent-child example applies to cording with siblings and with other relationship as well. It also applies to the child, however old, releasing the cords with parents. It is a great step towards liberation and the release of so many filaments eases our recapitulation work with those to whom we are corded. Once de-corded, we should experience an immediate lightening of the load within these relationships and an easier flow of memory. It does not preempt recapitulation, but assists it.

As recapitulation proceeds we will be enjoying an overall lightness of being, and freedom from the self-imposed tyranny of an unconscious life. At first, memories flood our consciousness and we make lists of scenes and recapitulate them. Eventually, the memories floating in and out of our field are easily recognized and recapitulated in the moment. To our surprise, some deep remembrances will surface from time to time for our conscious assessment and instant recapitulation. We will be enjoying some mastery over the unconscious. The work in this chapter can form a seamless bridge to our formerly unconscious self, changing completely the world in which we live.

All too often, filamentous exchange is the end result of dramas in our lives. Because scenes from our dramas will be replayed as we proceed with recapitulation, we are also providing the perfect research arena for deciphering our behavioral and mental patterns. Assigning a special notebook to this work, we can begin taking notes of the memories as we do the exercises of recapitulation. We will likely see patterns emerging in those memories. Those patterns are held in place by core beliefs. Breaking those core beliefs will be our next "take charge" step of liberation.

It is important to remember that this exercise is not a public confession. It may sting our egos to admit that our own wants, needs, and desires caused us to hook into others. It may also be humiliating to admit that we allowed our selves to be hooked. Vulnerability is not a crime. It is simply unconscious. The courage needed to take responsibility is the mark of the spiritual warrior – a warrior for our own truth and light. Each of us has one of these warriors ready to step forward on the quest for consciousness. It is no small thing to embody that warrior – truly a leap into the unknown. However, as long as we blame others for the misfortunes of our lives we are paralyzed on the spiritual path. By taking responsibility everyone wins.

Changing Our Reality

The reality we perceive is limited only by our beliefs. When we were born, we believed our selves to be a soul seeking reunion with all that God is. Soon after birth, that reality began to diminish, to be replaced by the reality of life on earth. That is to say, life on earth according to the beliefs of the family and culture into which we were born. The impact of childhood on our assemblage point is enormous. We call in our families and all that comes with them, but because babies are helpless/powerless, the free will is compromised and a reality is forced on us without our third dimensional consent. As we have already discussed, this is the result of the amnesia present on the earth.

When we acquire beliefs later in our life, they come to us through our life experience. If we need to change them, to alter our stand on human rights, for example, those beliefs are easy to change. However, childhood and the years of educational indoctrination are profoundly impressionable times – the whole idea behind early education has to do with conformity and uniformity of beliefs. This is the reason to begin reweaving the filamentous fabric of our assemblage point by revisiting our childhood. We find that many beliefs, forming part of our reality in those early years, continue to serve us while others support the painful patterns that are so hard to break.

Core beliefs are incorporated into our assemblage point in two ways. The core belief can be imposed on us directly. For example, when a parent repeatedly tells a child "You can do better than that," that belief enters the child's field. The core belief can also enter our field indirectly as we observe life. A child's assessment of their family life might be "If you want to be loved in this family, you need to be a good boy, and please your parents."

There are two ways to access these deeply embedded core beliefs. One way to access them is by telling our story. When we are doing this work together in circle, we tell the stories of our childhood. In the telling, we can see where beliefs may have entered our field. For example, in the

Emotional Fitness

telling of a story involving childhood abuse, we may find the that beliefs like; "It is not safe here," and "People cannot be trusted" – are still with us. These beliefs limit participation in life if they cannot be broken. Many of us were not overtly loved as children, leading to beliefs like "I am not worthy of love," or "I am unlovable" - and no amount of love as adults seems to fill the empty spaces left by these wounds. We must heal these wounds our selves, by changing our core beliefs, then love can flow to and from us unabated. Many children were berated with resulting core beliefs like "I can't do anything right," "I am not good enough," or "Why bother to try to please Mom (or Dad, or anyone)?" The poignant experiences of depression era parents planted the seeds of poverty consciousness in many of us with beliefs like "There is not enough," "I can't afford it," and/or "I will never be able to afford that."

These beliefs are deeply embedded and difficult to live with, but not impossible to change. Though none of us has had a perfect childhood, in all fairness, many have only praise for their parents, and beliefs like; "I can do anything I set out to do," "I am loved and appreciated," and/or "I feel so loved and supported." These are testimonials to good parenting. In childhood we can find the roots of most of our fears as well as our judgments against others. Our story will shift and change over time to uncover more core beliefs that no longer serve us. For this reason, it is good that we continue telling it. If we are not in circle with others, we can write this story out in our notebooks to help uncover the deeply held beliefs that continue to limit us.

A second way to access these childhood beliefs is through self-observation. The discipline of self-observation will alert us when we feel a limitation in our life or discover a pattern that binds us to behavior we are ready to change. We can use the limitation or pattern as a catalyst to journey back into childhood (or later in life) to discover the core beliefs in which it is anchored. Our lives are the laboratory of self-awareness. We must constantly remind our selves to find the core belief at the root of the problem and change it.

Our greatest challenge in changing a core belief – a reality-altering event – will be to research the source of limitation or resistance. Once we have arrived at the core belief, and know what we would rather have in its place, the work is simple. The research – accessing memory and observing patterns – requires that we bring our unconscious into consciousness. Like cognitive therapy, we are downloading information from our fourth dimensional memory bank, our own unconscious (our subconscious) into third dimension. This gives us awareness but not the ability to break the core beliefs.

Remember that the core beliefs make up the luminous body which is anchored somewhere in our fourth dimensional (mental) bodies. The assemblage point, where the core beliefs (luminous filaments) converge, defines our reality. Cleaning out all we have stored in the fourth dimension (our accessed memories) is critical to the work and no small task, but to actually change the core belief we must enter into our personal fourth dimension. How can this be a simple matter?

The simplicity lies in the ease with which energy moves in the fourth dimension. Once changed, the core belief is gone from our luminous field. The healing is immediate and permanent unless we chose to adopt that belief again or have a complex of related beliefs that will all need to be changed. The skills of the shaman lie within fourth dimensional navigation. Here is the missing piece of conventional psychotherapy. We can train our selves to be our own shaman by using the shamanic journeys[1] recorded to accompany this work. These journeys provide spoken guidance and vibrational access to the fourth dimension. In time, we will be able to hold this space for our selves, shifting core beliefs in a heartbeat. With each changed core belief the assemblage point becomes more a part of our conscious awareness, and we become more of its master.

It is a good time to honor all of the magnificent changes we have already made in our lives to create realities much different than those of our families. Those of us who engage this work have generally attained a certain degree of autonomy and self-consciousness in our lives. Now it is time to search out the remaining beliefs that limit us in our attainment. We will find, as the work continues, that every step requires that we relentlessly track down our core beliefs because they comprise the luminous body we are intent on mobilizing. When our childhood work eases up, we can approach the recapitulation of adolescence, sexuality, parenting, being parented, our work world, and our bloodlines.

Emotional Fitness

On Stage

By far, the earth experience that taxes our energetic system most thoroughly is drama – action/reaction. There are those who, in unconscious service to the predators, continually create drama around themselves because, in dramatic reaction, energy is released and predatory energy thrives. We may think that the drama king or queen is the one taking our energy – that is what it feels like – but they are only serving as open conduits to the collective fourth dimension. The important thing is, in non-judgment, to recognize that we feel whipped after encounters with such people. Because they are in our lives to teach us about energy loss, judging them would be counterproductive to our growth.

Qi, the life force melding the first three scaffolds of our rainbow bodies (physical, etheric and emotional) into our physical presence, is not part of fourth dimension, which is thought form. As a speculation, we can assume that the stolen Qi is converted to an energy currency in the collective fourth dimension because it is a sought-after commodity that sustains the predators. Intent, the prevailing force of the universe, is likely the means of conversion, and unconscious thought form is likely the resulting currency. The predatory thought form entities can use that thought form energy to sustain and expand their influence over fourth dimension. In this way, much of the predacious energy in the fourth dimension was created directly from the unconscious lives of humanity. Prior to the amnesia of "The Fall," predatory energy was not able to influence humanity because all was conscious. We came and went from earth as fifth dimensional beings and beyond. The amnesia necessitated the creation of a collective unconscious for humanity, which attracted the predators who could move freely and undetected within it.

However they arrived in the unconscious, the predators are there to challenge us. The only effective method of banishing them from our lives is starvation through awareness. If we are conscious of energy loss and refuse to participate in it, the predators will leave us alone. They are not looking to be challenged. Let's face it, there is plenty of unconscious negativity in third dimension to nourish them. What we participate in doesn't have to be major drama-trauma either – any drama at all will suffice. Reactions come in all styles and sizes. Self-observation will allow us to

Awakening and Healing the Rainbow Body

see our own tendencies to energy loss and participation in unconscious drama, because it will make the unconscious conscious.

At this stage of the work we are actively engaging in the water initiation - getting out of the drama. Leaving drama and emotional reaction behind will give us some mastery over the emotional body scaffold, thus providing a clear line of communication from our own unconscious into the third dimensional world of the physical-etheric-emotional body complex. We will take plenty of notes as we unravel the dramas in our lives, and as new opportunities for mastery present themselves – the universe will not let us slack off once we are aware.

We may find our selves moving away from people in our lives who seem intent on engaging us in their dramas. Perhaps we have already lost friends from projecting our own dramas. We need not have guilt over these situations. This is the universe dishing out life for our lessons. Guilt is a religious institution. Let's replace it with sensitivity and find a gentle, sensitive way to end the relationships – burning no bridges behind us. Sensitivity is a quality of the open heart. It comes to us through this consciousness training. Though few are capable of freely giving it, everyone responds to love.

When we are bound to reaction we cannot be sensitive. Instead we will be repulsed, disgusted, outraged, scared, and so forth. Sensitivity sees the God in all things, which means that the ego has no vested interest in the outcome. That may be a bit down the road for most of us so, for now, let's keep an open mind allowing the heart to follow suit. As we gain experience seeing through the dramas, our hearts will grow in power. Emotions such as guilt, shame, jealousy, betrayal and self-pity (to name a few) will lose their power over us. There is no power in unconscious emotional reaction. It is enslavement. On the other hand, we will have feelings. We can, and should, acknowledge and express feelings consciously with no consequences to our rainbow body. Feelings and emotions are two different things.

The Observer

We cannot engage the drama consciously without good self-observation skills. At the heart of the work of self-observation is the observer. In cultivating an unbiased observer within us, we will come to

Emotional Fitness

know our selves as separate from the "person" acting out our dramas. Our observer will provide us with a wealth of information needed for awareness and self-correction. Ultimately, the observer will be the part of us that makes contact with our higher self, because the observer exists outside the lower ego – it is not part of our personality at all. Cultivating our observer becomes the subtle and painless way in which we master the lower ego. Lower ego has value because our paths are in the world where personality is useful and powerful – as long as we have mastery over it.

Many spiritual paths regard the ego with disdain – a beast to be tamed or exterminated. This path asks that we befriend the ego and use a little coyote, or trickster, medicine to bring it into alignment with our spiritual quest. Fortunately, the ego loves this work and has no hesitation participating in it. Ego is more than willing to engage this process and to discover more about itself – egocentricity.

In this part of the work, we begin to understand who we are as a collection of our personalities aspects, called sub-personalities, who rarely have any awareness of each other. Over time our work will transform these personality aspects into conscious aspects of self with spiritual awareness. The culmination of the self-observation work is our fully integrated personality – one capable of connecting to higher self, which is the higher ego. To understand the psychology behind personality integration, called psychosynthesis, we can find and read the work of Roberto Assagioli who was a student of Jung. Reading the work of those who have followed Assagioli's principles in applied psychosynthesis may be less academic than Assagioli's writing, and the content may be more easily absorbed. We can search our libraries or well-stocked metaphysical bookstores for related material.

To understand how we can become astute observers is simple. We look at our life as if it were a play being acted out on life's stage. Our personality aspects take on different roles in the play, which is all about us engaging life. Our observer becomes the director of the play - though most of our observer/directors have been on lengthy sabbaticals. With the director back on the job, we can position him/her in the orchestra pit where keen, objective observations of the ongoing play can be made.

Awakening and Healing the Rainbow Body

Within these observations, we will see our patterns of drama/reaction and identify the subpersonality playing the role.

Whereas we previously had no consciousness about the role-playing, using our director's unbiased observations, we can now make some changes. Perhaps the drama occurs because the subpersonality who habitually takes on the role is miscast completely. Once we have identified all of the aspects of lower ego, we can turn our attention to consciously directing another personality to assume the role. When the director gives the part to another aspect of self, less prone to that typical reaction, the outcome of the scene could be non-reaction. The power of this work lies in the director/observer's ability to recast the parts, rewrite the script, hire and fire the actors, and even close the show.

Identifying our company of thespians is the first task of the observer. We need only watch our selves as we participate in life to arrive at four or five strong personality aspects. We often find one aspect still acting out dramas from our childhood or adolescent years. These subpersonalities are living in the past. These aspects can be nurtured to maturity with some attention from other personality aspects having adult skills. Easing them into adulthood will be helped through our work of recapitulation (soul retrieval) and changing core beliefs. Often times, a new reality must be created to sustain their maturation. The easiest aspects to identify are those who play the roles of our greatest reactors, perhaps a victim, a warrior, or a defensive know-it-all. We can and should have fun with them, giving them amusing names that fit their playing-out.

Once an aspect is "caught in the act" by our observer/director, how do we approach the necessary recasting of the role? It is a matter of backtracking. When we begin this work of self-observation, our observations will be retrospective. Initially we may struggle to isolate "scenes" from our lives but the work of recapitulation actually helps us begin seeing life in scenarios. In time we see the scenes clearly, but after the fact – "Oh no, I've done it again!" With this recognition, the director is able to name the subpersonality and make some keen observations that we can add to our notes. Awareness expands until we find our selves conscious of the scene when we are fully engaged in it. Though it is too late to gracefully shift roles, this awareness is important. We don't want

Emotional Fitness

to beat our selves up over a lost opportunity because it is all good consciousness work.

In time, our skill increases and we reach a point of knowing we are going to engage the scene – it feels like we are standing at the edge of a precipice ready to fall into the abyss. This is our "golden moment." It may seem like a nanosecond when we first arrive there but an astute director can alter the course of our life in a nanosecond. Having had plenty of opportunities to contemplate recasting, the director can easily send in the chosen subpersonality replacement. For example, in a volatile situation, our "mystic" might handle the scene a lot differently than our "warrior." The transition may be awkward, even embarrassing, at first – small ego pain in return for a big consciousness gain. Patterns of reaction will be increasingly easy to pinpoint for scrutiny and can be transformed through the emotional body work. The universe will joyfully send us a variety of similar experiences to assure that we hone our directorial skills. When we have gained sufficient expertise, those scenes, and often the people involved in them, will disappear from our lives. Then we can move onto the next challenge of awareness.

Feelings and Emotions

Within that "golden moment" lies a great gift – the gift of feeling. Feeling, a chemical reaction begun in a few cells, uses the nervous system and etheric body to become a whole rainbow body event. Upon reaching the emotional body "bridge" (the energetic connection between the emotional and emotional-mental scaffolds), the feeling triggers a release from the fourth dimensional data bank on the other side of the bridge. A flood of information relevant to the feeling (from past experiences, schooling, reading, and so forth) enters the emotional field and combines with the feeling to become emotion. Reaction quickly follows based upon this information, which supports the unconscious patterns and programs of a rigid assemblage point.

Within the space of awareness preceding reaction – our "golden moment" - attention to the feeling is hugely important. Awareness of the feeling can be a revelation because we generally only relate to the reactions and are unaware of our feelings - like the heat rising in our body that is signaling anger. As awareness of the feeling grows through subsequent emotional challenges, our consciousness comes to expect the feeling as the forerunner of our pattern. In addition to knowing the identity of the subpersonality in the reaction, we now know the feeling that triggers the subpersonality and its resulting reaction. If our director can assign the status of a red flag to this feeling, it can be used to avert the drama by recasting the role or rewriting the script.

An alternative approach, which offers a transitional level of expertise, has our director directing the subpersonality who is on the verge of reaction to enter a state of non-reaction. This does short-circuit the drama, and provides an internal laboratory for unexpected research into the explosive nature of feelings trying to become reactions. This exercise is only advised as a transitional technique because it creates stress within the combined fields of our physical presence.

Through this work, our director is accumulating the tools needed to transform the subpersonalities, to elevate the level of consciousness of the entire production, and, eventually, to integrate the subpersonalities into a powerful third-dimensional representation of higher self. Our soul's enthusiasm for higher consciousness will bring many such opportunities for mastery into our lives. Because this process has engaged lower ego, it will have its awkward moments - even doubts. When in doubt, we can reread the first chapter of this book to reaffirm our intent, and the last chapter to remember where we are headed. We are drawing Essence to us, and the drama stands in the way. We need our energy to complete our mission, and the emotional reaction allows our energy to leak away. Rather than dwelling on the idea that we might become social bores (the truth of this depends on our perception), let's intend that our enlightened approach to people interaction has a positive affect on the collective. Then, it will.

Archetypes

The collective unconscious, the collective fourth dimension that we are all connected to through our assemblage points, contains enormous behavioral thought forms called archetypes. These thought forms govern the behavior of humanity because they are continually reinforced by mankind's experience – the sum total of which ends up in the collective unconscious (the dark sea of awareness) in unconscious human death. Generation after generation, we are subject to these powerful thought

Emotional Fitness

forms until something happens to shatter them. The thought forms tell us how to behave – how to be a mother or father, how to be a wife or husband, how to fight for our rights (warrior), how to be spiritual, and so forth.

In western culture, the last big impact on archetypal thought form came with the patriarchal bid for domination thousands of years ago. At that point, our cultural myth shifted. The sacred stories passed down through generations began to change in favor of the patriarchy (they had been upholding the matriarchal culture for many millennia). The new myth evolved over time to become solidly embodied in the stories of the Greek and Roman gods. In *The Asteroid Goddesses*,[2] author Demetra George shows how this happened for some of the important goddesses, and how it is limiting our culture. Though astrologically oriented, this book is an eye-opener for all of us in terms of how myth has affected our behavior patterns.

Mythologist Joseph Campbell[3] often warned that we are a people without a myth. Because myth is the force guiding the future, we do not know where we are going. It is easy to see the truth in his thinking. The thought forms of Greece and Rome continue to govern our behavior. Even the powerfully emancipated life of Jesus was framed in a myth, which supported Greece and Rome. The women's liberation movement was one more battle of Athena, the warrior queen of Greece and Rome. At this time in our history we must create new myth through the conscious choices we make in our lives. Relationships can be autonomous. Warriors can be soft. Spiritual growth and enlightenment is not for the few. As we live more consciously, our own lives will gradually rewrite our myth, but other gifted people will take on the collective myth as their mission.

A good example of mythmaking as a mission is the creation of the Jedi Knights in the Star Wars series. George Lucas has created a new model of warrior whose qualities do not reflect the bloodthirsty warrior legacy of the god of war, Mars, who is more closely represented by the agents of the dark side. Master Yoda and the Jedi Council guide the Jedi from a place of wisdom rather than power abuse and hierarchy – an embodiment of the Grail Codes of kingly service to the people. Though our children are brandishing their light sabers in play fighting, the myth, the wisdom, and the right use of energy are establishing themselves in their subconscious fields. Warriors with integrity, impeccability, wisdom, patience, sensitivity, vulnerability, and magic could be part of our future, and the collective would shift accordingly. Leaders carrying, and acting on, the Grail Codes may one-day replace our Zeus-modeled heads of state. The choice to unconsciously live out archetypal patterning or to consciously change them is ours.

Perception and Mirrors

Our directors could benefit from some graduate-level training before we delve even deeper into the emotional-astral layer of the fourth dimension. We will call this perception. There are many ways to look at a single event. In fact, if twenty people observed a given event, there would be twenty different versions to report. No two hard drives contain exactly the same information. No two assemblage points are in exactly the same place. Without heightened awareness (indicative of a higher level of perception) life necessarily colors vision. What the witnesses believe they have seen is a function of their perception. One step in acquiring sensitivity is an awareness of this limitation and the resulting diversity of opinion. Instead of arguing over a point until someone wins out or dies in the process, perception sees the truth in the other person's conviction. Friendship reigns.

Another limitation of perception is our tendency to take everything personally. The good side to this social pitfall is the recognition of mirrors. The down side brings hurt feelings and self-pity. Mirrors are the work of the soul. At the soul-level, we have planned our life around the soul contracts made with others. It works both ways, since we have made contracts to bring mirrors to souls we will meet in this life, as well as to receive mirrors from other souls in our service. It is a wonderful system for soul advancement once we realize the value of it.

Until our director is in command, when people annoy us or push the buttons that trigger reactions, we project emotional reaction at them. The last thing we want to recognize in those people is our own behavior, but nine times out of ten that is the reason they are pushing our buttons. Lower ego does not like mirrors. They are painful. If our director can recognize the lesson in our face, a little self-correction will go a long way towards the elimination of such mirrors. Other mirrors will appear, but

Emotional Fitness

our consciousness practice will gradually cause reaction to be replaced by the curiosity of the director searching for the lesson; "What is this person trying to show me about myself?" These are opportunities for mastery. If we are ambitious, our soul will send us more. How do we get through this period of training without feeling like a punching bag? Discernment can save us a lot of wear and tear.

Projection

We will take our lumps recognizing mirrors until the director gets the upper hand, but much of what we receive on a day to day basis has nothing to do with us. It is called projection. We do it to others, too. Let's just say that projection is our ego's way of venting steam, which masks a refusal to take responsibility for our own actions. For example, Joyce's boss takes her to task for a transgression of business policy. There is absolutely no denying the transgression. But Joyce's ego cannot tolerate the guilt and shame associated with wrong doing, due to some deeply held beliefs about being perfect (perhaps religious-based core beliefs screaming to be changed). Instead of apologizing and being done with it, Joyce walks over to her associate's desk and berates Sue for something she has supposedly done.

Joyce's lower ego victimizes Sue with the backlash of her own undeniable reprimand. Like a missile launch without warning, the accusation hits its target with stinging accuracy. The innocent victim, Sue, is in shock, tears, emotional turmoil and mental agony, which could haunt her for some time if she doesn't recognize the projection. Alternatively, in reaction, she may rid herself of her initial feelings by turning around and projecting at someone else. This is the "hot potato effect." We have all experienced both ends of this ego play called projection. The attackers work is crystal clear, to own their own feelings and reactions, and self-correct.

What conscious options are available to "victims?" As recipients of projection, we do have ways to cope with such attacks that may not have occurred to us. Why do we let undetected projection flood our heart with pain? We can put filters on our heart, letting everything we take in every day pass through these filters before we take it personally.

Awakening and Healing the Rainbow Body

We need only become aware that these filters exist to begin using them. We can start with the "truth filter" which asks; "Is what I am hearing true?" If it is, we must own it and transform it. Then there is our "beliefs filter" which asks; "Do I believe what this person is saying?" If we don't believe it, it is not part of our reality, and cannot affect us. Our "rational thought filter" might ask; "Does this make any sense?" If it doesn't, we cannot even extract some good mirroring from it. It isn't ours. It is a discernment lesson. Ultimately, when life starts becoming transparent, our "wisdom filter" reigns with "What is this really about?" It is in wisdom that we can understand what the other person is truly experiencing and shift the energy to dissipate the projection for that person and our selves.

What of the attacker? In our example, with wisdom, and the ability to see life transparently, Joyce might recognize that her projection towards Sue was born of her need to be perfect. The emotional reaction triggered by her feelings of inadequacy is common for people having perfectionist beliefs. Her recognition of her projection would eliminate the need for future projection, and perhaps allow her to find the right words to heal the wounds inflicted on Sue. This is compassion in action. We will find more filters as we become adept at recognizing projection until, at some point, our heart will be nothing more than a field of loving power, *munay*, in need of no protective or discerning filtration.

---

[1] Deep Trance Shamanic Journeys, Volume I, Pachamama's Child, Jessie E. Ayani, Heart of the Sun, 2000.
[2] The Asteroid Goddesses, Demetra George, ACS Publications, 1986.
[3] No single reference suffices for Joseph Campbell. His books and videos are available in most libraries and bookstores.

EMOTIONAL-MENTAL FITNESS

As we move from the emotional body to the emotional-mental body (our first level of fourth dimensional awareness) it is a good time to assess our progress. Has the work with recapitulation, the observer and the changing of core beliefs had an impact on our assemblage point? Has reality shifted for us? Do we feel lighter, clearer, more capable and more energetic? We can keep a log in our notebooks of the shifts in consciousness that accompany the shifts in reality. Has the clearing of scaffolds allowed the return of some glow of awareness? Do we feel more connected?

We will experience more clearing of the scaffolds and an increase in overall energy and light as the water initiation continues. It is increasingly important that we not waste time and energy looking outside of our selves for energy/light meters. We must learn to trust our inner guidance and the "knowingness" that we are on the right track, gaining light in every way. Relying on the opinions of others, or our ego's need to compare our selves to others, as a gauge of our own progress towards enlightenment, is one serious limitation we can easily avoid.

Awakening and Healing the Rainbow Body

Within the light geometry of the fourth scaffold of the rainbow body (our emotional-mental body) is the repository of our life experiences. Some life experiences are more readily accessed than are others, but all of them have been spirited away in this layer of our hologram. In our department store metaphor, the least accessible memory is stored in the basement, while the more readily accessed memory fills the floors above the basement. Those memories with a big emotional charge or a sizable ego investment will have stressed the scaffold with their "weight" causing possible distortion, filamentous webbing, and even mutation of the light geometry (depicted in Illustration Four in Chapter 3). The filamentous webbing, like spider webbing, is common in our lower astral bodies, and, like all of the fourth dimensional field, it is thought form. At the level of energy/light, it represents stagnant energy, repetitive or addictive behavior patterns, and nests of life experiences that can be readily accessed to support reaction.

For example, all previous experiences of the suppression of personal power, and the resulting resentment, can have formed a nucleus of webbing in the emotional-mental body of a person who might eventually rebel against the status quo. This web of experience, as thought form, is accessed in emotional reaction when someone tries to control the rebel, and is then expressed by the emotional body as rebellious behavior. Whether we are working with a psychotherapist, writing our memoirs, or doing our own recapitulation, we must access memory from this holographic layer of self. If we can recapitulate the memory completely, the webbing can be removed. Distortions in the geometry of the scaffolding caused by the webbing can be corrected when we are in soul awareness – accessed in our spiritual-mental body. When the geometry of all layers of the rainbow body is restored in this way, the complete glow of awareness returns. We will encounter webbing throughout our fourth dimensional bodies, but especially in the lower astral bodies.

Many of the core beliefs contributing to our assemblage point are emotionally based and directly linked to this layer of our rainbow body. We will find that most of the remaining core beliefs comprising the luminous body of awareness are anchored in the next scaffold – that of the intellectual-mental body. In communion, these core beliefs, as filaments of light, define and color our reality. Do we live in a narrow, limited world

Emotional-Mental Fitness

or an expansive, limitless world? Are we grounded or ungrounded, or floating around somewhere between? Are we able to manifest for our selves or do we feel incapable of influencing our own reality? These two scaffolds, the emotional-mental and intellectual-mental body scaffolds, comprise our lower astral unconscious (subconscious) self. They hold the potential for magical transformation because fourth dimension is the realm of instant manifestation. When we work in our fourth dimensional bodies, we have the power to change things instantly. When we pass from this world into the fourth dimension of the collective, our lives and learning are very different because it is a world of thought form instead of material form.

Assemblage points can shift and change due to our life experiences or they can become further entrenched in the past. Our flexibility and willingness to change through self-correction are indicators of the degree to which our assemblage point can be mobilized. To do this we must make the assemblage point – our awareness – our own, by owning it, knowing it, taking responsibility for it, and then moving energy to shift it into new states of awareness. Again, let us invite life to be our teacher as we open yet another door to self-mastery.

Relationships

Life in any dimension is about relationship. Here on earth we are social beings, I think, in part, because we were collectively "abandoned" by "God" when we plunged into unconsciousness at "The Fall." There is nothing like a natural disaster to bring a community together, and that was a disaster of significant proportions. The beautiful part of our predicament is that the simplest path of return to God Awareness is through our reflective relationships with others. We are here to help each other. A simple shift in our core beliefs about others allows us to drop the adversarial aspects of relationships and see the mirrors through which we can engage self-reflection and then self-correction. Those who push our buttons, with the most expertise, are our greatest teachers. Though we are less likely to be aware of it, we push the buttons of others just as effectively.

Rather than cloistering our selves away to seek God within, this path asks us to engage the rich landscape of relationship to find God in others. In such a state of God Awareness, there is only love. Until we are walking in such bliss, any button pushed signals the need to self-correct. Any limitation signals the need to change a belief. Each correction helps to clear the scaffolding of our rainbow body contributing to its eventual restoration as a mirror of the soul template. Often, multiple scaffolds are healed through one profound insight, with the added bonus that the provocative issue dissolves forever and more energy flows through our energetic system.

With our observer at the helm, we now want to look at the richly rewarding spectrum of behavioral patterns that spring from our relationships with others. It is in our best interest to be flat-out honest with our selves to get the most out of each remembrance and every current experience. As we release the patterns that have kept our emotional-mental bodies from reaching their highest potential, the fourth scaffold in our rainbow body clears, allowing more energy to flow through our bamboo, and brings us one step closer to our purpose.

Agendas in Relationships

Agendas and expectations hold a powerful court in the realm of relationship. These common pathologies of relationship, rooted in core beliefs, are sustained through manipulation and control - two strong human tendencies springing from fear and driven by wants, needs and desires. Agendas and expectations represent the driving force behind the invasive art of emotional body filament exchange – the compulsive way in which we attach our selves to others and they attach themselves to us. All of this sticky business is so commonplace in relationship it is thought to be normal. Far from healthy, these distortions of personal interaction prevent us from experiencing enduring happiness and spiritual growth in relationship. It is obvious that they do not foster personal power and emotional well being either.

When those in our lives fail to meet our expectations or follow our agendas, we can experience disappointment or even stronger emotional reactions. The nature of our reaction depends on the strength of our attachment to the outcome. If basic survival needs have been threatened, it could be quite strong. It is here that the work of detachment and surrender begins. Perhaps the most difficult part of our journey is the process of coming to believe that wisdom beyond the conscious mind is capable of guiding and taking care of us in this life. If we have never been exposed to one living in the ways of magic, from their higher self, we are understandably reluctant to cut the lifelines of our fear-based control. We become our own worst enemy by blocking the flow of energy from our higher self.

For example, a great number of us tolerate jobs that no longer serve us. In fact, we might hate every minute that we are working at our job. The longer we stay at the job the sicker we make our selves. Why do we do it? Usually the answer is security. Most of us will not leave one job until a more suitable job is in place. Because we are sickening our selves with our own negativity, we lack the energy to find a new and better job. We probably don't look or sound too appealing to potential employers either; and so we remain trapped in the negative experience.

The patterning behind such behavior could be widely varied but the agenda is clear - we do not step out of a situation, even a horribly negative one, until our bases are covered for ongoing security. The agenda is held in place by a complex network of core beliefs like; "I will become a homeless person if I give up this job," "People will think I'm goofing off if I quit my job," or "I have to work hard to be a success – even if I don't like it." These beliefs may have been part of our childhood experience in our families or part of our own working life experience. As we adopted these beliefs, we brought them from our parents' words into the first person and owned them completely. They became part of our assemblage point. As part of our assemblage point, they will have formed a set of core beliefs that have operated throughout our working life – to our detriment, on all levels.

The work agenda in our example forms a nest of webbing within our fourth dimension scaffold. Our first step at unraveling the webbing is to become researchers of our own thought field. Investigating motivating factors, we can easily see the fear of survival and acceptance within community – two absolutely basic fears that are intertwined. Our research must uncover the history of survival issues within the memory of our emotional-mental bodies and recapitulate the "scenes" from those dramas. Step by step, we are disassembling the agenda – clearing the webbing from our emotional-mental bodies.

Awakening and Healing the Rainbow Body

Next, our research will allow us to identify the hidden core beliefs that have supported our work agenda. They may even have come down through our bloodlines, having been instilled in the familial heritage by traumatic conditions of survival. These bloodline beliefs would sound something like "Responsible people do not take chances with money," "There is never enough, so you must be careful," "You have to work hard and not complain to get ahead or even to survive," "Obey authority or be damned," and so forth. The latter two beliefs are usually accompanied by a great deal of private moaning, groaning and self-pity – or dumping on friends. This is just one possible scenario supported by an agenda. There is only servitude in agendas. We are seeking liberation. The agenda-based core beliefs limiting us must be change to core beliefs that will support liberation.

What we must realize about agendas is that they are already in place when an opportunity arises. We are great at manifesting, whether we are conscious of it or not. In our example, when we originally went looking for the job that we subsequently came to hate, the anatomy of our work agenda drew to us an exact match for our beliefs. To change the agenda, the core beliefs must be changed to create the assemblage point of a new reality. In the process of changing the core beliefs, we will be freed to quit our job under good terms, take a huge, deep breath - a sigh of relief - having called to us a job that will serve us. Core beliefs are the keys that open the door to a new reality.

Our belief-based expectations of partnership form other common agendas. Though current beliefs are quite different from the past, there are still many women who expect a husband to take care of their needs in return for taking care of his comforts, children, and home. If these beliefs were strongly held in a woman's family, it is quite likely that some form of that agenda was in place prior to her having met her partner. She will have attracted an old-fashioned man who expects the care taking in return for meeting her security needs. Throw into this milieu a new idea. She births a longing to prove herself in the business world (a common enough empty-nest idea). To her husband, who is living comfortably under the long-established belief-based marriage agenda, she may be regarded as unappreciative, and even irrational. She, on the other hand, is bored with her life and yearns to be free of their marriage-based agenda. Will she be responsible for the unraveling of her marriage, or will she find a way to shift the agenda? Both are possible.

In today's culture, our young people exhibit completely different agendas about partnership than previous generations because their parents' generation rocked the cultural assemblage point of marriage - affirmed by the spike in the divorce rate. It doesn't mean they have let go of agendas or expectations. It just means that their agendas are different from their parents. For example, one of the most obvious agendas affecting many partnerships now is the timing of careers and children. It is easy to see how the reformulated agendas of the previous generations have shifted values in the generation to follow through the changing core beliefs. Cultural core beliefs begin to change as a result.

One of the most obvious examples of an agenda is the life plan parents can have for their children – usually beginning in utero. Without allowing the development of talent and interest to occur, parents make plans for the child's future. This is an agenda. In instances where the parental core beliefs have been wholly embraced by the child, the child will experience gratification in the fulfillment of the parental agenda – until his/her soul consciousness begins to awaken. If they have not been fully embraced, the child may be force to live a life he/she abhors until enough personal strength motivates change. A third scenario finds the child as a rebel, breaking free of the parental agenda at an early age. Any way it plays out, the wounds from agendas are plentiful and deep. The webbing of the parental agenda is transferred to the child's astral field through suggestion and expectation (anchored in their field with related core beliefs) and controlled experience (no early awareness of choice). Parents who succeed with these agendas get tremendous reinforcement in their own astral webbing as their child fulfills their expectations. There is often an inability to distinguish the child's life from their own lives.

For our last example, let us take the teacher. From primary school lesson plans to the stringent requirements of the "guru," teachers have agendas. How strictly these agendas must be followed – a measure of the flexibility of the teacher – depends on the teacher's investment in a controlled outcome. Schools and teachers set uniform achievement goals for students who are tested and graded according to set standards. Because we grow up in these systems, we tend to pass information on to

Awakening and Healing the Rainbow Body

others in the same way – consciously or unconsciously. Thus the pattern of agendas is adopted and reinforced. We can see how this system is hurting the children among us, especially those children whose creative potential is not information-based. Perhaps as adults we have also felt misunderstood or unheard by teachers whose agendas are so strong that variations from the controlled outcome elicit angry responses with possible expulsion from the group.

Dropping agendas and expectations, as difficult as it may seem, opens us to the opportunities present in the now moment. When we contemplate the notion of trusting that there is an operative Divine Plan instead of our preconditioned agendas, we arrive back where this discussion began – detachment and surrender. We can begin by changing core beliefs that shift our assemblage points and our agendas into realities of higher frequency. At the threshold to self-realization, the webbed anatomy holding agendas in place – whatever the frequency – must collapse. Agendas do not fit through the eye of the needle.

Patterns and Programming

Next, let us look at the filamentous anatomy of reaction. As we have already discussed, reactions originate with a feeling which, almost instantly, combines with fourth dimensional information to provide us with an outpouring of emotion. The thought forms accessed from fourth dimension are both intellectual (information which we have incorporated into the database of the hard drive in our intellectual-mental body), and emotional (the experience-based thought forms in our emotional-mental body). Some of the information originated by deduction from experience, while most of it came through the various learning opportunities in our lives.

With programming, we are looking at repetitive unconscious behavior, which appears in the scaffolding of our mental body as filamentous webbing. Some of it resembles roadways because it is accessed so frequently. Riding a bicycle or driving a car are ordinary examples of behavior that becomes natural (unconscious) with repetition. Those who have ever traveled to a country where the citizens drive on the opposite side of the road know that driving safely requires constant and considerable attention – hyper-vigilance. If our driving slips into the unconscious and habitual for even a second, it could spell disaster. When faced with something new we will either have to learn new behavior or surmise it by comparing it to past experience and knowledge. One requires the input of data into the hard drive while the other will rely on the results of trial and error (experience). Once learned, the activity becomes unconscious. This is a program. The webbing is established.

The smallest children exhibit alarming skill when it comes to establishing patterns. These are tried and true ways to get their needs met, and who could be more "in need" than an infant or small child? Programming is established early on, which reflects the core beliefs of our families and culture – the status quo. We learn to play roles like the angel, or the disturber of the peace, or the sufferer, that might still be with us as adults. When identifying our subpersonalities, we may find a childish or rebellious aspect of self, which is still getting needs met in the same old way. The motivation, at all ages, is survival. On a superficial level, the patterns may shift over a lifetime, but getting our needs met - the art of survival – is still the priority. Self-preservation is the ego's way of staying in power and avoiding the unknown.

Our egos know themselves in terms of the experiences stored in our emotional-mental body. What if we were to experience an amnesia wherein we do not remember our selves by way of our experience, or from any information we carry, yet basic survival programming remains? We would be able drive a car, for instance, but we could not remember our families, where we lived (though we might automatically drive there), our jobs, and so forth. There would be people "loving" and "caring" for us, but we wouldn't know them. We would not understand their sadness over our memory loss. If they were to try pushing our buttons in old ways, we wouldn't know how to respond.

Albeit dramatic, this would be the equivalent of the complete recapitulation of our lives – a thorough housecleaning of the mental bodies. In that state, there is no alternative to the now moment. The clarity within the emotional-mental body would afford us insight and transparency. We would see through the motivations of the "loving" and "caring." In time, the pushing of buttons would cease without our reaction but would afford great understanding of those around us. Enough of reality would remain

Awakening and Healing the Rainbow Body

for navigation in third dimension, but the assemblage point will have been swept free of core beliefs that no longer serve us.

While we are imagining, let us think about the aftermath of spiritual psychosis, the momentary destabilization or dissolution of the luminous body of awareness and the assemblage point, which we have previously discussed. It is comparable in ways to amnesia, because eliminating a large number of core beliefs dislodges related programming in the emotional-mental field. Which programs are deleted depends on the factors that led up to the psychotic event, but the nature of reality and subsequent behavior should shift dramatically. The loss of supporting core beliefs allows for a considerable healing of patterns and programs in the rainbow body. Programs, like most everything in our third and fourth dimensional realities, are core belief–based.

We needn't go to such drastic measures to clear the emotional-mental hologram but the end result will be similar. The step-by-step nature of our work, and the subtle skill, with which we nurture our relationships, afford a more natural shifting of reality. We will find, through the self-observation of our patterned reactions, the lower ego's lifeline to drama and reaction. We can reduce every reaction to the emotion driving the lower ego, then shift core beliefs around that feeling-based emotional trigger. I believe that, ultimately, every reaction can be distilled to reveal a fear, and that the fear can be further distilled to the primal fear – the unknown. This primal fear speaks to nothing less than our perceived separation from God.

From the perspective of energy and light filaments, the belief-based programs that unconsciously guide us through life are the cataracts clouding the vision and remembrance of our true nature. Like cobwebs, they cling to the scaffolding of the unconscious, distorting the geometry of the rainbow body through repetitive reinforcement. They hold the interconnected rainbow body in a state of distortion, which stifles communication between the scaffolds and, as we have noted, restricts the flow of energy through our bamboo. As we detach from the programs, the rainbow body is cleansed of the webbing in preparation for our alignment with our Original Birth Template.

Autonomous Relationships

It might be a bit difficult for us to conceptualize an autonomous intimate relationship. We don't often see them depicted in movies, on television, or in books – probably because there is next to no drama associated with them. That is just the point. When we are not enmeshed with someone, we have nothing to win and nothing to lose. We maintain our own autonomy, as does our partner. We have interests in common and interests that do not involve the other partner. As partners, we work from a relationship assemblage point that does not compromise the integrity of the individual assemblage points.

Within this autonomy is respect and support. We do not need to be directly involved in our partner's activity to fully support them in it. In turn, we are supported for following our own dreams. In relationships there are a lot of levels on which to communicate. In enmeshment there is a lot of giving and taking, pushing and pulling, and some good exchange as well. In autonomy there is the opportunity for sharing, and emotional and mental accord. In mastery there is intuitive and energetic relating that flows from a radiant, open heart. Autonomous relationships have endless possibilities, whereas enmeshed relationships have endless work.

Addiction

When we become slaves to our unconscious programming, another element enters the picture. In addiction, the lower ego can no longer control our repetitive patterns because it has been sabotaged by an energy more powerful than itself. We have already established this energy as predatory.

Addiction is a dreadful energy drain on our present culture – a culture having the time and where-with-all to pursue addiction in its many forms. However, it is likely that humans have had addictive natures since "The Fall." Humanity's remembrance of God is no longer strong enough to propel us forward spiritually so we take the easy path of self-gratification. Wants, needs and desires have become our new "gods." What is more, we are natural creatures of habit. Though not all of our habits are harmful, they do indicate assemblage point stasis. An immobilized assemblage point is not going to help us on a path where fluidity opens the doors. In a small way, we can consciously try doing habitual things differently every day

Awakening and Healing the Rainbow Body

to exercise our flexibility skills. Even randomly rotating different routes home from work every day will increase our fluidity. We begin living life more consciously as we eliminate the unconscious patterns – especially those that are addictive.

As might be guessed, discipline – coaxing the lower ego into some sort of consciousness – is paramount to healing addiction. However we must be vigilant that a new addictive pattern doesn't slip into our mental field's landscape to take its place. Using an example, let us examine the genesis of an addiction from the perspective of the rainbow body.

Nell is a successful, highly regarded, real estate broker. Hers is a typically stressful occupation. Wanting to get ahead in her profession, she had taken night school courses to improve her understanding and position. Once in the position she desired, she maintained her high standing by bringing work home from the office at night and often worked a seven-day week. Her husband, who had been encouraging her to take it easy for years, finally convinced Nell that her position was secure enough for her to relax when she was at home and enjoy life more. He liked to come home from a long day at the office, pour himself a scotch on the rocks and turn on the sports channel. Nell was not attracted to liquor or sports, but did find it impossible to let go of work, and relax.

Nell's friends convinced her that a glass of wine in the evening might help her relax. Advertising in the stylish, intellectual magazines she liked to read reinforced their suggestions. She followed the suggested behavior and did find that a small glass of wine relaxed her. She felt relieved of the days pressure, and could actually flop in a chair and enjoy her husband's company. To make a long story short Nell's natural love for status and chic, coupled with her pattern of needing to be engaged in an activity, began to extend to her wine choices and the ritual of her evening glass of wine. When she walked in the door at six in the evening, the cork was withdrawn and the ritual began. When she was with her friends she found both fun and competition as a wine devotee.

Unfortunately, the glass of wine turned into half a bottle, and, before long, beyond that. Nurturing her habit had established it more fully in her unconscious mind and a little fortress of filamentous webbing was built to protect the habit. Core beliefs worked their way into her assemblage point like "A little glass of wine is not addictive," "I deserve

Emotional-Mental Fitness

to relax for having worked so hard," "I deserve the best when it comes to self-nurturing," and so forth.

The first alarm rang for Nell several years down the road, when she found that she was no longer able to think clearly after taking the first sip of wine. She was confused about having lost control of her intellect because she could remember thinking clearly when she had begun to use wine as a relaxant. The second alarm rang when she realized how much money she had been spending on fine wine and how susceptible she was to advertising in that regard. The third alarms rang when her marriage started to rock because she, who had been mindful of their home being clean and in order, was too numb to care. The fourth alarm rang when an old friend confronted Nell about the negative thoughts she had begun to project and the drama that resulted from them. Her friend did not want to see her any more.

How did something so innocent blossom into something so destructive? Keeping in mind that Nell's addiction was no different than any other substance used to alter mood, let's look at it from the energetic perspective to understand Nell's addictive behavior. Nell was an easy target for some heavy-duty webbing in her fourth dimension. She was already exhibiting an addictive personality with her work. She reluctantly broke the patterning of the workaholic but the webbing remained in her mental field making the transition to alcoholism both swift and seamless. Her hardest decision had been to give one up to begin the other. Nell was consciously influenced by her husband's regular suggestions to relax, as well as subconsciously influenced by his habit of drinking in the evening. Additionally, she had been supported by the suggestions and participation of her friends, and her own realization that she had trouble relaxing.

She had eliminated some core beliefs from her assemblage point – changing her reality about working at home – without consciously choosing replacement beliefs. The gaps in her assemblage point were immediately filled in with the newly acquired core beliefs, which were reinforced by her husband and friends. Without blame, we will refer to her husband and her friends as her enablers. Granted, no one forced Nell to drink. She made the decision herself and was well aware of that fact. The advertising contributed an important cultural validation of the addiction – a glass of wine in the evening was acceptable, even commendable, social behavior. Drinking alcohol was reinforced on the level of the collective, adding another set of core beliefs to her assemblage point. We can see that the anatomy of an addiction is very complex.

Nell's lower ego directed the shifting of her assemblage point. She had sabotaged herself into thinking her behavior was harmless. When we examine the scaffolding of her rainbow body, we see that the nightly repetition of her wine habit has created weblike distortions in her emotional-mental hologram. Her habit has become a form of self-nurturing. We can also see that these webs are filamentously linked to the intellectual-mental field's hard drive, where reinforcement comes in the form of mental justifications and her ego's investment in wine knowledge. Still other filaments link the webs down through the scaffolds of the emotional, etheric, and physical bodies where her actions and reactions take place, energy is lost, and emotional needs are met.

The state of relaxation she achieved with alcohol was justification enough for Nell to drink it. Others might have to quote scientific articles about wine's beneficial uses in heart health to justify their addiction, or they may need no justification at all. Her lower ego was directing energy from the rest of Nell's field to create and sustain the patterning of self-gratification (need fulfillment) in the emotional-mental body.

Unfortunately, it did not stop there. As the addiction continued and deepened, the filaments organized themselves into channels of energy flow and the physical body, as a manifestation of the first three scaffolds, became increasingly depleted of life force and will. The webbing in Nell's emotional-mental and intellectual-bodies became impenetrable. Once she engaged the pattern, her intellect could not function normally. The critical point to recognize in Nell's addictive patterning was the clouding of her intellect that occurred with one sip of wine. This meant that the webbing of addiction was a powerful enough plexus of thought forms to have greatly distorted her emotional-mental scaffolding. She had attracted the attention of predatory energy in the collective unconscious. Nell's ego lost its power to that energy, which felt like a loss of free will. She had to have her wine, even if it made her dysfunctional.

The distortion present in Nell's scaffolding invited the creation of a portal into the collective through an addiction-related sub-assemblage point (addictions usually have powerful and plentiful core beliefs to

Emotional-Mental Fitness

substantiate them). The portal was sustained by the core beliefs supporting the addiction and the predatory energy began to use Nell and her addiction to support itself.

The predatory energy attracted relevant core beliefs into the sub-assemblage point around the portal. This not only distorted Nell's luminous body; her consciousness no longer had anything to do with choices around the addiction. Her energy (life force) was lost through her self-created filamentous channel, which now looked more like a wormhole into the collective, mimicking the loss of life force at the moment of unconscious death. The predatory consciousness had full access to Nell's rainbow body. She was no longer acting on her own (lower ego's) behalf.

This example is deliberately extreme (though an accurate energetic picture of alcoholism), to demonstrate the progression from an innocent habit to the powerless state of helplessness and energy loss that accompany severe addiction. It can happen with any addiction, if discipline and consciousness are not present. Nell was no longer the one picking out the wine, opening the bottle and so forth. Activities related to sustaining the addiction, including supporting thought forms, had come under the influence of the predators. Their insatiable desire for energy, especially disturbed energy, is a force to be reckoned with. Is it any wonder that addictions are so hard to overcome, and that substitute addictions so often step in to continue service to the predators? The portal, supported by core beliefs, is wide-open. Even when the core beliefs are changed and the webbing is dissolved, the portal remains. Fortunately, it can easily be protected.

Though sometimes impossibly difficult to imagine, life without addiction is the only way to reestablish our glow of awareness. Not only is discipline required to accomplish the healing of an addiction, a precise series of steps must be taken to heal the rainbow body. It does not mean that Nell will never be able to have a glass of wine again. On the contrary, it means that she will be able to have a glass of wine consciously, without needing to have a second glass, or to have a glass every day. She can take it or leave it without attachment.

Awakening and Healing the Rainbow Body

Healing Addiction

We will work through those healing steps using a different addictive pattern, at the same time remembering that all patterns create a similar energetic pathology. Within this story we will weave Nell's healing journey as well. Our subject, Jennifer, is dangerously obese. She has steadily gained weight over the course of her adult life. Limited discipline has created a long history of fad diets – each one sabotaged by some mysterious force. She is addicted to high calorie combinations of fat and sugar, like cookies, baked goods, chocolates, and so forth. She will never run out of her comfort food because her cupboards are piled high with her favorites.

Jennifer has had her stomach stapled, portions of her small intestines resected, and still has not been able to control her weight. Her doctor, who has been monitoring her prediabetic blood sugar levels for several years, has just informed Jennifer that she is literally digging her own grave with each cookie she eats (she is compelled to bring them to the doctor's office in her oversized handbag). Jennifer's history of food addiction is a long one. She will, when healing, come face to face with childhood memories and the core beliefs of abandonment still in her luminous body from that time. Jennifer was raised by a single mother. Her mother worked during the day, and tried to juggle a social life with child rearing in the evenings. Television was used as a baby-sitter when Jennifer was still too young to be left alone. Her mother provided Jennifer with plenty of snacks, especially cookies, when she could not be there. Jennifer learned to associate nurturing with sweet food rather than with her mother.

We will find that all feel-good addictions have to do with nurturing and the fulfillment of wants, needs, and desires. For Jennifer, fears about being left alone became entangled with misconceptions about nurturing. The cultural acceptance of sweet treats was reinforced in commercials on the television used to pacify her. Outside of required gym classes in school, exercise – even playing - had no place in her life.

As a child, Jennifer developed a low-grade Candida Albicans fungal infection, which was sustained and nourished by the acid food she was eating and the direct feeding of the fungus with sugar. Jennifer was chubby as a girl and heading towards obesity as a teen. The infection had become systemic, manifesting in young adulthood as an occasional vaginal yeast infection, abdominal bloating, and lethargy.

In time, the cell population of the Candida outnumbered Jennifer's own cells. Candida Albicans are living organisms – with consciousness. In adulthood, the mass consciousness of the Candida gained enough strength to override Jennifer's own consciousness, undermining her own free will. This describes loss of energy and will to an internal parasitic consciousness. We could think of this as predatory energy from a parasitic internal thought field – that of her Candida population. From that point on, for Jennifer, the Candida were making the food choices, doing the grocery shopping, and stocking the shelves with goodies. Our third dimensional consciousness may choose to regard this as a metaphor. However, on the level of energy/light, this description of sugar addiction is not a metaphor. It is reality.

Because Jennifer's addiction was long term and severe, the webbing and channeling created in her mental body scaffolds attracted predatory energy from the collective. Like Nell, she was losing energy to those collective thought forms, but also to the internal parasitic yeast. Fatigue and depression had been part of Jennifer's life for many years.

The availability of low nutrition, high fat and sugar food has accelerated Candida Albicans to near epidemic proportions in our population. We can carry low-grade infections for years that need only the debilitation of an illness or injury, hormonal shifts, emotional turmoil and, most commonly, habitually poor dietary choices, to take hold within our bodies and gradually gain conscious control over our lives.

The first step of healing addiction is changing the core beliefs that have held the addiction in place – from the beginning to the present. Jennifer's started with abandonment and nurturing, while Nell's began with the need for relaxation and distraction. The core beliefs that had supported Nell's work addiction, which began around survival and success beliefs, had already been replaced by the relaxation driven beliefs. In addition to the investigation and identification of the core beliefs at the inception of the addiction, each must identify and change all of the core beliefs presently in place that support the addiction.

Cultural programming must be broken. That programming is also held in place by core beliefs. Jennifer will need to deprogram all of the television, radio and magazine commercials about nurturing oneself with goodies. She will have to break core beliefs that link junk food with loving one's self or others, and develop new core beliefs acquired from self-education about nutrition and healthy lifestyle. Nell will have to see the manipulation behind the ads and articles in the trendy magazines and the ego's attachment to the wine expertise she gained while drinking. These will also be found as core beliefs within her assemblage point. New core beliefs will be centered around healthy relaxation methods and relationships.

Next, for both women, the filamentous webbing present in the scaffolding of the rainbow body, which was created through repetitive behavior, must be dissolved through awareness. This work will gradually destroy the patterning in their addictive behavior. Some of the webbing formed channels through which energy was lost internally (in Jennifer's case) and to the collective (for both women). These channels can move between the dimensional bodies or can be linked to the collective allowing the predatory energies to help themselves to an individual's rainbow body and life force. Webbing and channels present within our rainbow body cause the distortion and imbalance we perceive as ill health, weakness, and imbalance.

In Jennifer's story, strong emotional links were forged between the scaffolds of the emotional body and the emotional-mental body through self-pity. Nell's emotional body links were connected both to the intellectual-mental scaffold vis-a-vis thought forms of trendiness and stylishness, and to the emotional-mental scaffold through related emotional dramas. These complex filamentous links must be dissolved and any core beliefs supporting the emotional or mental reactions must be broken.

It is then necessary to retrieve filaments lost or taken from those who enabled the addiction. Both women must recapitulate their life experiences with enablers. As with all recapitulation, the exercise must be done without blame – and in the spirit of love, forgiveness and compassion. This initial work of reclaiming personal power provides the foundation necessary to heal an addiction. If done thoroughly, it is tantamount to a brilliant piece of research.

Emotional-Mental Fitness

All of the above healing brings us to the point of entering the unconscious to confront the consciousness of the addiction. In Nell's case, she will confront the spirits of the grape plants and of the yeast that are the foundation consciousness of the wine. Jennifer will confront the Candida organisms. If, for example, they were healing an addiction to marijuana or cocaine, they would find themselves confronting those plant spirits, while those manufacturing or supply the drugs, as negative energetic entities, would be considered amongst their enablers. It should be said that most vintners and food manufacturers are not intending that people become addicted to their products, whereas those knowingly producing an addictive drug *are* intending addiction. Discernment must be used to arrive at the truth about enablers in individual addiction work. Breaking the core beliefs and the addiction patterning clears the webbing and channels from our rainbow body and dissolves the sub-assemblage pointed created by the predators.

If the addiction is severe enough for portals to have opened into the collective fourth dimension the predators must *not* be invited into the personal fourth dimension for confrontation. There is no need to confront them. The collective unconscious is not part of our field or our scaffolding. Therefore, we cannot repair the portal created by the predators. Damage to our own field can be restored after soul alignment. In the meantime, guardians can easily be stationed at the portals to provide a lifetime of protection from further invasive energies, and the scaffolding is freed of outside influence.

Once confronted and dis-empowered, the addiction-related parasites, entities, and spirits must be banished from our unconscious hologram. This can be done in a number of ways that suit the individual – like dissolving them, blowing them up, or sending them packing right through our assemblage point. Because each of our examples attracted predatory energy from the collective fourth dimension, guardians must be placed at the portals created between their collective and personal unconscious fields.

In addition to these confrontational steps, it is important that these women, and all those healing addiction, contact a higher part of themselves (higher self or higher ego) and ask for assistance in making all decision surrounding their addiction. By inviting in higher self, they are supporting their own shift to higher consciousness. When time stands between them and their addiction, they will find that higher self has helped to clear the webbing from their scaffolding easing the distortion and damaged caused by addiction.

To perform these steps of healing addiction we must be possessed of personal power and the intent to change. In other words, we must be in touch with discipline in a place of fearlessness. This is easier to accomplish than it sounds because knowing and owning the truth of our addictions should bring us to that place of fearlessness – even anger – about them. We would not be seeking help or doing this work if it were not the right time to embrace a more divinely inspired and directed future.

These insights help us to understand more clearly why our life force is gobbled up with our experiences at the moment of death. The predators' ability to tap into our energy through addiction assures them of that final feast. We have already discussed the energy taken through the creation of dramas, and here we see that it is taken wholesale through addiction as well. Addiction is a loss of consciousness because we no longer have control over our behavior or thoughts. We no longer have free will, and the soul has distanced itself from our earthly presence. Because it can restore our free will, discipline is needed to heal addiction. In the healing process, we can find our way back to the Divine Plan of our souls.

The second CD in our *Deep Trance Shamanic Journey* series, *Right Relationship*,[1] includes *The Journey to Heal Addiction*, which offers inter-dimensional assistance for the work described. After completing the foundational research and core belief work, the journey takes us within our scaffolding to complete all of the healing steps. Needless to say, the journey is powerless if the intent to heal the addiction is not present. In healing addiction, as in all healing, there are no quick fixes. However, with intent, we can make miracles happen in our lives.

Abuse of Power

Abuse of power is another way we humans get our needs met, but at the expense of others. We have already seen the abuse of power in the form of control and manipulation. For example, we can have a guru or priest using their position of authority to sexually seduce women or children. Add a charismatic personality to the situation and women will line up to be abused. Children, taught to respect authority, have no power in such circumstances – only memory to haunt them. It is our lower ego's emotional neediness and/or identity issues, our penchant for "specialness," that opens the door for the seducers. Most children are desirous of attention – especially those who do not receive it at home. Throughout our lives, we make wretched bargains with authority to survive. There are countless examples of power abuse in our everyday lives. That is the place to begin healing the strain put on our rainbow body by abusive behavior – theirs and ours. Obviously it is imperative to be in our power and to teach our children to be in theirs.

One component of power abuse is the betrayal of trust. Agendas are in place prior to the manipulative action – sometimes so cleverly woven into the fabric of life's illusion that hyper-vigilance is required for our observers to identify them. It is far easier to see the abuse of power in others and to disregard the mirror being presented to us. The more we need to self-correct the more intense will be the mirroring. We will need to look at our own agendas, dismantle them, and retrieve filaments to reclaim our power.

All institutions provide ample opportunities for authority to abuse power. We may be drawn to those institutions to learn about that power abuse and to self-correct our own petty tyrants. Casteneda's teacher, Don Juan, speaks of the petty tyrant within each of us. He could not have hit the nail on the head with greater precision. Those held in the grip of dictatorial leadership often mirror that dictatorial style in their family life. Either parent may assume the role of petty tyrant and hold the rest of the family under their masterful control. It may not be an easy mirror to see, but in their lives outside the home, they very likely draw the oppression of tyranny to them. It becomes a vicious circle.

People living under tyrannical leadership can shift the energy in their countries if they are able to shift the energy within themselves. Letting go of control is not a simple thing, but it is also not impossible. If accomplished within, that level of surrender can be applied to the families, and the workplace. Then government will shift accordingly. Without fail, we call to us that which we need to heal within.

Those living in countries with a leadership history of dishonesty, secrecy, subversion, and corruption need look no further than the mirror

Awakening and Healing the Rainbow Body

of their own lack of integrity. Institutions are held in place by thought forms/core beliefs – individual, group or mass consciousness. At this writing, we, in the United States, are watching the exposition of corruption and the overall absence of ethics in all of our institutions with corporate white-collar crime and sexually abusive Catholic clergy leading the way. We have witnessed the bending of truth, the self-consumed attitudes, the extortion, and an extraordinary amount of paper shredding. Abuse of power is so commonplace it plays like an ongoing television series. Dissociating our selves from the truth of what is happening leads to complacency – and the cycle continues. We cannot point the finger at our leadership if we have not lived ethically our selves.

We invite to us that which reflects us. Like the great lessons that the soul blueprints within the rainbow body of an individual, the soul of a nation blueprints lessons within its scaffolding for the healing of those who chose to be born in and/or live within that nation. It is for that reason that nations reflect to the world that which the souls of their people design to heal. For example when enough of the people in an aggressive nation embody peace, the nation will begin to make the transition to peace within the world. We acknowledge that sound leadership is necessary, but the grail codes of kingly service are still, unfortunately, incubating within our rainbow bodies.

The grail codes of kingly service are:

To put service to your constituents above service to yourself;

To honorably assimilate the traditions and character of those you must conquer into the existing culture for the enrichment of all;

To defend yourself well when attacked, but to attack no one without due cause.

We can add the paraphrased wisdom of the Ascended Master Saint Germain to the grail legacy – *make friends of all nations, and allies of none.*

We do have the potential leaders amongst us to embody the ethical codes of the grail. However, they will not become the leaders of their nations until the majority of the citizens of those nations embrace the consciousness of liberation, which would give them their necessary "electability." Liberation, on this scale, requires the dissolution of national assemblage points that have supported power abuse. These potential leaders cannot, and will not, flourish in the status quo political arena. As we will undoubtedly see, timing is everything.

Black Magic

Lastly, it is worthwhile to understand the basis of black magic and how people get hurt through its use. Black magic, though prevalent in some cultures, is not a common threat in ours. However, it bears scrutiny. We can learn a lot about the fourth dimension, thought forms, and intent from considering it. In truth, all manipulation is black magic because it invades the luminous field of another - but it is generally unconscious. Once consciousness is gained, we can move through our work to a place where any crossing of boundaries would, necessarily, be deliberate. Premeditation is required. Black magic is a deliberate and dangerous misuse of energy and intent. It works through the fourth dimension as projected thought forms. We might consider powerful thought projections as entities, not unlike predators.

To experience the infliction of harm through black magic several prerequisites must be in place. First, the black magician is a master of intent – as all true magicians are – whether black or white. It is with intent that thought is projected. Intent is always deliberate. Second, their character is mired by a lack of impeccability. Third, they are consummately devoted to themselves – a common enough ego flaw in an ordinary person but one of grave consequence in a magician. It is not uncommon for a white magician to be lured by the self-gratification of the dark side. So, the skill, the intent, and the consummate ego are present in the black magician.

Some people are greatly affected by deliberate thought projection and others seem to have immunity or at least resistance to it. What is happening at the level of the rainbow body – energy/light? From the perspective of the recipient, the following can be suggested.

(1) The projection cannot enter the rainbow body through the assemblage point. That interface with the collective is sacrosanct until death or its equivalent (psychosis, for example).

Awakening and Healing the Rainbow Body

(2) It is not difficult for a projection to enter through an open, unguarded portal. For this reason it is wise to clear our selves of addictive patterning and place guardians at all portals.

(3) It is not difficult for the projection to cause the creation of a portal if the recipient has had repetitive patterns related to the projection. For example, a male charismatic black magician wishes to use a woman to hurt other women. If this woman has had a history of hurting other women, the filamentous webbing is already in place to attract the projected energy and support the creation of a portal. The black magician becomes a principal predator.

(4) If there is no true foundation for a portal and no existing portal, the magician might try to surround the mental field with his intent in hopes that the recipient might become receptive to the magicians negative thought forms. If this should occur, the recipient begins to create the webbing necessary for a portal with his or her own negative thinking.

Fortunately, if the recipient is conscious of his or her thoughts and thought patterns, his or her mental field is impenetrable. That level of consciousness is a skill we will take up in our next chapter.

---

[1] Deep Trance Shamanic Journeys, Volume II: Right Relationship, Jessie E. Ayani, Heart of the Sun audio CD, 2003.

INTELLECTUAL-MENTAL FITNESS

Entering the intellectual layer of the astral, the fifth field of the rainbow body, our work of awareness turns to thought, or what is generally regarded as the mind. Because the word "mind" has been used in psychological and spiritual writing to describe a variety of the functions of consciousness, I have avoided confusion by not using the term at all. Instead, we will utilize the context of the consciousness of the rainbow body.

Our human capacity for thought and the storage of information is impressive. We have experienced an evolution of awareness over our long history on the planet. Mankind has been plagued by setbacks, genetic dead ends, and natural disasters grand enough to spare but a few. We must ask if all of this was intended for a greater Mission on earth – the Mission of developing a vehicle, the rainbow body, capable of embodying the fifth dimension in human form, and lifting humanity's amnesia. Time will tell if this is so, but the fact remains that we have evolved to a point where we could conceive of this embodiment. If we can conceive of it, we can manifest it. It is the nature of our reality, and, at the same time, that which will liberate us from it. Integral to this evolution has been the upgrading of human genetics (most importantly the increasingly complex brain), and the expansion of consciousness to embrace new potential within the super-conscious (the higher astral).

Primitive-type humans (not necessarily on a historical timeline) may have utilized gifts native to the mammalian brain: the gifts of emotional awareness, humor, feelings, interactions with other humans, animals and plants, and so forth. In that phase of consciousness evolution, humans were likely more aware of the plant and animal spirits, the powers of the natural world – for example, the devas, fairies, and gnomes. They may have been more in touch with their own feelings than we are today. Some may have evolved more quickly because they felt more secure with the processing of information into ideas and their manifestations, whereas those whose awareness remained instinctual and reactionary were likely more secure in the physical world. In either case, their assemblage points interfaced with a collective unconscious somewhere along the surface of their emotional-mental body.

When this phase of consciousness evolution was successfully completed, new genetics were introduced, either by direct seeding or genetic manipulation of existing humans (if we accept the idea of star-seeding). The neocortex appeared, and humans gained both brain size and function. This allowed for the conscious awareness of the intellectual–mental field to take place, expanding the unconscious to include thought as well as feeling. This was a great leap in consciousness that gave the assemblage point the potential to interface with the intellectual-mental field. Each step of this evolutionary process brought with it a more complex personality or ego.

We have yet to utilize ninety-five percent of the neocortex's consciousness potential. This leads to speculation about new frontiers in the evolution of consciousness including our ability to access the super-conscious. Are we already possessed of the ability to shift the assemblage point into the spiritual-mental body? Of course we are. It is happening every day to those who sincerely seek enlightenment. With this expansion comes the mastery of intellectual awareness and the exploration of the higher self. Higher self is possessed of inner truth, wisdom, and immense possibilities, including mastery of the unconscious and the awakening of the "lightbody." At the same time, it allows the seamless integration of

Intellectual-Mental Fitness

emotion, intellect, and our spiritual nature into one functional consciousness – fourth dimensional mastery. As part of this mastery, the ego is integrated and higher self is our guide.

We are clearly on the threshold of this great evolutionary leap in consciousness - already possessing all that is needed to embody expanded awareness. We will make this leap the topic of our next chapter and address, in this chapter, the mastery of the intellectual-mental body.

The Intellect

Our intellectual-mental body is a thought field. In addition, the mental body contains products of those thoughts (e.g. thought forms, ideas, concepts, core beliefs), pathways of the intellect (e.g., rational or irrational thought processes, repetitive programming), and, unfortunately, parasitic entities (e.g. miasms, predatory energies, projections from others). To more easily understand the intellectual-mental body, we will turn to a fitting metaphor – a computer. Because computers are designed to increase the capabilities of the storage and processing capacity of our intellects, they are the most appropriate metaphor to help us understand our intellectual-mental fields.

The Hard Drive

Computers were originally designed and built for the storage of data. Much like a library where information is contained in volumes, the computer hard drive stores information. The initial data storage systems utilized magnetic tapes. Huge machines have since been streamlined using silicon technology for desktop, laptop, and handheld simplicity. Originally, programs were written to guide the data storage and various pathways to access the data. Now, vastly more complex programming takes a far greater amount of memory but requires comparatively little space to operate. The current level of sophistication (vast internal memory and additional linked hard drive capabilities, as well as increased processing power – HZ) in computers touches upon genius.

The human brain and its intellectual capabilities constitute a first-rate hard drive. In that hard drive we have stored everything we have ever learned or experienced as memory. It is the unconscious intellect's data bank. Within that brain, we have also stored the programming needed

Awakening and Healing the Rainbow Body

to access that data. The hard drive wiring is analogous to the neuronal pathways – the electrical impulses that run our programs. Mental acuity is associated with unobstructed electrical wiring – clarity missing, for example, from the brain of a person with Alzheimer's disease. We confine ourselves to the pathways of learned behavior – trusted programming – that suffer the limitations of our core beliefs. In actuality, the limitations are self-imposed and reduce our brain function to a bewildering five-percent of the neo-cortex.

We must also look at the quality of information taking up space in our internal memory. Clearly, we place too much importance on information that fulfills wants, needs and desires – a throwback to the reptilian brain's need for security, and the mammalian brain's penchant for emotional fulfillment. Consequently, we assign little importance to the qualities that manifest innovation in thinking, like imagination, creativity and broader conceptualization. We have plenty of memory on our hard drives - we need only upgrade our system and begin including information, which has more possibilities, greater awareness, and magic. In this way, our mental capabilities can eventually access the exciting, though elusive, remainder of the neo-cortex – an evolutionary leap complete.

Programming

Hard drives are accessed through programs. That is to say, within the limits of our reality, we run programs that give predictable and repeatable results. If we add A to B, it is assumed that we get C. The programs are formulas for survival, safety, productivity, and success within the confines of our reality - our conception of reality as our assemblage point defines it. Our programs operate within the framework of certain systems and the systems are defined by core beliefs. If we want to advance in the world of computers, we must keep upgrading both systems and programs. If we try new programs in old systems, they often refuse to operate. When the system is upgraded it can accommodate new programs and often requires upgrades of existing programs.

The core beliefs (elements of the systems) must be changed first, then pathways more compatible with a new reality can be forged within the intellectual-mental field. Software is just that – soft and flexible. The

Intellectual-Mental Fitness

more complex the program becomes the more flexibility is required. We must determine if a program is working for us or not. If it serves us, we keep it and upgrade it as needed (as long as it works in the existing system) to reflect new levels of sophistication. When new systems are required, we upgrade our assemblage point accordingly.

Interestingly, if we try to delete programs, they remain on the hard drive even though we can no longer access them. In other words, we put things in the trash and our computer dumps what we delete into a landfill, but the landfill is somewhere on the hard drive. Computer specialists are able to retrieve lost material for us from the landfill. Erasure of the hard drive would empty the landfill along with everything else. This piling up of the trash in the landfill is analogous to holding tension or distortion in the geometry of our rainbow body through thought-formed (unconscious) filamentous pathways and webbing. When the assemblage point is actually shifted and old core beliefs have been released to the collective unconscious, we get some relief.

Once the assemblage point has shifted, the webbing can be cleared away and, eventually, the geometric integrity can be restored. The only way to truly clean house is to bring a new system onboard and reprogram accordingly – or to have the unfortunate experience a complete crash of the system (a psychotic event, near-death experience or similar collapse of reality). If the hard drive crashes as well, we experience complete amnesia where information cannot be accessed, systems and their programs have vanished, and a new computer, system, and programs are required.

Our programs are written in the language of core beliefs to be compatible with our current systems. We must learn that language to have mastery over our assemblage point by changing core beliefs. That language is a composite of our culture (both archetypal myth, and collective human behavior), our upbringing (bloodline and family experience), our experience (life experience, trial and error), and self-realization (soul-guided autonomy). While focusing on emotional fitness, we have learned how to identify core beliefs and change them. Soon we will delve into some of the pathologies apparent in the intellectual-mental field where the core beliefs are formed. But first we will carry our metaphor to completion.

Awakening and Healing the Rainbow Body

www.com

I can think of no better metaphor for the collective conscious/unconscious than the worldwide web. It has become a complete reflection of our highest aspirations and most sordid preoccupations. Modern systems have programming that allows us to connect through specific wiring and our hired server to the internet and world wide web. Metaphorically, our personal fourth dimension is connected to the collective fourth dimension through the assemblage point. This connection occurs in the emotional-mental and intellectual-mental scaffolding of both the personal and collective fourth dimension.

Through this connection we can control the receiving and sending of messages from and to others (thought projections) - either welcome (friends and issues of interest) or otherwise (spam or junk mail). We must keep in mind that our assemblage point is sacrosanct. We can access any aspect of the collective that interests us by searching for key words or using web addresses. However, conscious or unconscious permission is needed for anything to enter our field through our assemblage points. Metaphorically, this searching of the web represents the function of the emotional-mental or intellectual–mental fields' relationship with the collective, as guided by our assemblage point and free will.

This metaphor becomes even more interesting when we consider viruses and the hackers who infect systems with the viruses they have created. Antiviral programming has been designed to eliminate the possibility of infection – though the programs cannot keep up with the onslaught of viruses, and work only on those that can be predicted. Metaphorically, we can have vigilant programming within our construct of reality to help us discern and redirect energies and predatory thought forms that others project towards us. Conversely, when we project at others, we will either get through, be blocked, or get returned mail. Being able to discern and either redirect, deflect, or return transformed energy is standard protocol for anyone awakened. Viruses are continually evolving (mutating), and these simple tests of discernment now require heightened awareness and vigilance to avoid infection.

Let us take it a step further. The nastier viruses came originally as constructs meant to invade our systems when we opened an e-mail attachment. A serious glitch could be avoided through discerning interest

Intellectual-Mental Fitness

in the sender or subject presented in the e-mail in these cases. Oftentimes, the subjects are misleading, and we are mistakenly drawn in. Until intuition can replace discernment, we are required to reject everything we do not already know to be safe. The next generation of viruses caused havoc upon simply opening an e-mail - pushing discernment to new heights with clever disguises. At this writing, hackers are delving into organized crime through theft and resale of credit card numbers, and identity theft. These predators have now found a way into our computers through the convenience of continual internet connections like broadband. In this case, the glitch cannot be avoided as long as we have chosen to remain continually connected or happen to connect at the wrong time. Let's explore this as metaphor.

Returning to the energetic world of addiction, we can use this metaphor to understand how we make a choice to connect to the collective fourth dimension, either by "dial up" or by remaining continually connected. Before we succumb to predation through portals in our fourth dimensional interface, we "dial up" through repetitive behavior. When repetitive behavior becomes unconscious, we become continually connected through superhighways and portals just like broadband – and, as long as we remain unconscious, we are helpless to prevent what is taken from us. If we are not in our power, not conscious of the fourth dimension, we open ourselves to attack by fourth dimensional predators but also from black magicians who know how to send energy through fourth dimension.

On the other hand, when we have gained consciousness of our own fourth dimension, and are fully in our power, we can take advantage of all that this dimension has to offer without losing our power or energy to it. To do this requires awareness, integrity, and courage. Enlightenment *does not come* to those who have not mastered their unconscious. In this work, we are well on our way to understanding how to accomplish that. Now let us move from metaphor to pathology before we speak of healing and mastery of the intellectual-mental body.

Dysfunctional Programming
If we could see the scaffolding of the intellectual-mental body, we would likely be appalled at the amount of filamentous webbing, channels, and

Awakening and Healing the Rainbow Body

super highways distorting the original sky-blue geometry. Like those of the emotional-mental body, which were deposited through repetitive behavior, most of these will have been deposited by repetitive thinking. Many of the highways and channels are connected to those in the emotional-mental body as information is repeatedly accessed to sustain reactions. There are, within the distortion, filaments linked to stored data – the hard drive.

Whereas the webbing within the scaffold represents rational thought processes, obsessive thoughts, ego constructs that support identity, and internal dialogue, the channels and highways represent our core programming. The core programming has been written through the trial and error thought processing of information, which resulted in tried and true rational pathways for problem solving, creative processes, data recall and organization, and so forth. These old programs and the filamentous webbing distorting the scaffolding of this body serve to cloud the mental field and obstruct the smooth flow of energy through the bamboo that could bring insight, innovation, and inspiration – to say nothing of gifts ready to flow from the spiritual-mental body.

Our culture is highly invested in intellect. Perhaps this is an indication that we have immersed ourselves in the mastery of that mere five-percent of the neo-cortex's potential. Our obstructive programs may actually be inhibiting access to most of the intellect by focusing the mental process along these repetitive pathways or by trapping it in the webbing existing in this body's scaffold. If we are able to clear the webs and rewire/reprogram our mental processes, we might begin accessing more intellectual capability. At the same time we might begin to open ourselves to the potential power of the neocortex, which is now as inaccessible as the upper astral, or spiritual-mental body, with which it co-creates.

To elevate the assemblage point into the upper astral requires a complete clearing of the webbing, the downloading of useless information, and the upgrading of programs as well as systems (reality-creating core beliefs) that no longer serve us. *The Journey to Heal Addiction*[1] can be used to facilitate the scaffold clearing. We can master the intellectual-mental body with good energy flow and clear thinking. This allows us to transform an injured ego sustained by survival fears into an integrated personality sustained by love and compassion. Let's look at some of these pathologies in depth. Many more patterns may come into the realms of our understanding, once we see how patterns and programs work.

Negative Thought Patterns

The simplest place to start is negative thought patterning – a mental pathology so common as to be ubiquitous. If severe, this patterning will lead us into depression or a number of other mental health problems. Even in its mildest form, it will block positive occurrences in our lives. If our thought patterns are mildly destructive, our observer will easily pick up on them, especially if our observer has been honed through our work with the drama and subpersonalities. When asked to observe thoughts, most of us are stymied. How do we start? Sometimes it is easier to observe negative thinking through its verbal expression in those around us. Then we can apply the results, as mirrors, to ourselves.

These negative thought patterns can emerge as the gentle put-down, like "It's not going to work," "I can't do that," "I look awful," and so forth. They can also be character assassinations of others, demonstrated by turning any of the above put-downs on another person. They are also expressed as a focus on negative news items, defeatism, violence, any fear-based statements or warnings, catastrophic prophecies, and woes of all sorts. After we start picking them up in what other people say to us or around us (without correcting them, of course), we can take the mirror and begin monitoring our own thoughts. This exercise, if done properly, calls for hyper-vigilance – as if our observer were a detective hot on the trail of a seemingly invisible criminal. Unless we have a serious mental illness, once the negative thought patterns are observed, self-correction is simple. It is similar to getting out of the drama. Soon we will find ourselves thinking positively. Instead of living in gloom, life will be seen as the adventure it is.

Negative programming robs us of energy. We can waste time in patterns of worrying about the future that can become obsessive. Conversely, fixating about the past can lead to depression. A mild form of this pathology is processing. Processing is common in the spiritual work, causing some of us to get mired in the details of the work. We can waste time and energy trying to attach significance to the slightest event in our lives. Likewise, we can spend so much time trying to squeeze all of the

Awakening and Healing the Rainbow Body

mental juice from an experience that we fail to grow from it spiritually. We can get stuck in the muck. This path is about moving energy - letting go and flowing with the Divine Plan. Continual processing does not serve us. We observe, we self-correct, we are grateful, we let go, and we *move on*.

We can also be caught in old programs of assigning blame. It needs to be someone's fault for us to accept what appear as negative events in our lives. When something negative occurs, we access that old program and find someone or something to take the blame. Here is a program that inhibits our ability to take responsibility for our own lives - an absolute roadblock on the path to enlightenment. We can learn not only to take responsibility for everything that happens to us, we can, occasionally, take responsibility for the actions of others in service to ourselves and to them.

Perception becomes important when, as practiced observers, we cannot spontaneously accept responsibility. In some cases, perceiving the event or interaction from the perspective of the other people involved will help us take it on for transformation. Moreover, there will be times when incomprehensible conflict blocks our path. We may stand "falsely accused" of instigating or participating in a conflict because the perception of others is different from our own. To explore mastery and the real meaning of service, we can take these situations on for the person(s) involved. What does it cost, aside from the humiliation to an ego in need of mastering? If we have not yet become an astute observer, walked away from drama, and reprogrammed our intellectual-mental field, we may want to wait until we do to take on such opportunities for mastery.

Judgment, Opinion, and Criticism
Some specific programming that bears closer scrutiny is judgment programming, and the opinions and criticism that result from running these programs. Personal judgment is the internal sentence we impose on others because they do not share our assemblage point/reality. The core beliefs which support judging others can also support significant control mechanisms in our mental body. In a simple example, a woman can judge another woman because she is overweight. She may decide not to make friends with the woman, perhaps missing opportunities for

spiritual growth and friendship. Nothing is ever said (let alone understood), and avoidance results.

Within the judging woman's assemblage point, there are fear-based core beliefs relating to controlling obesity, her own appearance, the embarrassment of being seen with an imperfect woman, and so forth. This judgment program is reinforced by her circle of friends and family (like attracts like). Since the same program plays for everyone she judges to be even slightly overweight, those close to her who begin to gain weight may become targets for verbal abuse – judgment expressed as criticism. If she, herself, were to gain weight, it could lead to eating disorders, depression or some other manifestation of self-judgment.

Though simple, the example above is as complete as any when looking at the work to be done. Core beliefs must be identified and changed for attitudes to shift. The programmed pathways through the mental field must be dissolved through self-observation and self-correction. Thought patterning pathology can be thought of as addiction, since similar filamentous webbing and channels are created in the intellectual-mental body scaffolding. Again, *The Journey to Heal Addiction*[1] is a useful tool for clearing and healing the scaffolding.

Preconceived judgments and opinions of others offer substantial roadblocks on the spiritual path. Patterns of judgment and opinion can be passed on, generation to generation, in bloodlines and/or ethnic and/or national groups for years, centuries and even eons. Think about religious, racial, and ethnic prejudice, nations hating other nations, civil wars (any wars), conquest, class structures, sexual abuse, and so forth. We live in a fear-based world with many of our institutions overtly projecting fear. At the root of every core belief, which supports these fear-based realities, there is fear itself. If self-realization is our path, part of our work will be the internal transformation of these outwardly manifested fears. The need for fearlessness continues throughout the path – in time becoming more the art of transforming fear into love through the shifting of the assemblage point.

If our bloodlines hold patterns of judgment, our families will be extremely critical of others – what we might call a judgmental family. Seeing the light about the programming and changing our reality accordingly will require some deep work. The fears underlying the core beliefs may not be readily apparent, and we may not know the history of our bloodline to the point where it all began but we can imagine it using pieces of information. If our grandparents, parents, and their siblings have the same chip on their shoulders about some aspect of life, it may go back a long way. As we advance in our work, we can intend that the programming be healed within us, and through all the generations that embodied it. We can intend that the ancestor who originated the program be released from the reality he/she created out of fear.

This works for all programming. For example, if our family is greedy, our generous nature will not be able to express itself until we clear the programming. Looking at all manifestations of greed in our own lives, we can break the core beliefs, and heal the underlying fears that support them. Then, we can turn to our ancestors. We can question our elders about their elders and the family stories, especially around times of tribulation when hoarding might have taken hold. If we can pinpoint anything, we might be able to imagine our ancestors' fears and the resulting core beliefs. We can heal our bloodline through intent when we have gained that power, but initially we can begin to heal our ancestors by healing ourselves. If we cannot identify anything, we can heal what we see manifest in the living ancestors who hold the fears unconsciously, and who have unconsciously transferred their fears to us. Bloodline work requires perseverance as well as good detective skills. It is well worth the effort as we realize the effects of clearing on the intellectual-mental field.

Opinions, expressed or not, are the result of judgmental programming. We learn the art of expressing opinion first from our families, and later from our teachers, media, written material, and the many forms of mental stimulation present in our culture. People without opinions are thought to be dullards. Editorializing life is part of the culture but it has little to do with truth. If we were in our truth it would not be necessary to sift through the webbing of the intellectual-mental field to come up with an opinion or to make an informed choice.

Having opinions of others usually means that they have opinions of us. Judgments about others can lead to opinions, which act as darts – reaching out through the collective fourth dimension to energetically stab our targets. It doesn't take much skill to pull off this form of projection. Thought forms are easy to project at the intellectual-mental holograms of

Intellectual-Mental Fitness

others. If we add to that opinion, the verbal criticism, the dart can be projected in third dimension as well. One form is no less powerful than the other in mental combat or conquest. Why we use these tactics to survive, look good, stay in control, and so forth, is simple to understand. They are old programs with cultural (often archetypal) validity. They protect us and keep others in their place.

How many parents use criticism rather than love to guide their children towards self-sufficiency? Criticism is the most common form of control. And how many parents can cease criticizing when their child is a self-sufficient adult? Parents have validation for this behavior not only from their own parents, but also from the intimidating tactics of government, religion, economic institutions, and the rest of our social constructs.

We are living in times when fear, control, and lack of ethics are endemic. To change society we must first change ourselves. Our observers must get busy in the mental field by paying very close attention to our judgments, opinions, and criticisms of others. We must also observe our relationship with ourselves. Many of us have clever egos that can try to minimize the work of self-correction by indulging in self-criticism. By taking responsibility for our own lives, we can learn to love ourselves, and lose the need to project our self-criticism at others in the form of blame, judgment, criticism and accusations of stupidity.

When all of this ego-rattling overwhelms us, as it well might, we can pause momentarily by immersing our selves in the poems of the Sufi poets, Hafiz or Rumi. They will fill the imagined wounds created by detachment and surrender, with the laughter and love of the universe, and bring us back into balance.

Control

We use our system to control the programming on a computer. Control in our lives is a core belief problem. It is fear-based and fear-fed. Though already discussed in the emotional-mental body chapter, it must be noted that controllers run their programs from the intellectual-mental field. The easiest way to understand these programs is through their core beliefs. Our most often used controller core belief is "It's my way or no way." That is stated simply, for there are likely numerous core beliefs

Awakening and Healing the Rainbow Body

backing the thought patterns grouped to support strong control. It is a difficult system to bust. It likely took us less than a second to think of someone who operates predominantly under that belief system. They have no room for compromise, no time to listen to another way to approach a problem, and if we do not do it their way, they will refuse to help us.

The good news is that we do not have to change them. What we have to do is find the mirror within, because we are all controllers at heart. Our need to control began at "The Fall" – or perhaps as we left the Heart of God on this great journey of discovery. Control is an abandonment and survival mechanism. It locks tension and stress in the body until, having lost our natural fluidity and flexibility, we begin to feel like we are turning into wood or stone – that is if we can feel at all. Who did it ever help?

The bad news is that it obstructs the flow of the Divine Plan within our field. The Divine Plan is flowing whether we choose to be part of it or not. Some of us remain in control until we take our last breath – the most poignant factor in the terror of death faced by the unconscious person. The more we surrender to the Divine Plan, letting go of control, judgment, opinion, criticism, drama and everything else we have discussed in this book, the less we have to fear – and the more magic we invite into our lives. This is the embodiment of the attribute of fluidity. There is magic aplenty in the Divine Plan – more than enough to provoke amazement and awe for the rest of our lives, and to inspire us to surrender even more. Our mantra for this part of our work is:

"Let go. Let flow."

Injustice

Injustice can get our blood boiling. If we were to list what we regard as injustices in the world, it would likely be a lengthy diatribe. If we were to ask ourselves to go back to the list and dispel all judgment, opinion and single-minded perception, we would have nothing left. If each of us were to dispel those sticklers from our mental bodies, there would be nothing left in the world to provoke thoughts of injustice. The work is clear.

We can cultivate the wisdom to see beyond the greater picture and to understand the journey that each soul has embarked upon, through acceptance. If we truly understand the virtue of acceptance, and embody it completely, love and compassion will replace our sense of injustice. Our energy can be channeled into more spiritually oriented thinking and another obstacle to peace – within and without – will be jettisoned from our field.

Invasion

We know, from our work with addiction, that our personal fourth dimension can become fair game to energies, entities, predators, and thought forms that are normally unable to access our field. Most often, we unconsciously invite them in through thought patterns, repetitive stimulation, and destructive core beliefs. Seemingly harmless leaks occur through the many forms of distraction we employ to ease our boredom. We can call this voluntary invasion since we have invited it – conscious or not. Repetitive stimulation and distraction (addiction) through modern music, radio and television, video and computer games, cell phones, palm pilots, laptop computers and gambling machines, to name a few, create more webbing in the intellectual-mental field. Though potentially harmful in their clouding effect on the mental processes, and overstimulation of the nervous system, these forms of stimulation also cause enormous energy loss and constitute unconscious ways in which we give our power away.

The more webbing and clouding we have in the mental field, the more likely it is that our reliable programs will begin to falter. Rather than following rational thought patterns that have always served us, they will begin to randomize, causing misfiring of the system and what we might call irrational thought. It is irrational to deliberately kill another human being yet it happens every day, perhaps every second of every day on a global scale. In a less provocative example, we are led to buy things we don't need through commercial stimulation on television – much of it subliminal. We give our power (money) away. Eventually we are unable to think, imagine, conceptualize or even fantasize of our own accord.

This sort of repetitive and constant stimulation is likely engineered under the guidance of predatory energy from the fourth dimension to steal human energy. Individuals who are hungry for power, and regularly abuse it, can easily be invaded and manipulated by predators to facilitate the channeling of energy into the fourth dimension. This could be true of

Awakening and Healing the Rainbow Body

those who produce addictive substances as well because they prey on the human addictive nature. We must ask if they are agents of the predators and, as such, what they have bartered of themselves for power.

It would be most beneficial to avoid all forms of distraction and mind entertainment. Boredom is an illusion. This life is pure excitement; the earth a source of wonder and wisdom - when we fully engage life. When we hit our stride in our soul's purpose, there is rarely a dull moment. If, like Nell, we have trouble relaxing, we can take up yoga, tai chi, or meditation, for example. When we feel like being entertained, we can invite friends over for a good meal and an evening of stimulating conversation. We will want to avoid needless routines when at all possible. We are consciously gaining power, rather than giving it away.

Miasms

Miasms also enter into the intellectual-mental field but their source is internal. Miasms are thought forms of disease, which are passed down along the bloodlines to successive generations. Miasms hang out in the intellectual-mental body gathering strength and credibility as we age because we build filamentous thought form nests around them. They are passed on as thought forms through the "energetics" of our genetics, the telling of family stories, and experience. Over time, they become life threatening - supported by core beliefs with terminal prognoses.

For example, a girl child is born into a "breast cancer family." She may not know anything about the disease in her lineage until she is in her twenties, when her mother is diagnosed with breast cancer. Before the young woman can comprehend what has happened, her mother has had a double mastectomy, radiation treatments, and chemotherapy because her family history puts her in a high-risk category. The daughter is told that radical and immediate treatments are accorded those in "breast cancer families." She is also told that her grandmother had a radical mastectomy when she was in her fifties. Perhaps her grandmother died of a metastatic cancer. She has suddenly been assaulted by thought forms, stories, and her mother's experience of this deadly and aggressive disease, and comes quickly to believe that she will be next. This is how a miasm operates.

Her mother's familial miasm was activated by the grandmother's experience, and on back through the lineage of women. Breast cancer

Intellectual-Mental Fitness

families are breast cancer families because the miasms have been too strong to overcome. It becomes an inherited disease as the energetic genetic mutation imposes itself on the scaffolding of the lower bodies; specifically causing the etheric body to cease holding form in the physical breast tissue. Miasms, if not overcome, predict, then precipitate, our deaths. Homeopathic and radionic treatments can be used to help remove miasms from our mental field, but the obvious work of core beliefs and the clearing of the first three scaffolds of our third dimensional presence must be done as well.

Archetypes

Archetypes are another passive form of invasion. They are mythic by nature – important energies of behavior guiding the collective unconscious. In western culture, for example, we have the mythic stories of the Greek and Roman gods. We may think they are nothing more than stories but, on closer examination, we find that their behavior is templating human behavior in our culture. Our male warriors are modeled after Mars, the bloodthirsty avenger. Our female warriors are modeled after Athena, the liberated warrior woman whose latest conquest is the corporate world. Our model of marriage is that of Zeus and Hera so frighteningly depicted in the movie, *The War of the Roses*.

Our model of mother and daughter relationships springs from the myth of Demeter and Persephone, a story of the classical controlling mother. We can free ourselves from these archetypal patterns through awareness of our behavior and the shifting of our assemblage point. In that way, we help to change the collective. In addition, we can, in our own lives, write and live new myth that will guide us into the future.

Aggressive invasion from the collective unconscious occurs in addiction and black magic, as we have discussed. Like the hackers on the worldwide web, predators abound in the collective and will try to take advantage of our unconscious patterning. Our best defenses are viral scans (awareness), reprogramming (breaking negative patterns), rewiring (healing the intellectual-mental field), and upgrading our systems (changing core beliefs).

There are also invasive energies in some forms of mental illness, which may or may not have been brought on by abusive behavior, like

Mental Illness

How might we begin to understand mental illness from a fourth dimensional perspective, and, perhaps, help to facilitate the development of more effective treatment strategies? If we can apply the rainbow body model to mental health, with its luminous body's assemblage point, an energetic understanding of mental health disorders might be possible. We can look at a few mental health problems as examples.

Programming Errors

From the perspective of the rainbow body, the first group of mental disorders are those in which programming errors have occurred. These would include thought patterning, program content, and faulty wiring. In depression, a person has a tendency to negative thought patterns because negative core beliefs are projecting a gloomy reality. The negative thought patterns become programs that sustain the depression and often cause it to spiral downward as feelings and beliefs of hopelessness shift the assemblage point even further into low vibrational reality. We know that this can frequently lead one into the dark night of the soul.

Obsessive-compulsive disorder couples thought programming with repetitive behavior. It is enormously taxing energetically. It is quite likely that the long-term repetitive patterning of those suffering from this disorder opens portals allowing fourth dimensional predation, and even more energy loss. Thickly woven channels supporting this disorder transit through the unconscious, dominating the emotional and intellectual-mental fields. The thought patterns are clearly based on core beliefs but the programming is so dominant that the patient is bound to it in a kind of servitude. Prescribed medications, which restore the normal flow of brain chemistry in the majority of patients, may be allowing the patient to bypass the obsessive–compulsive program by blocking access to the thought forms, or by disguising the well-trod road of the pattern.

Intellectual-Mental Fitness

Internal dialogue ("mind chatter") resulting from repetitive programming can distract us, and deter us from ever feeling peace. It is a mild mental disorder but one that literally drives us "crazy." The thought patterns of the dialogue may be speeding along filamentous roadways created by the repetition of distracting stimuli, as mentioned above. Thought observation, breaking patterned distracting behavior, and core belief work could bring some much needed quiet time to those so disturbed.

Many of us fall prey to predatory energies because the breathtaking amount of stimuli we manage to sustain, including drugs, has poked holes in our fourth dimensional bodies. If we could "listen in" to our unconscious (subconscious) when it is so troubled, it would sound like a stereo blaring away or a tree full of magpies all squawking at once. It is quite difficult to focus on this reality when that level of distraction is present in the unconscious. As in the addiction work, we can ask the energies to leave us alone and place a guardian at the portal through which they accessed our mental field.

Assemblage Point Disorders

Next, let us look at mental disorders of the assemblage point. We have already discussed psychosis as the temporary or permanent collapse of the assemblage point and the reality it creates. If not severe, like spiritual psychosis, or a brief psychotic episode, the patient can be assisted in recreating their assemblage point through the incorporation of core beliefs. Though some psychotic events are very brief, in severe prolonged psychosis, often the result of drug abuse, a stable reality will be very difficult to regain.

Don Juan describes dreaming as the sliding of our assemblage point along the dark stream of awareness – the unconscious. It is no great leap, but a gentle slide wherein other realities are accessed, most of them variations on the theme of this reality. Is it possible that schizophrenics experience waking-state uncontrolled shifting of the assemblage point, most often to a repeated and, thus, familiar reality? They may have hyper-mobile assemblage points. Those experiencing concomitant paranoia may be accessing the predatory energies and entities of the collective unconscious.

Awakening and Healing the Rainbow Body

Paranoia is an understandable bedmate of schizophrenia from the energetic perspective. It is also the all too common result of drug addiction – even the experimental drug use of visionaries. It is common to find mild to severe paranoia in some spiritual people who have accessed "vision" and "truth" through mushrooms, hashish, LSD, and so forth. LSD is particularly powerful for opening us to the fourth dimension. Continued use can result in predatory leaks and reality shifts. Esoteric teachings suggest that LSD burns through the protective membranes between the chakras. Does that mean that it creates portals in our fourth dimensional scaffolding allowing predatory access? Those who have taken a tragically dirty dose of LSD could probably give us a good picture of the collective fourth dimension if they were not left paranoid-schizophrenic from the drug. This disorder is a high price to pay for rushing our natural capacity for vision.

What of anxiety, autism, attention deficit disorder, bi-polar disorder, mania, and the many other mental disorders? Perhaps mental health professionals will soon be able to help describe them energetically. As more and more of us move toward energy mastery, there may be ways to correct mental illness in our culture that are simple and heart-centered. For example, we could cultivate the ability to create a safe space where energy can move in the direction of healing, and the patients can, at their own pace, shift into stable and healthy assemblage points.

Healing dysfunction in the mental field, whether a serious mental illness or distracting thoughts of judgment, requires significant change. We must begin with self-observation then we can try to identify the fear, or whatever else, sustains the dysfunction. Shifting reality by changing core beliefs follows, along with a clearing of the webbing and channeling related to the dysfunction present in either the emotional-mental or intellectual-mental field. In diagnosed mental illness, the mental health professional also considers the patient's timing, their capacity to feel safe with each stage of the work, and their ability to maintain the desired outcome. Assemblage points can be shifted incrementally when stability is a question.

The mental health professional of indigenous cultures was the witch doctor. By our standards of "judgment" he would not have been considered sane himself. However, he was a master of the fourth dimension with the skill to heal fourth dimensional illnesses. What he could see when he journeyed into the patient's unconscious is exactly what we can visualize in our own fourth dimensional bodies – filamentous webbing, channels and superhighways, punctures and leaks in the scaffolding and assemblage point aberrations. We can do all of this for ourselves – and must do it as we seek enlightenment. If we are a mental health professional, we might also find ways to apply this work of self-awareness to assist clients with mental illnesses.

The witch doctor was also able to confront predators, disincarnate spirits who were either confused or who had malevolent intent towards the patient, self-predatory thought forms, and parasitic entities. This is exactly what we have done while working through addiction. On behalf of a cursed patient, the witch doctor fought with black magicians in the collective, cleaned up the damage they had done in the patient's field, and, on rare occasion, his consciousness never returned from the fourth dimension. He died to cure his patient. He was absolutely fearless.

Investments

One of the most potent exercises in the intellectual-mental body awareness work is to list our investments. What are we attached to? What is important to us? What would constitute a loss if it were taken from us? If we were to perform this exercise periodically, we would be able to see that our investments shift as our awareness grows. We would also be able to monitor our egos because it is the ego that clings to the past; that invests in the material world; that fears change.

This work will destabilize our egos but the concomitant exercises with our subpersonalities should counter the jolts to the ego, and help to integrate personality towards self-realization. Often, when we first engage this work, the ego is invested in people (signaling enmeshment), drama (the spiritual work trying to present itself), appearances (emotionally immature self-absorption), pain and suffering, and so forth. These are emotional body investments. When we look at the intellectual-mental body, the investments look more mental, for example I.Q., achievement, problem solving skills, compulsive teaching (usually lecturing), quick wit, position, earnings and all that they manifest, and so forth.

Awakening and Healing the Rainbow Body

Our beliefs have made our investments important to us. They support them. As we change beliefs, the attachments will loosen, and liberate us. We can have people in our lives without enmeshment. We can have all the nice things money can buy without being attached to them. We can have money without hoarding, comparing, or worshipping it because our assemblage point does not support fear-based realities. We are liberating ourselves from investment.

It is time to review our subpersonalities and see that all of them are gaining awareness and letting go of attachments. One very important consideration at this point in the path is the degree to which we have invested in the path itself. Initially, we search for validation from teachers on the path – one of the reasons we want teachers at all. This is a stage of "specialness" when we are engaged in the emotional aspects of the path. In this stage, it will be important to us to know the right people, attend the right classes, and buy the right books - and to make sure everyone else knows it. Usually, the most important investment is in the teacher. For this reason we place teachers on pedestals. When they fall off our pedestal – by showing us they are human – it can be our excuse for abandoning them and, perhaps, the path, or it can be the motivation for understanding how we have invested in the teacher.

When a teacher falls off our pedestal, we need to take a closer look at our selves. Why have we invested in the teacher? What are our personal agendas? What is our need for the drama that ensues? Do we need to devalue the teacher to others to make our selves feel good? Where does our need for validation come from? These are all the workings of the ego. This is not to say that there are not unethical teachers out there. They may outnumber those with ethics because discernment is such an important lesson for all of us at this time. But, when we are taken in by an unethical or inauthentic teacher, do we blame them for lack of ethics or do we look at our own ethics, and our motivations for working with them? Do we admit that that teacher has gifted us or do we write them off as a villain? What lessons can we learn from getting boxed around the ears a bit? Perhaps, more than we care to admit.

In the next chapter, we will see that a great transition is necessary to enter the upper astral consciousness – the spiritual-mental body. All of the work we have done thus far does not reach into that space. If we are

Intellectual-Mental Fitness

to move into that consciousness, the gateway to self-realization, we must have completed the work of the lower astral. Using all of the tools thus far presented, we can move forever beyond our stories, our mental processes, and our emotional and mental body ego attachments, to explore the gifts, the wisdom, the inner truth and the higher self encoded in the indigo scaffold of the spiritual-mental body. Are we ready to pursue the NOW moment?

---

[1] Deep Trance Shamanic Journeys, Volume II: Right Relationship, Jessie E. Ayani, Heart of the Sun, 2003.

NOTES

SPIRITUAL-MENTAL FITNESS

Imagine our egg of light filaments with its assemblage point surrounding us in either the emotional-mental or intellectual-mental field of our personal fourth dimensional space. The placement of the assemblage point as it interfaces the collective is determined by the overall (mean) frequency of our luminous body filaments – our core beliefs. Even though our assemblage point may be fixed to the collective in our intellectual-mental field, filaments of that luminous egg can extend in to the emotional-mental body or out to the spiritual-mental body. Our assemblage point will shift to interface with the collective upper astral when the mean frequency of our core beliefs aligns with the spiritual-mental field's vibration.

Entering the spiritual-mental body with our assemblage point is not like entering the end zone and scoring a touchdown. It is a gradual process engaging some of the most challenging work on the path. As the scaffoldings of the emotional and intellectual-mental bodies are cleared of the filamentous webbing, channels, and roadways that our life choices embedded in the geometry, we are able to flex the luminous field and begin shifting the assemblage point into the spiritual-mental body. However, clearing the scaffolding of the lower bodies does not automatically realign them – a process necessary to regain the glow of awareness. This can only begin to happen after we have reconnected with the soul. Soul connection begins when we integrate core beliefs of higher astral vibration into our luminous bodies. When fully connected (the entire luminous body in the spiritual-mental field), the soul geometry will realign the spiritual-mental scaffold through our intent. The spiritual-mental body scaffolding then becomes the template for the realignment of the lower body scaffolds.

Because this is a gradual process, some of the treasures awaiting us in the spiritual-mental body can begin to bleed through into our consciousness while we are still clearing the lower bodies. We are not, one day, astoundingly telepathic but we may notice that we understand our pets in a way previously unavailable to us. We may find that what was once a suspicion of someone lying to us has evolved into a clear knowing of not only the untruth but also the motivation behind it. This is not so much a gift as it is the regaining of our natural power of clarity that we have lost through the unconscious living of life. Reacquiring this clarity and using it without reaction or mental processing is part of conscious living.

The striking feature of this part of the path is the way in which we gain transparency. This transparency is naturally the result of our clearing work but also accompanies the reconnection with our inner truth, the ongoing integration of personality, and our director's every increasing connection to our higher self. This transparency allows the glow of awareness to penetrate our rainbow body. The final realignment of the rainbow body with the soul template brings the glow of awareness back completely with the concomitant flow of energy through the scaffolds – the full flow of energy through our bamboo. We are, once again, as little children. This brings to mind the words of Jesus who reminded us that passage into the kingdom of heaven (fifth dimension attained by passage through the eye of the needle) requires that we become as little children.

We will revisit the blessings that accompany the embodiment of soul as we complete this chapter, but first we will journey through the healing of our spiritual-mental body. This work has enormous focus on the ego, as one might expect. Ego is about all that is left of our connection to the unconscious everyday world as this point. As we move closer to the integrated personality, ego, fearing dissolution, assumes clever disguises and "highly evolved" roles of a more abstract nature. Our observer-director must be equally clever and detached to guide the course corrections needed to clear this field.

Primal Fear

Having worked at clearing emotion since this path began, it is safe to say that what remains of emotion as we enter this spiritual-mental field is very old. We can call it primal fear because it is ancient, but also because it is the fear behind all fear and all other emotional reaction. It is a fear held by the soul itself. It exists in the fourth dimension and not in the fifth. It must, therefore, have come from "The Fall." Every incarnation mimics "The Fall," reinforcing the imprinting of this fear. It is the fear of loss, abandonment, separation, being lost souls, and the lack (loss of abundance) that accompanies those fears. It is, in a word, huge. It separates us from God. It prevents us from completely letting go – losing control over life. This primal fear blinds the ego and gives our observer its greatest challenge. If we cannot overcome it, the eye of the needle, necessarily approached in fearlessness, will not manifest on our path.

The scaffold of this spiritual-mental body remains as the soul templated it until we are awakened spiritually - until our egos begin investing in our spirituality and we experience all that accompanies that investment. As we work through the emotional and mental work that clears the two lower fourth dimensional bodies, we begin making a mess of this one. The ego has no other place to go – no other place to invest itself. We will begin with investments because it is precisely where we were working with ego in the intellectual-mental field. We will see that the face of investment has changed.

Spiritual Investment

Having succeeded at detaching from emotional and mental investments does not actually complete the work of divestment. We find that our egos have been busy investing in things and concepts "spiritual." Our predilection for addictive behavior may have manifested in things "spiritual" as well. Furthermore, moving flawlessly into the spiritual-mental body rarely happens because it is a gradual and haphazard process. For example, if we have been very successful healing addiction and divesting from the third dimensional world of drama, it may have been at the expense of personality integration or our physical body health, and balance. The work we face initially in this realm is that of weaving the layers of our healed rainbow body together. An honest assessment of progress needs to be made – not by our egos but by our directors/observers. One way to approach this assessment is by looking back at our life in terms of our greatest wound, the personality aspect that embodied that wound, and how the healing of that wound has given us purpose beyond personality.

When we begin to walk the spiritual path a lot of options are open to us. Though no sanctuary from the emotional and mental work, we could decide to follow a guru or enter a mystical order. If we are so inclined, we might stay reasonably focused on the devotional path. Another option would be to find a type of spirituality that appeals to us and learn all that we can about it through books, workshops, various teachers and so forth. Or, like most spiritual seekers in today's world, we can have a rather more ballistic experience – often called the shotgun approach – and sample it all. It is a supermarket with all the pleasures, pitfalls - healthy choices and junk food - that the word implies. Whichever methodology we use, we will be tested aplenty. Whatever it is our soul wants us to learn will align us with the path of that learning. The supermarket of spirituality brings with it, for example, discernment. It seems a big lesson for the times in which we live.

No one begins walking the spiritual path with confidence. In fact, confidence does not come until one detaches from the path itself. In the beginning we are obsessed with the by-products of our ego's fears. "Who am I?" is the first, and it seems the last, such by-product. Since we used to be identified through emotional and mental investments, who are we after we have detached from them? The ego naturally invests in the spiritual path. It becomes necessary to know how we are doing on the path. Are we enlightened yet? At what stage of light body activation are we? Are we as "clear" as so and so? We will likely uptake similar patterns of attachment to those we had in the emotional and mental world – and they may still have the emotional and mental overtones of our patterning.

Spiritual-Mental Fitness

For example, if we have always measured our selves by comparison to others, that pattern will take on a spiritual nature. We will tend to compare our selves to those walking the path with us, and to those who simply refuse to get with it. If we have been people who seek validation from those around us, especially those who are leaders, we will expend vast amounts of energy trying to be special in the eyes of those leaders – and receive a lot of gratification when they notice us. This invariably leads to work around jealousy and self-pity as they turn their attention to others. If we have been people who have exuded self-confidence and superiority, we will likely walk the spiritual path in an exclusive way – our head held high and, perhaps, our nose in the air. Service in the community has no appeal. Clearly, our souls have been masterful in designing our lessons.

Judgment and opinion have shifted gears, but they have not evaporated. All of this is normal. It just means the ego is still possessed of considerable muscle and further subpersonality integration work is urgently needed. The subpersonality work tends to fall by the wayside as we feel clearer and more spiritually confident in our selves. However, it still holds the key to making that final connection to higher self, which we will discuss near the end of this chapter. It is important to turn to the subpersonality holding patterns of investment, and divest – change the assemblage point to a new level to support detachment. Now is a good time to revisit our subpersonalities, evaluate their progress, and identify ways in which they are limiting us – still attached to luminous body filaments (core beliefs) that have lower astral vibrations. Each subpersonality is on a path to mastery, which is full integration into higher ego. This evaluation will require that we appraise each subpersonality with respect to all the healing steps thus far described on this journey, then self-correct.

One way of dealing with this is to deny familiar territory to the ego. We can call this a jaguar leap into the unknown. It is at this point in the path that some of us need a radical change in lifestyle, for example, a move to a place where we are not known, or starting an entirely new 'career' that challenges the ego in every way. The soul will provide these opportunities as open doors to the future. We can take them or leave them, but we must be fearless to follow them, and open to magic. None of this is to the liking of the ego, which is invested in security and secure identity but it may be necessary to jolt the subpersonalities into a more complete integration. Detachment and surrender are the most important qualities of the work at this level. Remember that the eye of the needle, should we face it, is narrow indeed - not big enough to take anything with us.

In our cultural acquisition of discernment, we seem to have created opportunities for mastery that have never existed on so large a scale before. Spirituality has become big business and our gurus are those who have what it takes to promote themselves, their products, and their lifestyle. Our culture loves this and engages it with the kind of passion we ordinarily reserve for politics and sports. Contrast our journey through this diversionary, though profitable, realm with that of a young man entering a monastery in Tibet. How can we doubt that there are lessons of discernment and right action to be learned in our culture? Can each of us make our way through the quagmire of "spirituality" as it is marketed in our culture to find the path of truth and light that has always existed within us? We must.

The pitfalls are many – too numerous to list them all. If we have had a history of attachments, as most of us have, there will come an almost imperceptible shift in the nature of those attachments. Below are a few striking examples presented as essential constituents of the spiritual path as the majority of people are walking it in our culture. The truth is that all of these will fall away as we move more fully into our spiritual-mental body. *There is absolutely no substitution for doing our work.*

We put a lot of stock in astrologers, psychics, mediums, channelers – anyone but our higher selves. We want to know the future so that the jaguar leap will not be a jaguar leap at all but a triumph of planning. We want to hear about our potential rather than live it. We want to know about our past lives rather than be present in this one. We are willing to believe that a Master, like Sananda, is speaking through a channel but we do not believe that we are masters at levels of consciousness yet to be touched. Essentially, we continually find ways to give our power away, looking outside our selves, because we do not believe that we have power, or we fear power.

The intent is not to put any of this down. Many of us have walked through all of it – and out the other side. It was all meant to be part of our paths – most often for lessons that ricocheted off our "good intentions." However, there is a place or space free from the need to know, free from the fear of the future, in touch with truth and, most especially, at peace within and without. There are many tools, this book included, that we can use to find our way on our spiritual path, but *we must make the path our own*. If we can own the path, just as we have taken responsibility for our lives, it is ours to release when the time inevitably comes that we need it no more. If it is someone else's path, the only way to release it is to abandon it. A path is just what the name implies – a way to walk through life that resonates with our truth. But the eye of the needle is the end of all paths.

Consciousness is all that is required to see how ego has reinvested at the level of the spiritual-mental body. Unless we have been walking and investing in the spiritual path for all of our life, with the resulting webbing in our spiritual-mental body scaffolding, these are freshly laid filaments in the spiritual-mental body connecting it to the lower bodies. If the former is true, considerable clearing will be called for. Those who are relatively new to the spiritual path will have easier webbing to clear because they will not have invested so much of their wants, needs and desires in the this upper astral body. We can walk away from our spiritual crutches into the light of liberation. As we clear this "young" clutter from our spiritual-mental field, we have to take a look at the other ways we have come to identify our selves. Ego can be deceptive – a deft saboteur.

Abstraction

A curious thing happens to us as we walk this path. Our life takes on story form – a series of stories. These stories may be about abuses we endured and have truly forgiven; illness that could have killed us but we triumphed over it; meaningful events that propelled us forward spiritually; and so forth. The stories linger on. The curious part is that we did recapitulate and we have, in truth, let go of the past. We forgave, got the lessons, and moved on. We divested our attachments but why are these stories still with us? What purpose do they serve? It may be that the ego has abstracted the life events and created what we could call a work of fiction. We can actually be somewhat detached from this work of fiction, yet it keeps reminding us who we were, are, and will be.

Awakening and Healing the Rainbow Body

Though it is not my intent to raise doubts about the path, this curious occurrence with the life stories is a bit troublesome. Since ego has condensed the life events and abstracted them into story form (so easy to repeat and repeat), the conscious person has no alternative but to become consummately bored with their story (we hope not to death), or consummately obsessed with their story (everyone else's turn to be bored). If severe, the former will lead to implosion while the latter will result in explosion. What can be happening except the explosion or implosion of a history as ego has constructed and perceived it? Rather than becoming doubtful, we should be hopeful at this turn of events. It may not be pretty, but energy is moving. If we can self-observe at this level of self-absorption, we might be able to detach from the entire book without imploding or exploding.

It seems inevitable that the final struggle with ego will end up looking a lot like ego development – only in reverse. Part of the risk of walking this path of self-observation and self-correction is that we can lose threads in our weaving. We needn't have the path come to such an intense climax but those who have lived intense lives may find it so. Knowing that this can happen, let us not lose the keen observation of self that can prevent it. If we find our selves telling our stories, we can ask our selves "why?" Are we trying to teach? Are we bragging? Are we having an identity crisis? Do we have an agenda? Is it a manipulation – "my way or no way?" The ego is up to something. Where are our assemblage points, and what core beliefs are supporting the behavior? It must be said, without an ounce of judgment, that for many of us, this will be the jumping off point on the path.

If we have been diligent enough in our work to pierce through into the spiritual-mental field, others will be looking to us for inspiration. Will our egos grab for the kudos or will we recognize the test, and learn the lesson? All those watching us have souls guiding them. Our own experience may inspire them but it is not and will never be their experience. It is not meant to be. Can we be sensitive enough to the path of another to provide subtle guidance as a garden of choices, or do we force our success or failure on them? Compassion is more at home in the fifth dimension but here is where the seed of it begins to sprout and grow – sensitivity, and softness likewise.

Spiritual-Mental Fitness

There may be a beneficial way to use our stories to assist others. If we are asked to or are expected to help others, it may be relevant to use our stories. We will have to use discernment to know if they are relevant in service or an ego trap with big lessons. Then we can make abstractions of the stories by assigning them to infinitely more interesting but fictitious people, which, by the way, is not so far from the truth. This is a step in the right direction since ego is forced to detach to some degree. However, it is not a solution that supports higher self.

Metaphors put our story in the context of parable without attachment to our history. Cliche, by the way, is not metaphor. Teachers who learn to use metaphor rather than telling stories of their own or other's experience are more effective teachers because they have abstracted one step further than story - one step closer to a universal appeal.

Beyond the use of metaphor lies the art of extracting the essence - the wisdom juice - from our experience. With this level of detachment, our experiences fully enter the universal and are available to anyone, and are meaningful to everyone, without personal attachment. These are the ultimate ego exercises when we find our selves ready to quote from that big book of fiction we are carrying around. Once we are firmly anchored in our higher self, a book burning has a lot of appeal.

Spiritual-Mental Body Healing

We have had some big hints of the healing that must take place in the scaffolding of the spiritual-mental body. Detachment and surrender are our most useful tools. At this point on the path, we have had so much experience detaching that the act of detachment is not the problem. Finding the investment is the challenge. Once found, we know how to move the energy - detachment on all levels. Self-observation will reveal the investment and give us the information we need to shift our assemblage point by changing the core beliefs that support the ego's investment. There will be fears to face, and beliefs around them to change.

Naturally, we can expect the fear level to increase steadily. We are walking a path of fearlessness. We do want to regain our glow of awareness, don't we? Healing at this level will include facing our fears. Again, reviewing our life wound may help us with this. We must understand ego's need for the fear, and identify the fear-based control mechanisms that ego is clinging to? Then we can sidestep the ego and go right to the boss – higher self. Higher self will become more and more familiar to us as our new power center.

Miasm Healing

Though most miasms are intellectual constructs, we are still operating in thought field as we clear the spiritual-mental body. The psora miasm is an upper astral thought form construct. The name of the miasm associates it with skin disorders, like psoriasis, which can manifest to demand this clearing work, but its origins are in leprosy. If we cannot clear this miasm, we will not be able to fire our "lightbody," and without our "lightbody" we will not survive the fire initiation, the small death, at the eye of the needle. This miasm, also known as the leprosy miasm, is about lack. It seems less connected to bloodlines and more connected to soul lineage. Lepers have always been banished from society. The stories of those who courageously served the lepers are filled with references to having been banished as outcast with the lepers to inaccessible places. Any story of lepers is a touching metaphor for "The Fall." The leprosy miasm must be about separation – separation from God. As we stand before the eye of the needle, it is an awesome, but totally appropriate bit of healing to let go of those primal fears acquired by our souls at "The Fall" – abandonment and loss. This loss is manifest as lack in life as well – there is not enough money, opportunity, love, and so forth. The fears do not exist, as such, in fifth dimension where we reconnect with a part of our consciousness that is more familiar with the Divine. Love and fear cannot coexist. Fifth dimension is about learning to open our hearts and live in love. How much easier it is to understand life when we have the hard-won clarity of true spiritual work.

Our Benefactors

If we are lucky enough to have soul-contracted with another human being who will breeze into our life to poke holes in our ego (hopefully overlooking none of the ingredients germane to utter humiliation), we must remember two things. First, we would not have contracted the ego-assailant if our soul had not seriously intended our enlightenment. That is a good sign. Second, no matter what our initial

Spiritual-Mental Fitness

reaction (usually not pretty or gracious), when consciousness dawns about the importance of this person and the events they have precipitated, we must shower gratitude upon them in a myriad of ways until they insist that we cease and desist with our adulation. These are the most important people in our lives at this stage of the path. We are trying to overcome human nature, which would spontaneously project the whole affair back on this important person; this benefactor; this great ally of our soul. If we make a mess of the "assaulted ego" work the first few times around, we can take heart. If we are going to walk this path to completion, our soul will provide us with as many humiliating experiences as we need to arrive at the eye of the needle.

Thus far, the healing work is little different from that of the lower bodies. In fact the techniques will be much the same – we know them and no longer need anyone to tell us how to change our lives. Let's move into some uncharted waters with a few concepts that will increase our awareness and help with the spiritual-mental body clearing. These have to do with the way we have walked the path and how that might be improved to help support our efforts at enlightenment.

Non-Linear Expression

We are accustomed, in our culture, to walking through life linearly. That is to say we have an idea; we make a plan; we follow the plan; and we get what we want. On the spiritual path, we climb the mountain of spiritual awareness one step at a time, removing the obstructions we encounter along the way with consciousness. When we get to the part of the path were the path itself falls apart, the linear protocol ceases to make any sense to us. What will work instead? We are moving out of linear time and into circular time. Linear values will not work anymore.

For example, we have been working as individuals. We have cleared our barriers, removed our problems, got out of our dramas, and have become open and clear. Then we apply the principles we have learned and attempt to connect with the Divine. Our Divine connection is intercepted by ego which says, "I have no problems," "I will work on everyone else's problems," or "I will have to move this group to community." We have entered the lonely world of sacrifice and spiritual ego gratification. It is a trap. Everything is still "I" – self-absorption.

Awakening and Healing the Rainbow Body

Unfortunately, this is the norm. Someone is in control and everyone else needs the help of this spiritually superior being. It supports a kind of hero or messiah complex - an absolute hierarchy - which provokes the ego into absolute gloating. How could we do this differently? We know that we are to move outside the hierarchy. We know we are to move outside the linear. Suppose we tune into our self and listen intently. Then we tune into others in our group (an essential component), and listen intently. Then we connect our selves to others as an equal saying "I am part of all the problems," "Let us work on them together," and "Let us work towards community." Not only have we gone circular, we have dissolved the hierarchy, and we have healed the leprosy miasm doing it. Then we connect as group to the Divine and we work with the Divine. The group philosophy is "We all have problems," "We all have dramas," and "We are all capable of removing them."

We have exchanged the semi-enlightened path of cleansing and clearing with the enlightened path of sensitivity and spiritual growth. When we walk this more enlightened path there are no convolutions. Action is direct, and with intent and we are all growing together. By sharing problems, knowledge, and concepts, we begin to receive insights and gain sensitivity. This is how the mystery schools of ancient times evolved and how they could evolve again. It is a perfect marriage of the masculine and feminine within. It is how we could bring enlightenment to anything we pursue as a group. In the enlightened state, this non-system operates out of group heart. When self-glorification and self-absorption enter this non-system, the non-system expels them and they tumble back down to the linear world of third and fourth dimension. It seems the only way we can begin to affect the course of human history - by changing our governments, our churches, our corporations, and our families into heart centered organizations. It does begin with self-service, attending to our own spiritual work without indulging in the ego-trap of needing to fix others. However, in the enlightened state, self dissolves into the awareness of our oneness.

Living Virtuously

We can accelerate and refine the journey to the needle's eye by working with our energy systems instead of against them. Remember

Spiritual-Mental Fitness

Essence? Essence is that part of us that is never touched by life on earth. It holds the original blueprint of the God-consciousness we are. What separates us from Essence are randomized energy patterns created by our wants, needs, and desires. We connect more and more with Essence as we release drama, clear our mental field, let go of our history, and try to harness our egos. It may feel like we are engaged in a cosmic battle, with contestably unfair odds, but there are simple ways to make the path easy. Rather than projecting our fears, anger, and sadness out into the world, we could be projecting love, joy, and hope.

"Not easy" we might say. That is the rhetoric of an abandoned human being. We, who have the universe at our disposal, have slipped into negativity. It happens all the time. In fact, it is the odd time out when people are positive these days.

Granted, we have forgotten we are masters, but have we also forgotten that we have guides, our higher self, and angels - supporters who want us to succeed? We also have virtues to guide us in the living of life – all of them positive, like acceptance, patience, kindness, gratitude, and fortitude. We can use them to guide the ways in which we express our energies. They were given to us as gifts – and who can argue with their quality? We have choices as to what informs us. We have power to re-inform every aspect of our being with Divine Light. We are the hope of Mother Earth.

Soul Connection

The inevitable culmination of our healing work is the full connection to our soul. However, as soon as we begin our spiritual work, our soul perks up and moves closer to us in anticipation of union. Let us picture the soul as the consciousness/template that blueprinted our original rainbow body in this life. That is the rainbow body that shone with the glow of awareness when we were born. Imagine soul's excitement as we finally begin working in the spiritual-mental body. It opens the possibility that our spiritual-mental body will become clear and that it can then be re-templated by the soul. That is soul alignment. It is after the completion of this important event that we can begin using intent to realign the lower body scaffolds as well. Understandably, keeping them clear is of utmost importance.

Awakening and Healing the Rainbow Body

When the soul connects with the spiritual-mental body through the assemblage point, and the process of alignment begins within the rainbow body, we are in for wondrous revelations. It is, during this process that the mission of our souls will become strikingly clear to us. We will know it. Why? Because it is a perfect fit. It will be something that we have been preparing to do for all of our life – and it will be an infinitive: To _____. It will be very specific - tailor-made for us. Generalized infinitives like "to teach," "to heal," or "to create" are not specific enough to be an individual soul purpose. Soul purpose sounds more like: To Awaken; To Illumine; To Bridge; To Balance; and so forth. What is more, it will give us bliss to engage it. Our soul purpose is what we came here to accomplish, over and above our own healing, yet our healing journey encompasses it. Often our soul purpose reflects the healing of our greatest wound, for that healing has given us a level of expertise in the school of life.

With mission alignment we will experience passion for our work, passion for our play, and passion for the privilege of being on earth in consciousness. It is a just reward. We will understand that we are not alone in our mission but are part of something greater – a group soul on a group soul mission. Life is exhilarating – fun, and the Divine Plan unfolds like magic. Enough cannot be said for surrender – to soul, to the mission, and to magic. Retirement is out of the question!

Another bonus of the alignment of scaffolds to the Original Birth Template is the gradual opening of our gifts as the geometry encoding them is realigned with original intent. All of our gifts will help to support our soul mission. The nice thing about knowing our mission, our soul purpose, is that discernment work is finished. All we have to do is ask our selves if the choice before us will assist our mission. If it will, we go for it. If it won't, we don't. Of course it is not always easy to pass up what is being offered, say a tidy piece of income, but it is crystal clear that we must. And guess what? Magic will happen because we have aligned with inner truth. Our new mantra will be:

"More flow. More glow."

It is inner truth that sharpens intuition, one of the more universal gifts we can hold. It is also inner truth that steers us through the attainment of discernment. Inner truth is aligned with soul and with higher self.

Spiritual-Mental Fitness

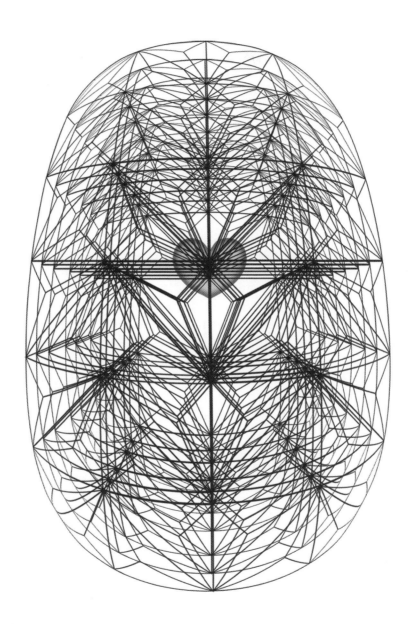

A Soul-Connected Rainbow Body

Awakening and Healing the Rainbow Body

Whatever our gifts, we will use them in an atmosphere of wisdom and infinite possibilities.

Soul alignment is a time when the integration of the subpersonalities comes to completion and our director/observer merges with higher self. Higher self is mission control and our core beliefs, all with the spiritual-mental body frequencies, will have aligned to support higher self and the mission. As joyous as this time is, it is still work, but it is clearly work originating from the upper astral where intent can be used to move energy quickly and effectively. Let us remember that this is the place where the sorcerers have their power, the mastery of fourth dimension. Remember also that, as we attain mastery, the edge of the sword (the balance we walk between white and black magic) becomes thinner and, consequently, sharper. Integrity and impeccability become paramount qualities with which to approach the eye of the needle.

Mastery of the fourth dimension (self-realization) is not full enlightenment. Fifth dimension is full enlightenment. Alignment with the soul is but a step toward union with our Christ potential. The soul's memory is clouded but not so clouded as the incarnation on earth in third dimension. The soul says to this world "This is who I am," in inner and outer voices. Discovering what qualities and motivations are behind those voices is part of the journey back to soul. Essence also says, "This is who I AM," but not to this world – to the universe. These are the inner and outer qualities and motivations at the core of our superconscious being awaiting discovery on the other side of the eye of the needle. We will find that on soul level "who I am" relates very much to this incarnation and this journey back to soul, while on the level of Essence "who I AM" will speak to the nature of our journey back to God.

Expansion

We move through schools of learning on the spiritual path. There are many. They sound like the many mansions reported beyond death. They are the many mansions of a conscious life. It is normal to master one school and move on to another – meaning that we might find the way we approach life, our spiritual path and our mission shifting over time. For instance, we may have been very firmly anchored in the school of Knowledge during our life and most of the spiritual path. But then we are

Spiritual-Mental Fitness

suddenly finished with that school - it no longer serves us - and we move on to the school of Consciousness, for instance. In this school, information is not what is important. Levels of consciousness and expanded awareness are important. Knowledge was likely our soul's inner "who I am." Consciousness is beyond the soul's design. It is new. This is good.

There are many more schools that we may or may not become interested in mastering as our quest for Divine Union continues. There are schools of Energy, Light, and Love, for example. Many who have had near death experiences have been awestruck by the choices of learning beyond death. That is but a small taste of the infinite. They have also felt something of a loss returning into the body. This could be related to the degree to which light must compress into human form. Remember, as consciousness, we are ever expanding geometries of light compressed into the human experience. Here, working at the level of the spiritual-mental body, we have expanded well beyond the physical form – and yet we are still in it. That is the nature of the rainbow body.

In this atmosphere of wisdom, inner truth, and infinite possibilities, our assemblage points have shifted completely into the spiritual-mental body. We are now interfaced with the upper astral in the collective unconscious or fourth dimension. In addition to our own soul, there are great teachers in the upper astral that are ready and willing to connect with us. Our higher self can exercise the choice to learn from these masters and will often draw meetings with these masters to us in dream time or the waking state. Inspiration has many sources and these teachers are one of those sources.

The recently described crystal children are nothing new, though there may be more of them incarnating at this time than previously. They are little masters incarnating through assemblage points in the upper astral. They are neither fully ascended nor enslaved to the lower astral. Their enlightenment work is in the spiritual-mental field, and the avoidance of distortion in their lower body scaffolds. Their wise paths seem old upon the earth. Their paths are not so heavily laden with lower chakra work as most of us but their human "falls from grace" will be worthy tumbles, because masters fall harder than do neophytes. We all experience unconsciousness upon incarnation. Their advantage is to be connected to truth and wisdom from birth. Their road to mastery should look very familiar to them.

Intent

At last, we come to intent; mastery of intent; and intent as a palpable power. Intent is how we can work with our scaffolding, move energy within it, align it with the soul template, and work with our energetic and physical DNA. Intent can shift the assemblage point in an instant, and by now we should be pretty good at changing our core beliefs. At the beginning of this book, we talked about becoming self-realized and how that meant being a master of our assemblage point. At this actual point on the path, that mastery is within our grasp.

Part of that mastery includes the ability to move energy within our scaffolding with intent. Intent is focused consciousness. It is exactly what we will need to die consciously, walking through the eye of the needle, and ascending in death. Ascension in conscious death presupposes a rainbow body aligned with the soul. How can we make that happen, once we have made soul connection? We have already discussed the work necessary – keeping the lower bodies clear, moving into higher self from ego, and so forth. But how do we use intent to align these scaffolds? What can we do with intent while still among the living?

The templates of our rainbow body scaffolding are crystals because crystals are uniform geometry of light. These crystals inform the DNA of each body because they hold information. The energetic DNA then gives the body its function and form as does the physical body DNA. If we have spent a lifetime informing our DNA with drama, entangled relationships, mental pursuits, and ego investments, we have lost our original geometry. All of the work we have talked about in this book will clear out those scaffolds of the filamentous webbing, channels, and so forth, which caused the distortion in the scaffolds and the loss of the glow of awareness. However, clearing alone does not restore the original geometry – it opens a space for that to happen and for soul to connect.

What is left of our work in the rainbow body is to re-inform our DNA at all those levels using intent. The DNA is responsible for the form and function. The scaffold is the crystalline transmitter to the DNA. The information passed from scaffold to DNA is transmitted as waveforms.

Spiritual-Mental Fitness

These waveforms speak in different languages like magnetics, light, energy, bloodlines, and so forth, depending on which body we are working with and what language we prefer to use. We have the potential to regenerate tissue, increase our life spans with quality of life, and, in continuing our work of self-mastery towards the right use of will, consider resurrection, immortality, and merging with our Divine I AM Presence.

In self-mastery, we use our intent to re-inform our DNA. Casteneda speaks of intent as the prevailing force in the universe. It is Source energy applied by focusing our own consciousness. Using it requires discipline and all of the qualities discussed in our first chapter. Wanting to use it requires an overwhelming desire to complete the work of the soul and step through the eye of the needle. When all of this comes together for us, we will know what to do with our intent, and the first thing we will do is to step off the path in liberation. The Divine Plan makes use of our talents and does not ask more of us than our spirits are capable of giving in this life. The most difficult part of this path is to step off the path itself, and to trust that we will always be taken care of and loved.

NOTES

THE PENTHOUSE

Finally, we have arrived at the penthouse of our metaphorical department store, the pinnacle of the fourth dimension. This is where everything comes together before the eye of the needle. The rarified atmosphere in the penthouse is that of surrender and detachment, but also peace and joy. It is a place of true paradox. What does that mean?

Take for example the yin and yang. If we have surrendered our yang nature to walk the path from a more feminine, receptive place, when we reach the penthouse, we will find yang awaiting us. There will be some integration work to weave our masculine and feminine together in a balanced whole – the middle road. Both are important to our mission – whatever it is. If we expect paradox, we will not be disappointed.

Another example is the discipline we have used to clear our rainbow body – to heal and awaken it in every way. When we arrive at the penthouse, we find equal value in the enjoyment of life without attachment. This *joie de vivre* is in keen contrast to the discipline – paradox. In the penthouse, wouldn't we expect a ruby glass of Chateauneuf-du-Pape or a well-sung aria like Nessun Dorma to wrap our joyful hearts in bliss? Of course! So often, we deny ourselves as a spiritual practice. This self-sacrifice is clearly linked to pain and suffering, and is not related to

Awakening and Healing the Rainbow Body

discipline. Paths of sacrifice and pain are exclusive - meager in heart. The other side of the eye of the needle is not on another planet. It is in our blossoming hearts, right here, right now. Discipline means we are paying attention, we are aware, we are present, and we are fearless.

Let's be here NOW. Let's feel the love and caring that began with the planting and pruning of the vine, with Puccini's genius, and the training of the gifted soprano's voice, and with the sowing of the seeds from the stars that has made it possible for each of us to reclaim our soul in liberation. Many times every day, we can feel gratitude for all that comes our way.

Life is so good.
Life is magic.
Life is most definitely worth living.

GLOSSARY

Assemblage Point: Our personal fourth dimensional point of attachment with the collective fourth dimension; our view of reality; the focal point of our beliefs.

Astral, Higher: The higher level of the collective unconscious or fourth dimension, corresponding to our personal spiritual-mental body; the highest layer, in frequency, of our mental body.

Astral, Lower: The lower level of the collective unconscious or fourth dimension, corresponding to the two lower bodies of our mental field, the emotional-mental body and the intellectual-mental body.

Attention: Being present, in the NOW moment, with vigilant awareness.

Autonomy: Self-governance and self-sufficiency attained by taking responsibility for our thoughts and actions through the practice of self-observation and self-correction.

Awareness: Expanded consciousness; an awakened state.

Bamboo: A metaphor for the unobstructed flow of energy in and through our rainbow body.

Bardo: The immediate after-death realm as described in the Tibetan Buddhist tradition.

Black Magic: The misuse of power (energy as thought form projection) in the fourth dimensional thought field.

"The Box": A metaphor for third dimension with its limitations of time and space.

Collective Unconscious: A term used to describe the collective fourth dimension containing both the lower and higher astral.

Consciousness: Coalescent light/energy that is both mutable and immortal.

Core Beliefs: Fourth dimensional thought forms that reflect or shape our reality.

Detachment: Letting go of wants, needs, and desires.

Director: The objective observer within us that is not part of lower ego.

Discernment: The art of conscious choice, from truth and wisdom with transparency, rather than from wants, needs, and desires.

Divine Plan: The plan conceived by our souls and encoded into our rainbow body for this incarnation.

Divine Self: Our I AM presence; the consciousness associated with Essence.

Dark Sea of Awareness: A term from sorcery, which seems to fit our description of the collective unconscious; the collective fourth dimension.
Ego: Personality, how we outwardly express ourselves in any dimension outside the Heart of God.
Ego, Lower: The ego of our base nature, connected to wants, needs, and desires.
Ego, Higher: The ego of our higher self; a fully awakened, integrated personality.
Ego, True: The ego of our Essence.
Enlightenment: Attainment of self-realization, or the mastery of fourth dimensional awareness; complete awareness of the luminous body and first six scaffolds of the rainbow body.
Essence: The part of us (templated-consciousness) that has never been touched by this world or any other. Essence holds the Original Divine Template of our God presence; our I AM Presence.
Essence (Chinese Medicine term): The fluid phase (cellular) of inherited life force.
Essential Consciousness: Consciousness of the complete Essence – the yin and yang of Essence united.
Eye of the Needle: The fiery passageway into the fifth dimension, transited in our body of light – "lightbody."
"The Fall": The dropping of the veil upon the consciousness of mankind and subsequent creation of the unconscious, both personal and collective. At that time the soul came into being - a remnant consciousness of our pre-"Fall" awareness.
Fearlessness: The absence of fear = love.
Fluidity: Flexibility, primarily of our assemblage point/reality, which contributes to our mastery of fourth dimension.
Glow of Awareness: The flow and embodiment of energy/light that comes with self-realization through the complete healing and alignment of the rainbow body. The light present in a newborn baby whose rainbow body is still aligned with the soul's template.
Golden Moment: The nanosecond preceding reaction, wherein our director/observer can expand time, evaluate outcomes, and reorganize the ego to avoid the reaction.
Hanaqpacha: Andean term for the fifth dimension, higher consciousness.
Heart of God: Like the eye of a hurricane, the place of stillness and non-dualism where all universes originate.

Higher Consciousness: Consciousness beyond the fourth dimension; generally used to describe fifth dimension, or Christ Consciousness.
Higher Self: Our incarnate higher ego - an outward expression of the soul's consciousness.
Impeccability: The complete accountability for our actions; walking our talk; integrity and living our truth.
Incarnation: The soul's manifestation into the third dimension.
Intent: In sorcery, described as the prevailing force in the universe; beyond the power of thought, intent works at the level of energy/light; part of fourth dimensional mastery.
Internal Dialogue: Mind chatter that does not allow silence within the mental field.
Kaypacha: An Andean word to describe this reality, third dimension.
Knowingness: A marriage of feeling, wisdom and truth that precedes intuition.
Liberation: Freedom from the influence of the unconscious; the unconscious made conscious.
Lightbody: The full incorporation of light/energy that accompanies the healing and realignment of the rainbow body to its Original Birth Template; self-realization; enlightenment.
Light Codes: Energetic encodements within the scaffolding of the rainbow body that are activated and released when the rainbow body is restored and frequency is raised. Some light codes provide consciousness gifts for those carrying them while others contribute to collective energy. Mental body codes will be manifest as thought forms, for example.
Luminous Body: A body of light filaments, core beliefs, that limits our awareness through the placement and frequency of its assemblage point.
Matrix of Light: The God Matrix – the geometric matrix of light/energy that is All That Is.
Monadic Consciousness: A level of soul consciousness that is more collective than group soul, which is more collective than individual soul consciousness. Missions exist at all levels of soul consciousness.
Munay: An Andean term for the power of love.
Observer: See director.
Original Birth Template: The sacred light geometry created by the soul as a template for the rainbow body at birth.

Original Divine Template: The sacred light geometry of our Essence, or I AM Presence, that remains always as our template of God-consciousness.

Original Soul Template: The light geometry of our soul that is reflected in the Original Birth Template but does not suffer the distortion of life on earth. It holds the intent of the soul for this incarnation.

Paradox: Seeming opposites that can co-exist in our reality. For example, we resent and care deeply about someone at the same time.

Planetary Ascension: The Mission to raise human consciousness. On a cosmic level, the Mission to create an evolved human capable of lifting the veil of the unconscious that was the result of "The Fall," through the embodiment of fifth dimensional frequencies. Thus the earth's own frequency can raise and she can shed the collective fourth dimensional veil as well.

Predators: Energetic entities of the fourth dimension (can be thought forms) that parasitize humanity to acquire energy for their survival. Emotional energy, negative thoughts, and unconscious death sustain the predators.

Predatory Energy: The manifestation of predation in this reality; examples of sources include drugs, pornography, violence, gambling, addictive substances, and so forth.

Psychosynthesis: The work of Roberto Assagioli. The spiritual work of integrating our subpersonalities into a seamless personality with the potential of ascension, and the expression of higher self.

Qi: Life force energy as defined by Chinese Medicine; gifted to us at conception and replenished through vibrant food and air.

Rainbow Body: Our multidimensional energetic body. As light, the holographic layers of the rainbow body appear in the colors of the rainbow (Hindu Chakra colors), red, orange, yellow, green, sky blue and indigo.

Rainbow Body Scaffolding: The sacred geometric matrices of light/energy that template or blueprint the holographic layers of the rainbow body.

Self-correction: The behavioral or mental changes that result from self-observation.

Self-observation: The art of observing one's own behavior and thought processes through the objective "eyes" of the observer or director.

Self-realization: Enlightenment; attainment through the healing and realignment of the rainbow body; the mastery of fourth dimension, the luminous body, and this reality.

Soul: A fourth dimensional "self consciousness" created at "The Fall" that has a dim memory of pre-"Fall" awareness, and thus a motivation to regain higher consciousness; our re-acquired working consciousness in the spiritual-mental field.

Spirit: A state of consciousness, akin to the vapor state of water that has the ability to connect and exchange with other Spirit in all dimensions.

Subconscious: A psychological term used to describe an accessible aspect of the unconscious. In this work, subconscious refers to our personal fourth dimensional field.

Subpersonality: An aspect of ego that can be observed "acting" in this reality.

Surrender: The act of letting go of control that accompanies the acceptance of the Divine Plan; dropping expectations and agendas.

Template: A blueprint.

Transparency: The ability to see through this reality, including the motivation of others and self.

Ukhupacha: An Andean term that describes the unconscious; the dark interior world of shadows.

Unconscious: In psychology, it is used to describe the inaccessible part of the unconscious. In this work, it relates to the collective unconscious, which can be understood and selectively accessed in self-realization.

Vigilance: To be ever watchful. In this work it is the focused attention needed to self-observe. Hyper-vigilance is sometimes required in more advanced ego work.

Wiracocha: An Andean term that describes the luminous body of light filaments. Wiracocha was also a mythic leader of higher consciousness who promised to return to the Andean people.

photo: Javier Casapia Salas

About the Author

A scientist turned shaman, Jessie travels internationally training women and men to awaken their true power - the power of a focused heart. She was awakened by the Andean Elders, the open-hearted people of Peru, and the Ascended Masters. Jessie is the author of The Lineage of the Codes of Light and The Brotherhood of the Magi, as well as Awakening and Healing the Rainbow Body. She has recorded two audio CDs to support the healing of the rainbow body with a third CD planned for 2005.

Jessie leads sacred journeys to Peru/Bolivia and Southern France each year for those who have studied in circle with her. For information about working in circle with Jessie, travel opportunities, her annual Mt. Shasta Retreat, and current publications, visit our website. If you would like to sponsor a circle, email inquiries to info@heartofthesun.com.

Heart of the Sun
http://www.heartofthesun.com

MAIL ORDER FORM

_____*copies of* Awakening and Healing the Rainbow Body @ $16

_____*copies of* The Lineage of the Codes of Light @ $18

_____*copies of* The Brotherhood of the Magi @ $18

_____*copies of* Deep Trance Shamanic Journeys: Volume One Pachamama's Child Audio CD @ $16

_____*copies of* Deep Trance Shamanic Journeys: Volume Two Right Relationship Audio CD @ $16

Name _____

Address _____

City _____ **State**_____ **Zip**_____

email(optional) _____

Book Total $_____

CA sales tax (if resident) 7.25% $_____

Shipping ($3 1st item, $1 ea add'l.) $_____

Total $_____

Send a copy of this page with checks made payable to:
Heart of the Sun, P.O. Box 495, Mt. Shasta, CA 96067
We do not accept credit cards. Allow 10 days for delivery.
To use credit cards for shipped books, order from Village Books in Mt. Shasta (linked to our website or 530-926-1678) or Amazon.com.